Advance Praise for *IMAGINE*

"*IMAGINE* offers a fresh approach to leading from the inside out. Its combination of science and stories will spark new ideas — and open your eyes to the hidden possibilities around us."

— **Daniel H. Pink**,
#1 New York Times bestselling author of
The Power of Regret, *Drive*, and *To Sell Is Human*

"Einstein called Imagination *"a preview of life's coming attractions."* He went on to add that it's *"more important than knowledge."* This book is a fresh take on how to make better use of it. I highly recommend it."

— **Dr. Daniel Amen, MD**
CEO and Founder, *Amen Clinics, BrainMD*, and the *Change Your Brain,*
Change Your Life Foundation

"*IMAGINE* offers a grand tour into the realm of imagination. Whether you're creating a vision for yourself or for your team, organization, family, community, or nation, let this invaluable resource be your guide."

— **Dr. Gloria J. Burgess**
Author, *Flawless Leadership,*
Dare to Wear Your Soul on the Outside, and *Pass It On!*

"Paul Gustavson uses the power of story to take us on a journey to recognize and grow in our imaginative abilities. He provides us with practical examples, tools, and exercises to cultivate the power of imagination that is within each one of us."

— **Dave Cornell**
Speaker and Author, *Cultivating Courage*

"Paul is a student of leadership and growing systems and people. In his newest book, this passion and commitment comes through with clarity and competence."

— **Kary Oberbrunner**
WSJ & USA Today bestselling author, and
CEO of *Igniting Souls*

PREVIOUS PRAISE FOR *BREAKING AVERAGE*

"*Breaking Average* is a skillfully-crafted, insightful resource for anyone who seeks to develop a high-performance team. Written from experience, wisdom, and a deep understanding of how leaders develop collaborative cultures, Breaking Average is approachable, refreshing, and empowering! It is filled with actionable tools that inspire and activate business success through team performance!"

— **Joseph Michelli**
Bestselling author,
The Airbnb Way, and *Driven to Delight*

"*Breaking Average* offers a fresh perspective on what it takes to build a team. It's a difference maker. The Seven Critical Factors alone, are invaluable. But this book goes even further. It offers relevant stories, practical tips, and tools to help score you and your team."

— **Bonnie St. John**
Bestselling author of *Micro-Resilience*,
Paralympic Medalist and CEO, *Blue Circle Leadership*

"Everyone knows that teamwork is essential to success, *Breaking Average* provides practical guidelines for building above average teams that will lead to above average results."

— **Ken Davis**
Author, Speaker, Communication Coach

"Interesting stories and actionable ideas will help you create a successful team or lead the team you have more effectively. Break average by reading and using this book!"

— **Mark Sanborn**
New York Times best-selling author of *The Fred Factor*

IMAGINE

IMAGINE

The Surprising Truth about Hope and
The 12 Powerful Ways to Invent the Future

PAUL GUSTAVSON

Lead Edge
PRESS

Imagine –
The Surprising Truth about Hope and
The 12 Powerful Ways to Invent the Future

by Paul Gustavson

Published by LEAD EDGE PRESS

LEAD EDGE PRESS
c/o Paul Gustavson
43 Town and Country Drive, Suite 129
Box #112
Fredericksburg, Virginia 22405

Lead Editor:	Joe Dutkiewicz
Spanish Support:	Daniel Hammond and Carolina Batres
Cover design:	Darko Bovan
Cover image copyright:	© Adobe Stock #464217233

Published in the United States by Lead Edge Press

ISBN: 978-0-9976872-5-5 (Hardback)
ISBN: 978-0-9976872-6-2 (Softback)
ISBN: 978-0-9976872-7-9 (Kindle)
ISBN: 978-0-9976872-8-6 (ePub)
ISBN: 978-0-9976872-9-3 (Audio)

First Release – Dec 20, 2022

http://theimaginebook.com

To anyone who is a
Dreamer,
Designer, or
Implementer.

You are a force of nature.
A game-changer.

You help shape the future and
make this world a better place for others.

This book is dedicated to you.

Never stop imagining.

With one idea, you can change the world!

TABLE OF CONTENTS

Author's Note	1
Foreword – By Mark Batterson	3
Ground Zero – The Starting Point	7
1 – Become Something More	9
2 – Equip Yourself	19
Phase One – OBSERVE	35
3 – Trace Your Path – *The Power of Patterns*	37
4 – Hunt Down Misconceptions – *The Power of Curiosity*	45
5 – Evaluate The Gains – *The Power of Assessment*	67
Phase Two – ORIENT	79
6 – Imagine The Possible – *The Power of Belief*	81
7 – Minimize The Distractions – *The Power of Boundaries*	97
8 – Align Your Steering – *The Power of Values*	113
Phase Three – DECIDE	127
9 – Get Bulletproof – *The Power of Resilience*	129
10 – Increase The Amplitude – *The Power of Today*	155
11 – Notice The Resistance – *The Power of Discipline*	171
Phase Four – ACT	187
12 – Enter The Matrix – *The Power of Movement*	189
13 – Engage With Others – *The Power of Encouragement*	209
14 – Reinvent Continuously – *The Power of Growth*	227
Epilogue – Let Imagination Speak Life	235
Acknowledgments	247
Appendix A – The Imagineer Assessment Tool	249
Appendix B – What About Faith?	259
Appendix C – Quotes That Inspire	273
Appendix D – Recommended Resources	277
About The Author	283

Author's Note

This book is written from an observer's standpoint. It is based on three decades of observation exploring how our imagination works independently of age, theological beliefs, or leadership title. In my research, we looked for stories and supporting science. While I wouldn't classify myself as a researcher by academic standards, I am an engineer.

Using inductive and deductive reasoning, I have tried my best to curate data, validate theories, and provide practical guidance. My goal is to offer you thought-provoking and relevant stories, coupled with some of the related brain health science, so you have a clear guide and tool to better leverage this amazing tool we call imagination.

I hope you enjoy this book as much as I have enjoyed bringing it to life. Now that it's finally written, I can honestly say it reflects what I hoped and imagined.

Enjoy!

FOREWORD – BY MARK BATTERSON

I am fascinated with discovering ways to make each day count. One of my mantras is to *"imagine unborn tomorrows."* Why is this important to me? Because I believe there's something bigger than the comfort zone of today. A critical step is to take time to imagine our tomorrows.

What does the future hold?

I've learned that if we don't ask that question ourselves, someone else might answer it for us. The future is already coming, so we might as well help create it.

A few years back, Paul Gustavson and I bumped into each other in the hallway of a conference we were both attending. It didn't take long for the two of us to connect. We share a passion for leadership, and over the years, we've swapped a few stories, including a common interest in the power of our imagination. For me, imagination is what fuels my faith and shapes my passion. I'm not sure how I could live life without it.

The book you are about to read, *IMAGINE*, captures the essence of what it takes to be future minded yet situationally aware of the present. Both are critical to how you live and how you lead. Think of this book as an invitation to uncover your gifts and experiences so you can offer others hope.

Mark Twain has a quote that says, *"if you want the fruit, you have to go out on the limb and get it."* There are two things at play here. One, you must see the fruit before you get it. Two, you must have the courage to go out and get it. The vision and the courage start in your imagination. It begins with the belief that there is fruit out there, which spurs the desire to reach for it.

Your desire to change must be greater than your desire to stay the same. That's where this book shares hope. It offers a means to understand how you are wired, including what makes you tick and what actions to take to go out on the limb and get the fruit.

I like how Paul also identifies that this is a foundations book. The Bible says God created man on the sixth day, in His image. That means that if you and I can better understand how we are designed to work, we might better understand how God works through us. After all, every feature unique to the human mind is a facet of the image of our Creator.

I wrote a book a while back called *Whisper*. In that book, I share that nothing is more mysterious or miraculous than the three pounds of gray matter housed within the human skull. This includes part of the brain that I call the locus of imagination. This is where our God-sized dreams reside. Aka, our hopes and desires. I believe the size of our dreams can remind us of the size of our God. If that's true, we ought to take full advantage of this tool called our imagination.

What will you imagine?

Mark Batterson,
New York Times bestselling author,
The Circle Maker,
Lead Pastor, *National Community Church*, Washington, D.C.

GROUND ZERO

THE STARTING POINT

Prepare Yourself

GROUND ZERO – THE STARTING POINT

"The beginning is the most important part of the work."

—Plato

Welcome to Ground Zero. The starting point and base camp for your imagination.

Ground Zero often refers to the point of explosion, where things start. When it comes to understanding imagination, we need a Ground Zero – a beginning point to our journey.

Your imagination is like a muscle. It can be the most powerful muscle you have. It can lift and influence you and those around you. But it needs to be developed and used.

While imagination is formidable and powerful, it can be wildly unconstrained. Like a bronco, the imagination can be hard to calm and control. Yet, if you train and settle your imagination, you will discover the beauty, power, and trust it offers.

Let this base camp be a place of preparation for you as we explore two prerequisites for the journey:

- The call to Become Something More
- The tools that Equip You for the Journey

Those that hear the call, and leverage the tools are the ones who take imagination to a whole new level.

1 – BECOME SOMETHING MORE

"A vision is not just a picture of what could be;
it is an appeal to our better selves,
a call to become something more."

– Rosabeth Moss Kanter

I sat glued to the television, watching one of the most thrilling winter sports I had ever seen. One by one, athletes would strap on a pair of skis almost seven feet in length and jettison down the side of a mountain slaloming from one gate to the next.

Each raced against a clock to see who could get to the bottom the fastest. There was a rhythm to how they skied that was mesmerizing. Each gate was almost like a punching bag as they maneuvered and sliced their way down. The sense of urgency and purpose captivated me.

On this night, it was one of the last competitions of the Winter Olympics. My family and I sat glued to the television; part of me felt like I was there. As they skied, I could almost feel the energy. Between runs, the commentator would rattle off the finish time for each skier. I kept track of the leaderboard to see who was in contention. My interest was in America's hope for a medal, and that was Phil Mahre. He was just ten minutes away from his final run, and I couldn't wait.

After a commercial break and just before the race, they aired an exclusive interview featuring Mahre with one of the reporters covering the Games for ABC Sports. Earlier that day, the reporter had a chance to talk to Mahre at the top of the mountain, and he asked him what it was like just before a race and how he prepared.

Mahre responded with an insight that left a lifelong impression. He described how he mentally imagines the run beforehand. He visualizes skiing from the starting gate to the finish line and pictures what he'll experience from one turn to the next. I remember him saying, *"If I don't race that mountain in my mind ahead of time, I won't have my best run."*[1]

New Awareness

The Phil Mahre interview was in 1980 when I was 13 years old. That moment created for me a new awareness that fascinated me. I realized there's something powerful about our imagination, and maybe, just maybe, we ought to learn more about it.

All these decades later, I still have that same impression. I believed then, and maybe even more strongly today that **imagination should be the most powerful tool in the toolbox.** Used right, it will move you from your current state to a future state. It's a tool of influence that offers vision and shapes your life and those around you.

However, for many, imagination might be underutilized, unappreciated, or misguided. As tools go, it may have gotten dull or dusty. But what if we dust it off, sharpen it up, and get more comfortable with it. What if we can learn to use it better? How much better might our world be?

Better

What excites me most about imagination is the power it gives us to see new possibilities. **Imagination is the birthplace of innovation.** It is where great ideas come to light.

Innovation is about bringing to life something that adds value and impacts others. These innovations typically come in three forms: better products, better processes, or better people. The operative word here is *better*. Better is better than best. Better is about inventing the future and never getting complacent.

Better starts in the imagination.

The Powers of Imagination

In the decade of the 80s, Phil Mahre was clearly on to something. Using the powers of imagination, he raced well enough to take home the silver medal in 1980, narrowly missing the gold by half a second. Think about it – in as little time as it takes to say the simple phrase *"Hello"*, you've already burned up almost a second. Just the physical time it takes to blink is 300 to 400 milliseconds. Phil Mahre was less than two blinks away from a gold medal, yet he might not have been in contention if he had not imagined racing that run ahead of time. By visualizing the race first, he likely shaved off several seconds, putting himself in a position to medal.

Using this technique, Phil Mahre would become one of the greatest American skiers of all time. His most significant stretch was when he was crowned the World Cup Overall Champion three consecutive years in a row: 1981, 1982, and 1983. This would be a feat no other slalom skier would accomplish again for another thirty years.

To cap off his career, he and his twin brother Steve took medals at the 1984 Olympics finishing 1–2 in the slalom. Phil won the gold; Steve took the silver. Think about that accomplishment; two brothers sharing the podium on the biggest stage in the world.[2]

More interesting is a video clip discoverable on YouTube of Phil and Steve just before the start of the competition that day in 1984. They are on the mountain sitting next to each other; both are in a zone. They are taking a moment to imagine the race beforehand. Each of them uses the motion of their hands as a tool to paint their path, navigate the gates, and pre-ski their race using their imagination. Frank Gifford, commentating for ABC Sports, looks on with fascination, remarking about the Mahre Twins' use of *"visual imagery."*

Your imagination is the mental representation of the past, present, and future. It represents what was, what is, and what can be.[3]

Think of imagination as your own personal *multiverse*. It allows you to see endless possibilities. It creates a space for exploring those *"what if...?"* scenarios. Think about it, imagination gives sight to your hope and can bring the future to light. It can also provide hindsight from your experiences and insight into your opportunities.[4]

Einstein adds that the imagination is a *"preview of life's coming attractions."* And a clear imagination creates a narrative your mind, body, and spirit will want to follow. The opportunities and possibilities are endless when your imagination is tuned just right. When it's not tuned right, your imagination will take you off course.

We learn from neuroscience that much of the brain can't distinguish imagination from reality. According *to* best-selling author Olivia Fox Cabane, *"Imaginary situations cause your brain to send your body the same commands as it would for a real situation."*[5]

Your imagination is formidable and involved in almost every aspect of your being. You use it when you reflect, read, watch, write, think, explore, learn, plan, create, perform, and even connect with others.

Imagination is to living, as oxygen is to breathing. You use it for nearly every life decision, even subconscious ones. Just as the quality of the air you breathe makes a difference in your well-being, so does the quality of your imagination. Get it right, and good choices and decisions will follow. But if your imagination is off, unfortunate things can happen.

Jordan Rules

Have you ever heard someone tell you, *"Don't miss!"* in the game of basketball, golf, or any other sport? What inevitably happens when the thought of missing is planted in your head?

You miss!

However, if you can focus your imagination in the right direction, you prepare for "the make."

Basketball great Michael Jordan attributed the powers of imagination to his success in *The Last Dance* documentary series, which originally aired on Netflix. He commented that *"things tend to slow down"* when using his imagination.

Jordan adds, *"As I go into situations that people don't know the outcome, I've already experienced them in my mind. Just playing tricks with myself, so it didn't seem new to me. I wasn't afraid to fail. Once I began to understand [this power], I became a master of the game of basketball."*[6]

Like Mahre, Jordan used his imagination as a means of preparation.

Jordan's coach, Phil Jackson, added, *"Something we talked about a lot as a team was how to be in the moment. Being able to visualize what might happen in those times. Michael so embraced this. I think that was the beauty of his game – he had all these abilities to adjust, not force his own predetermined idea but allow those things to come together for his game."*

Center Brad Daugherty, who played with Jordan at the University of North Carolina, shared how he visualizes every free throw before taking a shot. *"All that goes through my mind when I'm at the line is seeing the ball go through the bottom of the net."*

Likewise, in the game of golf, the legendary Jack Nicklaus shared, *"I never hit a shot, not even in practice, without having a very sharp, in-focus picture of it in my head."*

Years later, golfer Brad Bryant would add, *"The clearer you can visualize the shot, the greater chance your body has to producing it. If you don't have a real clear picture before you hit, then the shot will come up fuzzy."*

It didn't take long to realize that the powers of imagination help in sports and other things like business, relationships, life goals, leadership, and innovation. If you are a person of faith, then your imagination is vital. But remember, there's a slippery slope to the imagination too. Imagination without hope can lead to danger.

The Wall

Imagination, when combined with doubt, can throw us off. For example, when I play the game of basketball or golf, unlike Jordan, Daugherty, Nicklaus, or Bryant, I sometimes tend to imagine missing the shot – not making it. I let doubt creep in.

That might be why I am often ready to chase down my own rebound after a shot, or I have a knack for finding orphan golf balls in the woods when I am out looking for my own. ☺

All kidding aside, sometimes we use our imagination the wrong way. It reminds me of what happens when a race car driver goes into a spin on the track. They say your car goes where your eyes go. A common quote is, *"The driver who cannot tear his eyes away from the wall as he spins out of control will meet that wall."*[7] Our imagination is the same way.

If we don't learn to get our imagination tuned just right, it can lead us into real trouble. We might hit the wall.

But what if you could learn to be more present with your imagination? What if you could learn to imagine the possible like Phil Mahre or Michael Jordan? Don't you think that might make a difference?

That's the opportunity in front of you. Imagination is not just beneficial for sports; it's helpful for all of life. Any of us can get better at leveraging our imagination. It can be a game changer, but only if we put in the mental preparation.

Think of the imagination as a tool that can offer you greater clarity, understanding, and confidence. What you imagine is what shapes future wins.

The Win

With winning comes confidence, but what if you can get to confidence before the win? What if confidence starts in the imagination?

Confidence is something we all want more of, isn't it? For confidence to happen and to experience the win, sometimes our imagination needs to be flipped upside down. Rather than see the potential failure – the miss, the wall, and the doom and gloom – choose to see the goal, the shot, the hole, and the track in front of you.

We can employ a simple life equation to tell the story. The Future you shape is the product of four key observable components: Imagination, Experimentation, Evaluation, and Integrity. Each one builds on the other. You really can't leave one element out. Think of it this way:

The Future =
imagination x experimentation x evaluation x integrity

This life equation leads to greater clarity, understanding, confidence, and success. Yet, under the hood, there's more.

What's interesting about this equation is that the multiplier that you see in the formula – the x – is something significant too. The multiplier is HOPE. We need hope to make this equation work. Hope literally is the "x-factor."

Hope in this equation is more than a wish; it's a desire. It's important to understand the subtle difference. A wish can be well-meaning, but it is often a proclamation of something you want without personal action. A desire indicates a strong aspiration or yearning that you are willing to commit to.

According to author Napoleon Hill, *"Desire is the starting point of all achievement."* Hope at this level is a seed that gets Imagination started and can keep you going. Hope then leads to Experimentation, which gets you to a state of Evaluation, even if you experience failure. Integrity is what keeps you honest, trustworthy, and focused.

- Imagination is about thinking. *It's choosing to dream.*
- Experimentation is about doing. *It's designing the dream.*
- Evaluation is about assessing. *It's refining the dream.*
- Integrity is about character. *It's honoring the dream by staying ethical.*
- Hope is the multiplier for each part. *It is the dream!*

HOPE will deserve credit for your future success. We'll explore this concept of hope throughout the book – not just any kind of hope. Real hope is tied to real strategy.

Imagineering Types

There is one more important matter that we need to address upfront. It turns out that not everyone imagines the same way; there are different types of Imagineers.

The term Imagineer was commonly used by Walt Disney to describe a team of visionaries who can ideate and bring the future to life. Ultimately, they implement creative ideas into practical form.

Not all Disney Imagineers are of the same ilk. It turns out there are three different categories:

- Dreamers
- Designers
- Implementers

This book is laid out to empower Imagineers like you independent of your Imagineering Type. But seeing yourself as an Imagineer is essential.

Which Imagineering Type do you believe you are predominately?

- Are you a Dreamer who can come up with and formulate brand-new ideas?
- Are you a Designer who can intuitively expand on an idea and figure out how to make it work?
- Are you an Implementer who can take a designed idea and bring it to life?

Dreamers are visionaries, but casting a dream is never enough. Dreamers need someone who can shape the idea. This is where Designers come into play. They are prototypical engineers.

Once a pattern is thought out, another class of Imagineers is needed with the skill and ability to bring the design to life. This is where Implementers come into play.

Seeing all three types of Imagineers in one person is possible but rare. Most people find themselves as one type more than the others.

Which is your predominant Imagineering Type?

You'll find a helpful tool to assess your Imagineering Type in the back of the book and even more tools at TheImagineBook.com, including how to evaluate your Imagination Quotient (ImQ).

Chapter Summary

In this chapter, we've explored what imagination looks like and how it might satisfy our desire to become something more.

Becoming something more is the first step of innovation – including personal innovation. When you are bettering yourself, you are making yourself more valuable to others. To help you on the innovation journey, there's a guiding formula that defines the essence of what it takes to invent the future.

The Future =
imagination x experimentation x evaluation x integrity

To invent the future starts with imagination. Your imagination can take you almost anywhere. This means we should be chasing a better version of ourselves. The person you are today is not the person you once were, nor the person you can be. Each day offers a step that gets you closer. Imagination is the launch point to better.

Einstein once said our imagination is more powerful than knowledge. He believed in it so strongly that it made me wonder, *maybe we should too.*

Over the last few decades, ever since that day I watched Phil Mahre chase a medal, I have quietly made it a mission to study the powers of imagination so that people like you and me can make more sense of this gift that we have.

We've identified the Imagineering Types: Dreamers, Designers, and Implementers. You are at least one of them; the question is, do you know which type?

- **Dreamers** formulate brand-new ideas. They think of something new or novel that can change the game.
- **Designers** expand on an idea and figure out how to make it work. They are strategists who identify a pattern or a plan.
- **Implementers** help execute the patterns and bring something new to life. They are builders, creators, and developers.

Those that chose to become something more are empowered by what they imagine. **What do you imagine?**

Recognize your imagination is a gift. This gift of imagination is what allows you and others to become *"Better. Stronger. Faster."*[8] But it starts with desire. **Without desire, we limit our ability to shape the future!**

This book is for anyone who wants to become something more.

❖ ❖ ❖

Additional tools and resources focused on
Becoming Something More are available at
theimaginebook.com/ch-1

---

[1] The Phil Mahre Interview was aired on ABC Sports during the 1980 Winter Olympics. I was unable to find an archive of the interview to transcribe his actual words. I have done my best to reflect the intent and impression that the interview had on me when I was 13 years old. I did reach out to Phil, and he confirmed the account. I share more of what he said in the concluding chapter.

[2] There are a number of siblings that have competed in the Olympic games. The only other 1–2 finishers in the same event that I could find besides Phil and Steve Mahre were two sisters, Canadian Olympic skiers Justine and Chloe Dufour–Lapointe in 2014. They competed in the women's moguls.

[3] Imagination is also defined as "a mental representation of things that are not immediately present to your senses." This definition is attributed to Scott Barry Kaufman, a psychologist at the University of Pennsylvania. Definition discovered in an article written by Mike Lewellyn, titled *Can Imagination Be Measured*, discover more at https://ideas.ted.com/can–a–test–measure–your–imagination, published August 12, 2014, last accessed June 28, 2022.

[4] The term multiverse was first introduced by the American philosopher Williams Janes in 1985. He used it to describe the *"confusing moral meaning of natural phenomena to other possible universes."* The recent Marvel superhero movies and other recent movies and TV shows going back as far as Star Trek have leveraged the concept of the multiverse to show the possibility of other different potential narratives of history. The imagination offers the only true verifiable depiction of a multiverse.

[5] Olivia Fox Cabane, *The Charisma Myth* (p. 24), Penguin Publishing Group.

[6] ESPN Films, *The Last Dance, Charting the rise of the 1990s Chicago Bulls, led by Michael Jordan*, NBA Entertainment, Madalay Sports Media (MSM), 2020, https://www.youtube.com/watch?v=If0aH6MbqOE, last accessed June 28, 2022.

[7] Garth Stein, *The Art of Racing in the Rain*, https://www.goodreads.com/quotes/259828, last accessed June 28, 2022.

[8] This line can be attributed to the opening narration in the iconic TV show, *The Six Million Dollar Man*.

2 – Equip Yourself

Have you ever noticed that your brain is wired for hope? In its default state, it wants to believe the future might offer something better. And one thing that triggers hope is the word *imagine*.

- Imagine one day ...
- Imagine being able to ...
- Imagine if you could ...
- Imagine what it will be like ...

IMAGINE is a power word. A trigger. A prompt to persevere. IMAGINE activates hope.

As Aristotle shares, *"hope is a waking dream,"* and sustained hope is what gives us confidence. You could see this clearly in the Mahre brothers, and if you go back in time, you might see this in two other brothers whose hope and imagination would change the world!

The Flight Brothers

History will tell you that the future they invented was man-machine flight; they conquered the impossible and changed the world. But success doesn't come without failure.

Multiple times the brothers, Orville and Wilbur, tried unsuccessfully. One low point was when they prepared their prototype glider for flight, but an unexpected gust of wind threw Orville twenty feet away. Once the wind died, they found their plane had been smashed to pieces. I can't help but imagine a back wheel spinning in a heap as they looked on with disappointment.

The Wright brothers photographed the wreckage right after it happened. It was as if they valued failure.[9] Then, with some help, they dragged the damaged airship back to camp, feeling defeated. They were devastated! Most people would have just given up. In fact, according to their written accounts, they talked about packing it up and heading home. However, **a**fter a short night's sleep, they realized they still had hope. They were still confident.

When your *why* is big enough, you find every reason not to quit.

Repairing the damaged plane took three days, but a pattern was built. Every attempt, whether successful or not, was evaluated by a lens of imagination. The question for them was three-fold:

- What do we hope to learn from this experiment – this test flight? Pass or fail?
- What do we hope to accomplish next time?
- What ultimately is the hope we want to achieve? What's our long–range desire?

Let's take a moment and understand what hope is again. Hope in this context reveals their desire. If hope wasn't a strategy for the Wright Brothers – or the Mahre Brothers – then I'm not sure what hope is.

Hope was the basis for their *why*. It motivated their imagination, propelled them to experimentation, and drew them to healthy evaluation. The key was to keep the end goal in mind. That's where we learn about Orville and Wilbur's sister Katharine. If it wasn't for Katharine Wright, you may not have heard of the Wright Brothers.

Katharine Wright

In my research for the book *Breaking Average*, I discovered that Katharine Wright was the one who would often keep Orville and Wilbur's hope alive. She was the younger sister, the only one with a college education, and she had an imagination that echoed that of her brothers. This would play a significant part in their success. Katherine was the one who would respond to every letter of discouragement from Orville and Wilbur and offer hope and encouragement. When an experiment went awry, she would either write them or visit them. She was the supporting voice – what today we call a life coach. That voice would reignite for them their desire. **The urge to quit fades away when a desire is made clear.**

Katharine Wright deserves as much credit as her older brothers in ushering in the age of aviation. After all, as best as I can tell, she was the first female aviator ever. Katharine learned to work the controls as she flew over the fields of France and helped her brothers show the world that what we imagine can be made possible. She also advocated for the rights of women to vote and equal pay. She inspired a state of hope.

Note: From this point forward, I will use the phrase "Wright Trio" to reference their story instead of Wright Brothers. I believe Katharine deserves as much credit as her famous brothers.

Why This is a Foundations Book?

Before diving any further, I want to clarify where this book is taking you. What you hold in your hands is a foundations book. This book is meant to help you no matter what your belief or background.

I call it a foundations book because it's centered on our common human physiology, not a competing theology. This book is based on how we are all built and wired as humans. In the research, I wanted to find and present elements of belief that were irrefutable no matter your faith, ideology, or religion.

The logic is simple. We all share the same wiring system regarding our brain's design including the processes we use to observe, orient, decide and act. These four states, referred to as the OODA Loop, are the behavioral guidance components of your imagination. Knowing our everyday makeup gives us the underpinning for achievement and fulfillment.

Regardless of your faith or conviction, you can leverage and use your imagination. **Imagination is common to all of us.**

If you happen to be a person of faith, the foundations laid out in this book will offer you greater clarity and confirmation of how your faith and imagination are knitted together. Imagination is a gift. And no matter what your belief, imagination is *"the principal tool from which all creativity and artistry comes."*[10]

I want to share two components to that tool that you'll need for this journey right out of the gates. One is based on your physiology (your brain), and the other is based on your psychology (your mind). These components include:

- The Reticular Activating System (RAS)
- The OODA Loop

The Reticular Activating System (RAS)

Let's face it, we all want things. We are wired and created with this desire. Our passions express our areas of interest that move us forward. It's what makes us unique. What's remarkable is how it all works in our brain.

When I was training for a 10K race a few years back, I made it my routine to listen to an audiobook to help maximize the time. The book I was wired into was Mark Batterson's *The Circle Maker*. One of the chapters late in the book stopped me dead in my tracks. I halted my run to bookmark the audio location. Up to that point, I had been enjoying the incredible story of Honi and how he transformed a drought-scourged nation through the power of imagination–led prayer.[11] Batterson was sharing other stories of powerful prayers that had come to pass – including some in his own life. It was mesmerizing. In the middle of a chapter focused on shaping our Life Goal List, Batterson dropped a nugget of knowledge that has forever changed my awareness.

He shared a bit on how we are wired physically, describing how our brainstems have a unique processor that sits between the spine and the brain called the Reticular Activating System – or RAS.[12] The RAS is represented by a cluster of nerve cells. These nerve cells work together to take in all the incoming stimuli and help figure out what should get our attention.

When we create goals, lists, or express earnest prayers, our RAS sets a trap that allows us to notice things that align with those goals, lists, and prayers. Our RAS is like a radar system on the hunt for meaningful tracks – both threats and opportunities. When we express the desires of our heart – it wires up the RAS and readies our brain to be on the lookout for the resources and experiences that support our desires.

How the RAS works

Imagine a scenario where you are in the market for a new vehicle, but you want something unique. It can't be gray, white, or black, so you choose dark blue. In addition, you want something with black alloy wheels. Something different.

The next day you drive by a car lot and happen to see a blue pickup truck that has black alloy wheels. It's perfect—one of a kind. Before you know it, you secure a loan and drive it off the lot.

The very next day, on the way to work, you notice several other trucks on the road a lot like yours. By week's end, you see blue pickups with black alloy wheels everywhere. Soon your friends and family notice them too.

Clearly, the world didn't magically have an influx of dark blue pickup trucks. What's changed is your acute awareness through your RAS. Your RAS is alerting you. It's an arousal system that also gets you going in the morning. It is set by marking beliefs and wants with mental visual pattern matching. It scans and looks to prompt you when something related pops up. The RAS is like an internal smartphone alerting you with notifications.

As another example, if you've ever played the game *I Spy with My Little Eye,* you would have activated your RAS – at least for a short period. You'll have noticed that things with different colors magically come into your awareness. But it doesn't have to be colors. It could be shapes like squares or triangles. Or it can be objects of nature like trees and water.

Next time you play the game, watch and see how your RAS fires up.

The Two Sides of the RAS

That same RAS that alerts you of related opportunities that map to a desire is also looking to confirm your fears, doubts, and myths. The RAS is a sensor system that is a sentry for your imagination. The sensor looks for related signs and signals to validate a desire or verify a doubt. The RAS triggers both positive thoughts and negative thoughts. Therefore, depending on how it's been set up, it can work for your betterment or determent.

The RAS is also a pre-processor for many things. It controls your sleep, waking, response to fear, and more. It works as a signal – like a traffic light – prompting you along the way. But do you know who programs your RAS?

Here's a hint, it's the person that looks back at you in the mirror.

There's even more science behind the RAS, including how it activates the cerebral cortex with bursts of energy and taps into other parts of the brain, like the thalamus. But here's what you should know. Your RAS is customized by you and for you. It serves you and you alone. It is what activates your response and your awareness. It behaves like a genie – not the kind that grants a wish – but it makes you situationally aware of the opportunities you are looking for. You want your RAS tuned right and to be ready.

How to Wire Your Desire

The RAS loves lists. Lists done right identify your goals and aspirations and can drive you to success. If you are a person of faith, this is where prayer fits in too. Without getting theological, prayer is expressing the desires of your heart. That's it, plain and simple. The challenge for you and me is getting clear on what we desire. When trying to get clear on what you want to see realized, ask this question:

What do I desire?

In the *Circle Maker*, Batterson reveals how the RAS system works in conjunction with lists and prayers. Throughout the world, prayer is one of the most common practices to identify a goal and activate the RAS. The practice of praying is good for your brain. Batterson shares why.

> *"The brain is a goal-seeking organism. Setting a goal creates structural tension in your brain, which will seek to close the gap between where you are and where you want to be, who you are and whom you want to become... If you don't set goals, your mind will become stagnant."[13]*

By identifying your desires – your goals – your prayers – you are pre-setting the RAS to be acutely aware of the opportunities, decisions, and experiences that will help you achieve a goal. In other words, it allows you to see something into being.

If you are a person of faith, recognize that when you earnestly pray, you aren't just mailing a letter to the Creator of the universe with something you wish for and want. You're also preparing your mind to discover the answer to that opportunity. They go together. Batterson adds, *"The greatest tragedy in life is that some prayers go unanswered because they go unasked."*

If you don't ever ask, you may never get it – so go ahead and ask. I recommend a journal – capture your heart's desire on paper. This way, you have an instrument you can use to revisit your goals, lists, desires, and prayers. You can see how those hopes and prayers are realized as part of your RAS.

What's Your Moore's Law?

Moore's Law is one of my favorite examples of how we can influence the RAS and shape the future. Gordon Moore, a pioneer in the computing industry, predicted the future growth of the microprocessor and its impact in a white paper he wrote in 1965. It changed the game!

His groundbreaking paper titled *The Future of Integrated Electronics* created an expectation that set the RAS for all stakeholders in the tech industry. It created a new awareness of what could be. Moore predicted the doubling of transistors on a microprocessor would happen every one to two years. Initially, some scoffed and laughed at this, but others begin to wonder and believe, *"well, why not?"*

Transistors are switches, that regulate the flow of information. The more the transistors the more information can be processed.

Moore's Law proved to be prophetic. A comparison of Moore's prediction against the actual evolution of the microprocessor stack year by year is mind-blowing. He was on the money.

Knowing how many transistors a microprocessor stack would contain offered a competitive advantage for anyone in the business. *Why?* Because *you know the future*!

Moore himself admitted that fathoming the impact of this before his observation was beyond belief.[14] However, once your RAS gets set, the mind looks to prove it possible. For almost 60 years, Moore's Law has demonstrated that **expectation creates anticipation.** Therefore, we should be clear on our expectations.

Incidentally, did you know that one neuron within the human brain is approximately equivalent to a thousand transistors of a microprocessor stack? Knowing that the average human brain has 86 billion neurons, using Moore's Law we can foresee that by the year 2042 a multicore microprocessor stack will have enough transistors to be functionally equivalent to the processing power of the human brain.

The lesson to learn is simple. By setting clear expectations, we set our RAS and become compelled to achieve those expectations. Clearly, Moore's Law speaks to the value of casting a vision. A vision is vital! Your brain is wired for it. The question for any leadership team is intriguing:

What Moore's Law-type vision
do you have for those you lead?

The follow-on question challenges us to optimize our RAS:

How do we leverage our imagination to bring this to life?

This is where we need load an operating system for the hardware of our brain to work at its best. This reflects the same type of mental model that allowed Gordon Moore to predict the future.

The OODA Loop

Less than 50 years after the Wright Trio brought aviation to the world, Colonel John Boyd, a United States Air Force Pilot, mapped out a powerful yet simple tool known as the OODA Loop.[15]

OODA stands for Observe, Orient, Decide, and Act. It represents a repeatable decision process for how we can best react and respond to events. While it was designed for aviators and military strategists, it has proven beneficial in other domains like law enforcement, litigation, cyberwarfare, business negotiation, and more.

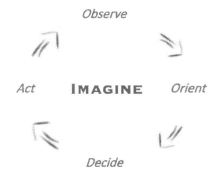

Figure 1 – The OODA Loop

The OODA Loop is a powerful tool to help you leverage your imagination. It offers a process model not unlike what the Mahre brothers used to master the art of skiing, or the Wright Trio used to birth the aviation of flight. The OODA Loop is designed to help you "get inside" and understand opportunities, perspectives, and decisions. It gives you a framework to leverage your imagination.

We will use the OODA Loop throughout this book, but here's the essence of the process:

- **OBSERVE** – What is the situation? What is going on?
- **ORIENT** – What are the options? How do they create impact?
- **DECIDE** – What course of action is best?
- **ACT** – Make the move!

The Kayak Scenario

A quick way to understand the OODA Loop is to picture yourself in a kayak on a body of water.

The Observe part is about identifying where you are presently at. What are the conditions of the water? What are the other elements surrounding you? This is about information gathering and awareness of the environment. Here we are sharpening the RAS to be more conscious without emotional attachment.

The Orient part is about interpreting the information and exploring your options. What are the routes available, and what are the ones you should avoid? This is about evaluating scenarios, deconstructing your information to what's important, and seeing your viable choices. Here we are bridging our RAS with other parts of our brain, plus those around us. I call this *perspective thinking*.

The Decide part is evaluating the best course of action. When you are in a kayak, consider the routes and then pick a path. *What choice will you make?* This is about evaluating the best options based on the information you've observed and oriented, then selecting.

The Act part is executing the decision. You are making the kayak move based on your choices seeking to align with your decided course. This is the phase that brings your imagination to life. It's where intention and action come together. This is an important step that many unintentionally fail to pursue.

There is an old riddle that helps put into perspective the importance of this final phase. Imagine five frogs sitting on a log, and four decide to jump off. How many frogs do you think are left?

The answer is that all the frogs are left. Just because four decided to jump doesn't mean that they did. Always take action – but look before you leap.

The OODA Loop is a constantly repeating pattern that gives your imagination a fresh foothold every time. Each decision might expose other nested OODA Loops.

For example, let's say you are about to encounter some river rapids and choose a line between two jutting rocks that look like the best and fastest path. After you decide and act, you encounter an unforeseen obstacle like a hidden log, where you immediately OODA your way through that challenge. In this example, you may recognize that the best choice is to pull hard to the right to clear the log and still achieve the original goal.

The Water–Paddle Metaphor

The kayak scenario triggers another word picture that helps us better understand the powers of imagination.

Think of imagination as water. It quenches your thirst, refreshes your spirit, and opens your mind. It's renewing. But imagination doesn't just represent the water you drink; it also symbolizes the water you explore.

In this boat called life, your imagination is the water beyond the present. It's the vast-open lake, ocean, or river in front of you. It offers you a place to explore and pursue your desires. Your imagination portrays your aspirations, and it works with your RAS. The question is, *how will you move in this water?*

It turns out the paddle to move you is hope. Remember that your RAS is looking for things you are hoping for. But it might also be looking for something to confirm your doubts too. We need to be careful with the thoughts we set in our RAS. Doubt without hope can paralyze and limit you.

False hope might be just as dangerous. For instance, whenever you put a deadline on hope, you introduce the opportunity for doubt to take over. What if the date deadline passes by? That's when hope often turns to doubt. But real hope that identifies the possible can take you places. That's the space you want to imagine.

Interestingly, as metaphors go, the Bible identifies hope as an anchor. This is because an anchor gives you a feeling of safety amid a storm, but I don't think of hope as just an anchor only for storms; I think of hope as a paddle good for action. While it is undoubtedly helpful to buffer a storm, an anchor will keep you from moving if you never pull it up. It can hold you back. Worse, it might make you think you are always in a storm. On the other hand, a paddle gives you a tool to move you forward and get you out of the storm before it starts. Never lose your paddle. Leverage hope.

With a paddle, you can steer, propel, maneuver and pivot. Even when it feels like you are facing troubled waters, the hope founded in belief is what leads you someplace better.

The Star Trek Analogy

Growing up, one of the things my dad and I enjoyed watching together was reruns of the classic show *Star Trek*. As I think of the OODA Loop, my mind is transported to the bridge of the starship Enterprise. Captain Kirk, Spock, Uhuru, Scotty, Bones, Chekov, and Sulu are in front of us. These were the show's main characters, and my dad loved how Captain Kirk often involved the whole team in his decisions and actions.

You can learn a lot about the OODA Loop by evaluating the roles and behaviors of these main characters.

Spock and Uhura were always on the watch, listening and looking for information to share with the captain and the crew. They personified the Observe Phase of the OODA Loop. Both characters were focused on information gathering.

Great leaders orient before making decisions. Think of how Captain Kirk would lean on Bones or Spock to support the Orient Phase. Bones, as the Doctor, would typically have an empathetic sense of the options and impact on others. He was more on the emotional side of the orientation spectrum. In comparison, Spock would typically use a systematic evaluation of the options. He was more on the logical end of the orientation spectrum.

Next, Captain Kirk would consider those inputs in his decision. He knew the responsibility was upon him to decide what to do. You might also say the same for Captain Picard in The Next Generation series. Both captains knew their decisions would mean life or death, so they needed to be armed with the information gathered from the Observe and Orient Phases. Otherwise, they were more likely to make a fatal decision.

Once Captain Kirk decided, the action was incumbent upon those he commanded. In the case of the original series of *Star Trek*, it might be his engineer Scotty, his helmsmen Sulu, or his navigator Chekov. Once again, the captain relies on others to execute the orders.

Next time you watch an episode of *Star Trek*, look to see if you can spot an example of the OODA Loop.

Chapter Summary

A strong imagination is exhibited by focused attention. In the bestselling book, *The Seven Habits of Highly Effective People,* author Stephen Covey lays out a core principle that helps activate our imagination and invent the future. His advice is to *"begin with the end in mind."*[16]

This chapter introduces some core tools to equip you for the task and invent the future. Your RAS sits ready, it just needs to be primed, and the OODA Loop offers you a strategy you can use in collaboration with others. What's left is to understand the powers of the imagination.

What's essential about the RAS and the OODA Loop is that they activate your imagination. When both systems are in play, you look for viable, compelling scenarios and successful outcomes. The RAS and OODA help you invent the future!

Consider it this way; your imagination is ready to play a movie trailer of what life can be. The question is, what kind of life trailer will you choose to see?

We also shared how imagination is like water offering you a place to navigate and explore, and hope is the paddle that will get you there. The key is to keep paddling. It requires all four repeated strokes: Observe. Orient. Decide. Act. Don't ever stop in the middle.

Finally, don't be the frog that decided to jump but still sits on the log. Visualize yourself progressing to the other side of the pond despite the fear and doubt. You are more equipped for the journey than you realize. To take the next step, remind yourself that success favors the bold.

❖ ❖ ❖

Additional tools and resources focused on
Equipping Yourself for the Journey are available at
theimaginebook.com/ch-2

---

[9] David McCullough, *The Wright Brothers* (pp. 49–50), Simon & Schuster.

[10] The quote is attributed to author Erwin McManus.

[11] Wikipedia, *Honi HaMe'agel*, https://en.wikipedia.org/wiki/Honi_HaMe%27agel, last accessed June 28, 2022.

[12] Edgar Garcia–Rill, *Waking and the Reticular Activating System in Health and Disease*, (pp. 1–16), Academic Press, 2015, https://doi.org/10.1016/B978–0–12–801385–4.00001–X, last accessed June 28, 2022.

[13] Mark Batterson, *The Circle Maker* (p. 178), Zondervan.

[14] Gordon Moore, *The Future of Integrated Electronics*. Fairchild Semiconductor internal publication, 1964.

[15] Robert Coram, *Boyd: The Fighter Pilot Who Changed the Art of War* (p. 327), Hachette Book Group.

[16] Stephen R. Covey, *The 7 Habits of Highly Effective People*: Powerful Lessons in Personal Change (p. 102), Rosetta Books.

OBSERVE

See the Path

PHASE ONE – OBSERVE

"There is some good in this world,
and it's worth fighting for."

—J.R.R. Tolkien

Now that we are past Ground Zero, we are ready for departure using the OODA Loop as our plan. The first phase is to OBSERVE, which is about seeing the path – it's about awareness.

When it comes to your imagination, this may be the phase most often missed, misunderstood, and mistreated. I've learned first-hand that you don't want to neglect this phase. Slacking off in this area will hamper you – especially if you are a leader. It can be the difference between seeing a red light and a green light – not just literally but figuratively.

I've learned from experience that if you don't develop and maintain the strength of observation – or awareness, it's nearly impossible to possess a well-tuned imagination. **Observation turns ignorance into insight; it transforms apathy into empathy.** Insight and empathy are critical to your success. They prime the pump for your imagination. You can't have insight or empathy without observed imagination.

We learn from best-selling author James Clear that *"the process of behavior change always starts with awareness."*[17] His point is simple: if you don't take the time to observe and be aware, then you can't make the necessary change needed to increase your success. Without observation, we limit ourselves. Clear adds that *"awareness comes before desire."* So, if you are trying to "up" your game as an Imagineer, and you know *desire* is an essential component of imagination, then spend some time in the pre-think to get it right.

The question to ask is practical:

What do I see?

Observation skills are nurtured over time. Rarely is someone naturally born with it. You must work at it constantly. It requires intentional listening, learning, asking questions, and reflecting. In this section, we'll explore some helpful tools to help you with observation.

The Observe Phase is about taking things in without initial judgment or presumption. Observation is vital for situational awareness. You step forward with your imagination only once you take in the data.

In this section, we're going to explore three behaviors that every leader can strive for to increase their Observation prowess:

- Trace Your Path with the Power of Patterns
- Hunt Down Misconceptions with the Power of Curiosity
- Evaluate The Gains with the Power of Assessment

Let's explore these three behaviors further.

---

[17] James Clear, *Atomic Habits* (p. 67), Penguin Publishing Group.

3 – TRACE YOUR PATH
Understanding the Power of Patterns

*"The greatest virtues are those which are
most useful to other persons."*

—Aristotle

History books are packed with evidence of how imagination has changed the world. But did you know you can look back at your own life to trace the path?

- Do you remember learning how to drive?
- Do you remember that impossible project that you somehow got through?
- What about that first trip on an airplane?
- Did you ever learn to ride a bike or ski?
- Do you remember asking that special someone out on a date?
- What about the first time jumping through a big wave at the ocean or water park?
- How about landing that first big job out of school?

Guess what was in play for each of those experiences?

If you guessed imagination, you get the gold star. You guessed right. But think about how you had to get through a progression of steps to realize any of those experiences. Can you see how maybe you used the OODA Loop, even though you may not have known what it was?

Observe. Orient. Decide. Act. The first phase of Observe is critical; it's where you begin to discover the Power of Patterns.

French Revelation

A few years back, I took a business trip to Toulouse, France, which was part of the world I had never been to. When I arrived, I felt totally out of my element. The main reason was that I could barely speak the language. After a few hours of exploring the beautiful streets of Toulouse, my stomach started speaking its own language. I was hungry and desperately needed some food.

What appeared to be a grocery store was just a few hundred yards away, so I ducked in to see what I could grab. When I walked in, it felt familiar, yet I still felt like a foreigner. All the food was labeled and covered so it was hard to be certain of what things were.

I had a craving for a sandwich, so I cased the deli meat section. Using the Power of Patterns, I spotted something that looked like ham in a U.S. grocery store. The only difference was it wasn't labeled "ham"; it was labeled "jambon". Immediately I cataloged the term, committing it to memory, knowing it might help me later. I then found a familiar-looking snack labeled with the word "maïs". I guessed that they were corn chips. It didn't take long for me to fill a small handbasket with some everyday food items, even though the labels were utterly foreign.

The next step was to navigate the checkout. Not speaking the language was going to be a tricky thing. To adapt, I focused on noticing the observable behavioral patterns of those in the store. I watched how customers made their purchases. I observed the interaction with the cashier. I noticed that the cashier always seemed to ask each shopper a question right before the sale was final. The customer would either shake their head with the universal gesture of *"yes"* and offer something out of their purse or wallet, or they would shake their head *"no"*. I quickly analyzed the pattern; I realized the cashier was asking for a shopping store rewards card, which of course, I did not have.

The cashier also appeared to ask how they wanted their goods bagged. Plastic or paper? I noticed that the typical response for plastic bags was *"sacs plastique"*. Without being able to speak much of the language, other than a friendly *"bonjour"* and a few other words like *"merci"*, I was able to purchase groceries like a local. Because of that experience, my confidence grew, and I began using the Power of Patterns everywhere I went. It became a helpful tool in a foreign land. Every pattern I rehearsed and repeated activated my imagination and trained me how to adapt, even in a foreign country.

The Power of Patterns

Your brain learns quickly by observing patterns. This is true when you are young, but it's also true as you get older. For example, consider how someone might take in a YouTube video to see how something is accomplished. When our brain recognizes a pattern, we quickly learn and can try to mimic and reproduce it.

The present-day use of the term *pattern* is often attributed to architect Christopher Alexander. He reflected on the Power of Patterns in the architectural design and construction of homes, buildings, and gardens.

However, it may have been John Boyd himself, the father of the OODA Loop who helped influenced its use. He emphasized the term patterns with his landmark report titled *Patterns of Conflict*, which he orally presented in 1976 and then formally published in 1985. Boyd's presentation theorized about the mental and moral aspects of human behavior in war using the idea of patterns.[18]

Boyd used the term *patterns* to capture warfighting experiences and describe a theory of tactics and expected behavior in battle. Similarly, Alexander used the term *patterns* to capture and categorize reusable designs of structures and environments. Both these Imagineers had stumbled onto something revolutionary.

Alexander's landmark book on this topic, published in 1977, was titled *A Pattern Language*. He shares this perspective, "*Each pattern describes a problem which occurs over and over again in our environment, and then describes the core of the solution to that problem, in such a way that you can use this solution a million times over...*"[19]

Decades later, others began to see the value of Alexander's observation in their fields of interest. For instance, in 1994, experts in the software industry published a landmark book called *Design Patterns*. This revolutionized the software engineering industry. In sports, the top players, such as hitters in baseball and quarterbacks in football, use pattern matching to recognize the type of pitch coming or how a defense will defend the pass or the run. In a split second, these top athletes make calculated decisions through the Power of Patterns early in the process.[20]

Author and software pioneer Martin Fowler offers a clear pattern definition for each of us. He describes a pattern as *"an idea that has been useful in one practical context and will probably be useful in others."*[21]

When it comes to repeating success, finding achievement, or persevering, there's no better mindset than to begin to look for patterns. For example, any time you enter a new culture, especially if you visit a country like France, the best way to fit in is to look for patterns and then adapt to those patterns.

Tony Robbins encourages us to look for these patterns in others. He challenges us with this thought. *"Success leaves clues. Go figure out what someone who was successful did, and model it. Improve it. But learn their steps. They have knowledge."* He's talking about curating patterns.

Neuroplasticity – *How the Brain Rewires*

The brain is elastic. It's able to change – sometimes quickly.[22] When we experience something new, like visiting a foreign country, our brain grabs a bunch of neurons and starts to shape new neural pathways. The awkward first experience and encounter you might have in a new part of the world or trying something new eventually becomes easier with repetition. As things are repeated, we become more comfortable.

The hack to expedite the discomfort of new surroundings is to utilize your imagination with the Power of Patterns right out of the gates. By leveraging your imagination in the Observe Phase, you expedite the brain's neuroplasticity. You can learn by imagining yourself in the shoes of others as you watch them. Observation sets you up for mimicry, and mimicry shapes new behaviors, which in turn generates new beliefs.

Typically, we think beliefs drive behaviors. This is true maybe 80% of the time, but **sometimes behaviors drive beliefs**. For instance, think about something you once couldn't do but tried to do anyhow. For me, it was learning to jump off the diving board into the deep end. At first, I didn't believe I could. But my brother and friends encouraged me to try it and assured me they would be there to help me if anything went wrong. Despite my lack of belief in myself, I jumped into the deep end.

Why?

In my case, it was because of peer pressure. I didn't want to be the chicken brother. The good news is that it wasn't long before I was playing Marco Polo with my brother's friends in the deep end. The peer pressure that provoked my behavior was replaced with a new belief!

It turns out that you don't always need to have belief before you can do something. **New behavior can lead to a new belief.** The truth is that belief and behavior live on a two-way street, not a one-way street. While most times belief drives behavior, sometimes behavior drives belief. You don't always need belief first; belief can come after an awkward behavior gets repeated.

What's happening here is that despite a lack of belief, your imagination guides your steps – helping you find and follow the patterns. Your imagination paints enough of a picture for you to give it a go. The thing to remember is that you need imagination as much as you need water or air. When you are in an environment that's unfamiliar – look for familiar patterns, look for patterns that can lead you to a new belief.

Patterns Are the Way

Patterns often influence us more than people. The key for Imagineers is to introduce, shape, and demonstrate patterns. In this regard, an Imagineer is accomplishing one of three things:

(1) They are creating new patterns that may have never existed before. Recall that these Imagineers are called Dreamers. Dreamers seed new thoughts into our awareness.

(2) They are evolving and shaping patterns into a process or approach. These Imagineers are called Designers. Designers shape a new thought into a structure that others can follow.

(3) They are reusing existing patterns to support new instantiations. These Imagineers are called Implementers. Implementers show how a pattern can bring new things to life. They like to create.

As you can see, patterns play a vital role for each of the three types of Imagineers: Dreamers, Designers, and Implementers. Each of us is one or more of these three types of Imagineers. We are creating, evolving, or reusing patterns.

Chapter Summary

This chapter has focused on the Power of Patterns. A pattern is helpful because it describes the core of a solution to a common problem. By getting a handle on ways that work, you learn to better leverage your imagination and invent the future. That's the Power of Patterns.

Pattern discovery starts with tracing the path. Socrates and other philosophers like to use the term *"know thyself."* By understanding your behavior, you gain a better understanding of your brain. Likewise, by understanding your brain, you gain a better understanding of who you can be.

This pursuit of knowing ourselves – knowing who we are, how we work best, and the journey that we are on – can make all the difference. This component of observation helps transform your thinking. It's what neuroplasticity is all about.

Imagine yourself becoming even more proficient with the Power of Patterns. See yourself shaping new futures as you look for best practices and new methods, mold them into patterns, and then put them into play. If it helps, trace your own path; look at how patterns have already shaped you.

What new patterns will you discover?

◆ ◆ ◆

Additional tools and resources focused on
Tracing the Path are available at
theimaginebook.com/ch-3

---

[18] John Boyd, *Patterns of Conflict*, first was introduced in 1975, orally. The written report is dated December 1986, http://www.ausairpower.net/JRB/poc.pdf, last accessed June 28, 2022.

[19] Christopher Alexander, *A Pattern Language, 1977.*

[20] *Patterns of success: sports, language, and life*, https://randombrandles.medium.com/patterns-of-success-sports-language-and-life-b76912f235b6, last accessed June 28, 2022.

[21] Fowler, *Analysis Patterns: Reusable Object Models*, Addison-Wesley.

[22] World Science Festival, *The Nuts and Bolts of Better Brains: Harnessing the Power of Neuroplasticity*, https://www.youtube.com/watch?v=59ODYOaUbX4, last accessed June 28, 2022.

4 – HUNT DOWN MISCONCEPTIONS

Understanding the Power of Curiosity

"Curiosity keeps leading us down new paths."

—Walt Disney

Does your imagination lift you or limit you?

Before you answer, recognize the tug of war in your mind between hope and doubt, and faith and fear.

Our imagination can be easily misguided. When it's off-kilter, we might leap to assumptions or unintentionally make things up about the past, present, or future. This will fool you and might even confuse those around you. Rather than seeing things for what they are or can be, you might be seeing things for what they are not or believe never will be.

The bottom line is this. **Your imagination will lift you or limit you.** If it's off by just a degree or two, your imagination can twist the truth and convince you of something different than what's real. It can be simple, like misreading a situation, misunderstanding a person, time-slicing a memory, or believing a subtle lie.[23]

When it's not aligned right, your imagination will mislead you, confuse you, and even deceive you. Furthermore, a misaligned imagination can cause more significant struggles like low self-esteem, attention deficit, increased anxiety, anger, mistrust, paranoia, post-traumatic stress, or even depression. Having the proper awareness, boundaries, and accountability fosters an aligned imagination.

The good news is there is a way through it, but there are two important things we need to recognize and deal with first:

- Imagination Blindsight
- Watch Out for the Myths

Imagination Blindsight – *How Our Brains Get Confused*

Our imagination likes to fill in the narrative. It wants to craft a story to connect the dots, especially when some of the data is missing or misaligned. Left to its own devices, imagination will fill a lack of knowledge or echo a memory marker with such vivid information that we think it's real, and the rest of the brain can't prove it otherwise. This is something called Imagination Blindsight.

There are three examples of Imagination Blindsight I want to share. The first is a personal experience. The second is a lesson from the iconic movie Star Wars. And the third is the story of former NBC News Anchor Brian Williams. These stories show us that none of us are immune to Imagination Blindsight. It reveals to us the dark side of imagination and the myths that can trap us.

"The Light Was Green"

A few years ago, I was in a car accident that shook me up pretty good. I was sitting at a red light, ready to cross an intersection I face daily. When the light triggered green, I dashed across the highway, knowing that the light would not stay green for long. The only problem was that one other car was still going northbound through the intersection. Despite doing my best to stop, my car was t-boned at the right front fender. This caused my vehicle to violently spin in nearly a full circle. All the airbags were deployed.

Fortunately, I would walk away with no significant injuries other than a few bruises and a burned arm from the airbag. However, my car, which I just recently purchased, was totaled. Despite me being a bit dazed, I was sure of one thing. The other driver had run a red.

Within minutes a state trooper arrived; an hour later, after my ambulance ride to the ER, the state trooper appeared at the hospital and issued me a traffic ticket with a charge of "failure to yield."

I was bewildered. *"Officer, my light was green."* He nodded, hearing my plea but responded. *"Listen, all I have to go on is the information offered by eyewitnesses. And two of them stated that – from their perspective – they saw that the light was still green for the car that hit you."* He proceeded to tell me that I had every right to fight it in court.

The next day, after a sleepless night continually replaying the accident in my mind over and over, I went to the scene of the accident and strategized how I would fight the ticket.

The following Monday, I called a lawyer. Three months later, we showed up at court, and the state trooper was in the lobby waiting for us. He asked if he could talk to my lawyer and me before going into the courtroom. Hoping that he was going to apologize and possibly drop the charge, he instead pulled a ruggedized laptop out of a bag and said, *"I was recently given evidence that you may want to watch before we are in front of the judge."* He then asked, *"Are you open to watching it beforehand?"*

I looked at my lawyer, who whispered to me, *"We have nothing to lose; let's see it."* I agreed.

The officer then remarked that one of the witnesses had a dashboard camera that caught the entire accident on video. He paused, *"when you see this video, I anticipate that you might want to change your plea."* Then he added, *"I want to give you the opportunity to see some incriminating evidence I have before we meet with the judge."*

Honestly, that moment felt like I was in a dream state. It didn't seem real. I remember nodding my head and outwardly saying, *"I'd be eager to see it!"* But part of me was in disbelief that such data could even exist. I remember thinking, *"Why am I just hearing about this now?"* But I kept that thought to myself.

The officer then started the video on the laptop. Right before my eyes, as if I was watching a reality TV show, I saw a white 2016 Honda Civic sport coupe – with me driving it – quickly leaving the intersection from a stopped position, going left to right in an easterly direction. Less than two seconds later, my car was hit by a northbound vehicle. My car spun almost in a complete circle before it stopped amidst the flying debris.

While staring at the scene's frame immediately when I was hit, the dashboard camera revealed something startling. The light for the northbound car that collided with me was still green. I was aghast. That meant only one thing. I had jumped the light. I ran a red!

From the day of the accident until that moment, I truly believed that my light had turned green, but now, after seeing the video, my perspective instantly changed. I realized my imagination had fooled me. My mind made things up.

Five minutes later, I entered the courtroom and pleaded guilty to a traffic charge of "failure to yield" and then paid the fine. In hindsight, I am thankful for that dashboard camera view and the officer willing to show it to me. I would rather know the truth than live believing a made-up story for the rest of my life. If I had contested the charge and were found guilty, I would have likely lived with an *"I was wronged"* grudge and chip on my shoulder. I'm so thankful for that dashboard video. The truth, as hard as it was, set me free.

That experience taught me just how powerful our imagination can trip us up. I would find out later that the highway department changed the light cycle for the intersection a few days before my accident. That made me realize another truth; we need to stay watchful – otherwise, our Subconscious Mind will automatically take over. If we're not careful, imagination can betray us. We need to be in the ready state of observation.

"The World's Against Me!"

The revelation of my misperception of the light made me think about the character Anakin Skywalker from the infamous *Star Wars* saga. While Anakin Skywalker is a work of fiction, there's something we can learn from his story that portrays how blindsight can sometimes happen.

As a young Jedi, Anakin would grow discontent with the Jedi order. He didn't always like the rules. Partially, that was because he had a love interest in Padme, which was not in the keeping of the Jedi way. Also, he wanted more acceptance and appreciation for who he was from the Jedi Council, especially from the likes of Yoda and Obi-Wan. He often felt ignored by them. Subconsciously looking for empathy, Anakin befriends one of the more influential leaders of the day in Chancellor Palpatine.

Now Palpatine is a nasty dude. He seizes on Anakin's weak state by offering some of the affirmation and approval that young Skywalker craves. Those seeds of relationship trust transition into seeds of Jedi doubt. Slowly, Palpatine leads Anakin down a different path to the Dark Side. Anakin begins to see the world very much different than his Jedi friends. His imagination deceives him, and he begins to see most people as against him and his *cause*. Except for Palpatine, who has now become a father figure to him.

In one of the critical scenes, before Anakin takes on the infamous form of Darth Vader, Anakin is enraged that Padme and his mentor Obi-Wan are seemingly working together to betray him. However, the truth was they were trying to save him, not betray him. Anakin's RAS is off track; he sees it differently. Because of that, Anakin casts a Force chokehold on Padme, knocking her unconscious. He then engages with Obi-Wan in a duel almost to the death. This causes Anakin to lose his legs and nearly lose his life.

Like a page out of Frankenstein, Palpatine saves Anakin, bringing him to life in the form of Darth Vader. With his imagination now even more misguided but still intact, Vader carries on a mission to eradicate the Jedi and anyone who stands in the way of the Empire.

Almost two decades pass without Vader ever realizing that just before she died, Padme had secretly given birth to two children he had fathered. When Vader realizes that Padme bore a child, he lashes out in anger, tearing up the starship he is commanding. However, he only learns the identity of one child, Luke. Vader sets out on a mission to persuade Luke to join him, to be part of the Dark Side.

The battles between Luke and Vader are epic. When Luke learns that Vader is his father, he is in shock. In one of the final battles, Vader senses Luke's mind and realizes that Luke also has a sister – Princess Leia. Realizing the error of his imagination – that Leia was his daughter – Vader turns on Palpatine and renounces the Dark Side.

With new awareness and near death, he turns to Luke, no longer as Darth Vader but now once again as Anakin Skywalker. He makes one last request. *"Luke, help me take this mask off."* He adds, *"Let me look on you with my own eyes."*

Luke argues back, *"I won't leave you here. I've got to save you!"*

Anakin responds, *"You already have, Luke. You were right. You were right about me... Tell your sister... you were right..."*

Do you want to know what Luke was right about?

Despite the doubt of others, Luke held onto the belief that there was still good in his father and that he could be redeemed and brought back to the light. In that scene, we see that Anakin's imagination has been reset. When the mask comes off, he sees the truth and is no longer Vader. As for Luke, the fruits of his imagination and determination are realized. Father and son are reunited.

Think of the Force in the epic series of *Star Wars* as a metaphor for your imagination. Like the Force, our imagination is in a constant battle, and there are two sides to the conflict: a light side and a dark side. The light side seeks order, awareness, connection, and peace. The dark side seeks control, position, pleasure, and power.

Each of us needs to take an honest look at our biases, prejudices, and misperceptions. When dealing with the potential dark side pulls, ask yourself:

What am I doing to ensure I see what others see?

Asking this question will help ensure you haven't put on a Vader-like mask and are neglecting the truth. We all have blindsight. But look for ways to see what you might be missing.

"I Got Shot Down by an RPG"

In 2013, NBC News Anchor Brian Williams appeared on the David Letterman Show. He recounted a mesmerizing story of him getting shot down as a passenger on a helicopter ten years earlier. Williams was on assignment, covering the war being fought in Iraq. He was embedded with a U.S. Army battalion equipped with four Chinook helicopters. As they headed north through the country, their helicopters began to take on enemy fire. He described how two of the helicopters, including the one he was on, got hit. And all four birds were forced to land in the middle of a desert.

Watching the Letterman Show that night was Lance Reynolds, the Army specialist of the helicopter that went down. As Williams recounted the dramatic story on late-night television, Lance recalled a different memory. He quickly jumped on the NBC News Facebook page and posted a rebuttal.

"Sorry, Dude, I don't remember you being on my aircraft. I do remember you walking up about an hour after we had landed to ask me what had happened."

Within days, Williams's story was discovered to be partially fabricated, yet Williams never knew at the time that he was lying. His imagination – and his ego – got the best of him. Williams would be suspended by NBC News for six months for misrepresenting the *"events which occurred while he was covering the Iraq War in 2003."* He would eventually return as a newsman but was demoted to fill other duties at MSNBC.

Malcolm Gladwell shares a great podcast reflecting this story. He shows how Williams' story morphed over time; how it subtly changed and got richer each time it was shared. Our memories and imagination can easily misinform and redirect the narrative we tell ourselves and others – especially as it relates to flash event memories.

In reflection, Williams spent some time trying to figure out why he occasionally embellished stories of his work in the field. He concluded, *"Looking back, it had to have been ego that made me think I had to be sharper, funnier, quicker than anybody else, put myself closer to the action, having been at the action at the beginning."*

Hmm. Ego. Imagination. Memories. They all seem to be at play. Brian Williams never intended to lie, yet he did. The question to ask is, how do we keep ourselves from being deceived by the dark side and seeing the light as green when it really is red? Or that everyone's against us when they are really for us? Or that the events that we remember, and recount are not accurate or true?

It turns out that our imagination, which is the amplitude of the mind, needs a guidance system like the OODA Loop. Otherwise, our imagination wanders.[24] We need our RAS to be in good alignment, or we might fall prey to the dark side of imagination.

The Dark Side

Our imagination paints a path that we can navigate. However, these stories compel us to never forget about the dark side of our imagination. In the reimagined words of the great philosopher Huey Lewis, *"Imagination is a powerful thing. It can make one man weak, make another man sing."*[25] It's so true.

- How often do we create false narratives and see and believe wrong stories?
- How often does our imagination paint a story, embellish a truth, or change the message?
- How often does our imagination take us to the shadows of doubt and discouragement?

Our imagination can literally make us weak and delirious. It can foster fear and trepidation. It can amplify doubt and scare you from acting and moving forward. Worst of all, it can make you want to drop anchor and not paddle.

But when it's properly aligned, your imagination can make you strong and resilient. **Imagination can take you almost anywhere.** However, the one thing to watch out for is the impostor that loiters in the recess of your mind.

Impostor Syndrome

A Georgia State University study in 1978 discovered that over 70 percent of the population experience something called *impostor syndrome.*[26]

Imposter syndrome is simply self-doubt. It is believing that you lack the ability that other people think you have and that you will be found out as a fraud.

Self-doubt at this level clearly shows an imagination off the rails. We know imposter syndrome is an imagination problem because most people who experience impostor syndrome are highly competent.

In her study for the book *Charisma Myth*, author Olivia Fox Cabane found that *"impostor syndrome is worse among high performers."*[27] In other words, the further you grow as a leader, the more susceptible you are to impostor syndrome.

Anxiety, worry, fear, and self-criticism all feed the dark side of imagination and create blindsight. The good news is there's a way out.

Recently, I was watching a bit about basketball legendary Larry Bird. They were showing interview clips from opposing players. The one common thing they shared about Larry was his confidence in playing the game. He believed he would make the big shot and wasn't afraid to tell you how he would. One of Bird's comments reflects the connection of confidence and imagination that he had.

"When I go to the line, I'm thinking 'All net.'
When I don't think that, I'm likely to miss."

It sounds like Larry Legend found a way to tune his imagination whenever he took the court. I don't know about you, but I want to have the confidence of Larry Legend for all the shots I take in life too.

In 1979, one year after the Boston Celtics drafted Larry Bird, a poster was published featuring a statement that seemed like something you might see at a Disney Theme Park.

"If you can imagine it, you can achieve it.
If you can dream it, you can become it."

The clever line is often attributed to Walt Disney, but it's not Disney. It should be credited to American motivational writer William Arthur Ward. Over ten years earlier, he published a book titled, *For This One Hour*, with a slightly longer variant of this famous quote.

"If you can imagine it, you can possess it.
If you can dream it, you can become it.
If you can envision it, you can attain it.
If you can picture it, you can achieve it."

As it turns out, the words provide a process guide for overcoming imposter syndrome. Phil Mahre, Michael Jordon, Larry Bird, and many more whom all faced self-doubt provide proof of its validity. The question is, what are you imagining? What are you dreaming of? What are you envisioning? And what are you picturing? If those aren't clear, good, and worthy, then you'll see the red light as green, you'll miss the shot more than you make, you'll remember the story differently, you'll think the world is against you, and you might think you are an impostor.

The remedy is to create possibility narratives. See yourself possessing it, becoming it, attaining it, and achieving it. Possibility narratives allow us to see and believe in redemption stories. This is where the imagination can give you a glimpse of all that can be. **See yourself as what you can be!**

Recognize that your imagination is hard at work. It wants to be right, but it's also easily distracted. Imagination will tell you the stories your mind wants to hear. It either validates the hope or feeds the doubt.

What we need are ways to confirm our imagination – guide it. As for me, I don't ever want to be wrong – at least not for long. But I am still a work in progress. Imagination, while it's a strength, can throw me off.

There's a lesson in this for all of us. You don't need to experience a car accident for your imagination to get off track. It can happen at any time for anyone. Think about how easy it is to try to suppose someone's intention based on their facial response, the tone of their voice, or the murmur of whispers when you speak.

Our imagination wants to fill the gaps. If we're not careful, it can start to conjure up assumptions and stories that might be wrong. When this happens, we fall prey to *confirmation bias*, which is seeing what we expect even if the intention was different. Observation without Orientation leads us to make assumptions that can hang us out to dry.

Reconsider Ward's precept. *"If you envision it, you attain it."* This is true not just for hope but also for fear and doubt. It aligns with the proverb, *"As a man thinketh, so is he."*[28]

Here are some questions we should ask ourselves:

Will my imagination paint a story of light or dark?
What soundtrack will I choose to hear?

In your frustrations and regrets, your imagination can throw you off. The key is to get it right, to learn how to use your imagination to help you plan, prepare, and persevere. This is where the OODA Loop comes into play – especially proper observation. It can save you from self-doubt. The next step is watching out for the myths that can easily entangle.

The Myths

Myths also play into our blindsight. A myth is a widely held belief or idea that you think is true but is false. They can create a false comfort, a wrong impression, and influence your imagination.

Unfortunately, a belief that is a myth can be hard to detect. But as a rule, the ones to watch out for are preconceived thoughts or opinions that cast a shadow of doubt or keep you from moving forward. They can pull you to the dark side. To avoid the dark side, ask yourself:

What myths do I believe might be holding me back?

Myths that hold us back need to be challenged because they impersonate the truth by wrapping themselves in endearing qualities like safety, tradition, and truisms. However, when you identify the limiting beliefs, you increase your capacity to be more and do more.

To set the stage, I want to share a personal story of the battle of myths I experienced when a doctor told my wife and me that our one-year-old son had cerebral palsy. This was something that blindsided me. Yet somehow, it forced me to face the demons of disbelief and discover how truly incredible our imagination can propel us to be.

Michael's World

One of life's greatest moments was experiencing the birth of my oldest son, Michael. Over the next 12 months, we watched him develop like most other boys. However, there appeared to be a little hitch in his gate. While Michael's mental acuity and speech seemed okay, there was an unusual stride to his walk – he toe-walked on his left side. In addition, he often clenched his left hand up in the air. This concerned my wife and me, so we had it checked out.

The diagnosis that I anticipated was that he was going to be just fine. It would be a temporary condition that was growth-related and could be easily treated with some orthopedic rehabilitation – like stretching and exercise.

The news we finally got back almost two months later was much more severe. An MRI scan revealed a small lesion in the brain; it was something identified as left-sided hemiparesis. That's the day we learned that our little guy was a survivor of a stroke that likely occurred in utero right before his birth.

Like many stroke victims, some impairment happens that needs to be addressed through physical therapy, occupational therapy, and more. But one medical professional gave Michael a label none of us saw coming. He called it cerebral palsy – or CP. That's when our world turned upside.

My imagination went off the rails. As a dad, I was devastated and feared the worst. One of the beliefs that I previously had was thinking that any child with CP is someone who would be severely handicapped; that the inevitable for someone with CP is a wheelchair and possibly lifelong care needed to help with things like feeding and more. My heart was broken for Michael, my wife, and me. That's not what a dad dreams for his first-born son.

The doctor went on to tell us not to expect much. His medical diagnosis was that Michael's CP, even though it appeared to be mild, would limit him from doing physical things that other kids his age could do. Things like skateboarding, riding a bike, roller skating, and more. We were told that playing competitive sports – even little league – would be a 'non-starter.' The good news, I guess, was that he wasn't forecasting a wheelchair for Michael. That he would be able to walk, but it just would be noticeable, and we should limit and protect him.

I remember watching Michael play in the corner of the room with some blocks, and it didn't add up. Michael's gate and walk were affected, but it didn't seem to limit his drive. His imagination kept him going. He could throw, run, climb, and more. I wondered, *why would any doctor want to limit that enthusiasm?*

The Power of Curiosity

As the years went by, I would continue to see a *drive* in Michael to overcome the roadblocks in front of him. I noticed even more how his imagination could hold his attention. His imagination was fueled by curiosity, sometimes exhibited by him quietly questioning someone's perception when someone thought he couldn't or shouldn't. It might be a classmate, a teacher, a doctor, or a parent like me cautioning his ambitions. Whenever someone planted doubt in his mind, he had a knack of questioning it rather than accepting it.

When you face a barrier, **imagination brings possibilities to light.** Curiosity explores what can be by asking, *"why not?"*. This can make all the difference.

The adage is true. Where there's a will, there's a way. What's not true are the myths of CP. Every child diagnosed with CP is different. We should never presume the outcome for a child or stroke victim. For Michael, the difference for him was his imagination and his drive. Nothing was going to stop him.

What I've learned since then is that the brain is an amazing organism that can be reconfigured and learn to adapt. It's what neuroplasticity is all about. This refers to the brain's ability to change and adapt through experience. Our imagination holds our brain's attention bringing new things to light. It's experimentation where that new possibility gets tested and tried. Michael's approach to life taught me a valuable lesson; myths are meant to be challenged head-on, especially beliefs of doubt.

The Four Common Myths

Let's now dive into four common myths.

Myth #1 – It Is What It Is

Even though Michael could walk and run despite having a limp, we were told to lower our expectations. Most of the medical advice we received – including parental guidance from those who had children with CP – was for us to be cautious and keep him from being embarrassed.

This well-intended wisdom from "the experts" essentially said that the best course of action was to simply learn to live with the condition and have him shelter at home after school and on weekends. But for Michael, that was a myth that needed to be busted.

Michael wanted to be a kid like everyone else, and no one could tell him that he shouldn't try. One day when I came home from work, I found him riding his bike in the driveway alone. That wasn't necessarily unusual, but I noticed the bike looked different. *"Hey, Dad, look at me!"* He hollered with a smile as he rode in a big circle.

As I looked at him, I realized what was missing. There were no training wheels. I was blown away.

It turns out that he had taken the training wheels off himself and learned to ride. What was more incredible, when he biked, there was no noticeable limp. When he rode, he looked like any other kid.

Soon he learned to do other things like skateboarding, pogo stick hopping, rollerblading, skiing, and more. Despite his gate, despite his limp, nothing stopped him from trying. He instinctively believed that if you try, you can overcome. He was a curious adventurer.

It wasn't long before my wife, and I realized that this desire was more important than the diagnosis and direction of the "experts". So, we looked to find advocates – champions of those who could help him seize upon his imagination and experimentation so that he could make the most of life.

I could fill pages of his breakthroughs despite others saying he couldn't nor shouldn't. But what I need to tell you is what he taught me. Just because someone tells you what it is, doesn't mean it is what it is. *"It is what it is"* thinking may be a myth to be challenged.

Imagineers Think *"What Can Be?"*

Let's go back to the Wright Trio for a moment. Their words marked a mindset fueled by their imagination. In one of Orville's letters to Katharine, he writes, *"If we worked on the assumption that what is accepted as true really is true, then there would be little hope for advance."*

Please take a minute to think through what he is saying. In today's world, we hear and maybe even use the phrase *"it is what it is."* As harmless as it sounds, that type of thinking gives us an excuse not to push forward. Not seek potential. It says we are unable to change our circumstances.

But Orville and his brother refused to subscribe to *"it is what it is"* thinking, and we should do the same. This myth thinking keeps us from leveraging our imagination and not considering other paths to success. Taylor Manes, a blogger, shares, *"As innocent as these little words may seem, they could end up having a largely negative effect on our personal development and the way we live our lives."*[29]

Imaginers Live in Two Worlds

Think about how the Wright Trio, as Imagineers, had to live in two worlds. One world was the "here and now"; the other was the "world of potential". The temptation of the "here and now" is that what we see in the present is all that there is and can ever be. But the other world we pursue– the "world of potential" – allows us to see and believe in what could be. In the case of the Wright Trio, a world of flight is what fueled their imagination. That's what they desired.

The question is, *what hope fuels your imagination?* I can almost be sure it's not *"it is what it is"* thinking. Otherwise, if we worked on the assumption that *"what is"* is accepted as true and nothing more, it would keep us from moving forward. I know my son Michael wouldn't be where he is today with *"it is what it is"* thinking.

Go back and ask yourself:

What hope fuels my imagination?

Myth #2 – Hope is Not a Strategy

Perhaps you've heard someone say, *"Hope is not a strategy!"*

If you are like me, you've probably heard it – maybe even said it – more times than you can count. Well, if hope is not a strategy, then what is it? Wouldn't that mean that strategy is void of hope?

Story after story, you'll discover that **hope is the center point of every worthy strategy.** It's the foundation. It's what creates motivation. For my son Michael, hope fueled his imagination helping overcome his limitation. Yet, despite their best intentions, several medical professionals seemed willing to sabotage that hope by trying to curb his curiosity. It begs the question:

Who might be sabotaging your hope?

The follow-on question is equally powerful:

Do you remember what hope you have?

One of the great things I've seen my son Michael do is that he shares what he hopes for, and then he seeks out people that can help him execute that hope. Michael found one of those advocates in Wani when he was in college. She would be the girl he would end up marrying. She has been a rock of encouragement for him and all of us.

Without hope, we have no clear vision, we have no clear mission, and we have no clear purpose. Without hope, we are unmotivated. Even if we have hope, but don't share that hope nor find people who encourage us to pursue that hope, it ends up being sheltered and potentially abandoned. There's no legitimate strategy without hope.

Hope matters. Without it, we walk and lead aimlessly. Hope is the essence of the human spirit, a visionary's dream, the entrepreneur's drive, and the leader's life. We simply can't be as effective without hope. **Without hope, there's little reason to imagine.**

Myth #3 – All Hope is Helpful

Now, before you run away thinking that hope is all you need (like a song from the Beatles), let's be honest. Hope isn't always the saving grace we want or need. Hope can also disappoint. The belief that ALL hope is helpful may be a myth to be busted.

It turns out there are at least two types of hope: there's real hope, and there's naïve hope. To understand the real powers of imagination, we need to understand what real hope is.

Holocaust survivor and author Viktor Frankl, who endured a Nazi concentration camp during World War II, shares that holocaust prisoners *"who gave up on life [and] lost all hope for a future, were inevitably the first to die."* It's a difficult commentary to swallow, but it's clear. Without hope, we are more vulnerable. The key is to keep real hope alive.

Frankl also reveals something we need to squarely address that he calls *"naive hope"*, which may be the hope we're not looking for.

> *"The majority of the prisoners had lived in the naïve hope that they would be home again by Christmas. [But] as the time drew near and there was no encouraging news, the prisoners lost courage and disappointment overcame them. This had a dangerous influence on their powers of resistance and a great number of them died."*

When I first read this, it made me do a double take. It was a *"wait, what?"* moment. I remember reacting as if Frankl was in the room,

"You mean to tell me that they had hope, based on an expectation, and because the expectation didn't come by Christmas, they lost all hope?"

I can almost imagine Frankl whispering in broken English. *"Yea. It was naïve hope."*

I'm not going to lie; having my son being diagnosed with CP was something that initially took the air out of my sail as a dad. I found myself struggling to find real hope. In those early days, I grasped on too much of what I recognize now was naïve hope. Naïve hope had me thinking that by a specific date, he would be 100% better. But when those dates were unmet, my hopes were unmet, and I got down. If I can be honest, there were a few times I was angry with God.

Finally, something triggered in me that restored real hope. It was by learning to see his imagination still at play – the desire that he had – he never quit. That's all I needed. I didn't need hope to be like a wish assigned with a date. I just needed to see desire, and that desire was right in front of me. He imagined himself a better future with new experiences to grasp. It was seeing that imagination pursued with experimentation that made a difference.

The hope you have needs to be adequately vetted and evaluated. Hope, as good as it is, can get you into trouble if it's naïve hope. According to Frankl, naïve hope is creating an expectation of a miracle with some anticipated date or method of delivery. You can slip into a very dark spot when that miracle doesn't happen as you hoped.

In his book, *Man's Search for Meaning*, Frankl shares, *"Whoever was still alive had reason for hope."* Here he is talking about real hope.

What creates a reason for hope despite the challenges around you?

Frankl offers us a list:

"Health, family, happiness, professional abilities, fortune, position in society — all these were things that could be achieved again or restored. After all, we still had all our bones intact. Whatever we had gone through could still be an asset to us in the future."

Frankl is telling us to look at our résumé. You've made it this far for a reason. You haven't come this far only to come this far.

Look at what you've already accomplished. Look at the triumphs you have had. They can't be taken away from you. They can give you hope and encouragement. They are an asset.

Past performance is often an indicator of future results. Best of all, we can borrow experiences – and past performances – from others. This goes back to "Trace Your Path", which we discussed in the last chapter. True stories from those who persevere can offer others a lift.

Here's a thought to ponder:

What if your perseverance can offer the hope that someone else might need?

Myth #4 – My Story Doesn't Matter

I'll never forget my son when he was five, asking me how old I was when I learned to ride a bike, do a tic-tac on a skateboard, or ski down a mountain. He wanted to accomplish those things too because he knew I had. Who would have guessed that my actions and accomplishments as a kid would inspire my own child a generation later?

This leads me to ask another question:

What experiences have you had in the past that might inspire someone in the future?

Don't discount your past accomplishments; they might mean something.

There's a common myth that millions of people struggle with internally that their story doesn't count, but that's a myth that needs to be busted. Unhealthy beliefs about yourself may be the most important myth to take down. Thinking you are insignificant, nothing special, a disappointment, handicapped, or incapable will prevent you from being whom you were created to be. After all, "*If you have a heartbeat, there's still time for your dreams.*"

That's a quote from Sean Stephenson. Sean was born with osteogenesis imperfecta, better known as brittle bone disease. He stood three feet tall and was relegated to a wheelchair, but despite that, he began sharing a message of hope when he was 17 years old and soon became a therapist to help others through challenges.

His second book, *Get Off Your "But": How to End Self-Sabotage and Stand Up for Yourself* became a best-seller. In that book, he explains, *"I've learned that when people hide behind their limitations, they can't see anything else."*[30]

Can we just drop the mic?

Recognize you have a story of hope to share and a legacy to leave behind for others. Choose not to let your perceived limitation impair your imagination. Seize the life you imagine; it might one day inspire someone else.

In his book *Man's Search for Meaning*, Frankl quotes Nietzsche as if whispering us a secret:

"That which does not kill me, makes me stronger."

Building on this thought, Frankl speaks of the mindset needed to survive a Nazi concentration camp or any difficult situation.

> *"To the impartial the future must seem hopeless. Each of us could guess for himself how small were his chances of survival. I estimated my own chances at about one in twenty. But...I had no intention of losing hope and giving up."*

Can I encourage you with that? Live with *"no intention of losing hope and giving up."* That might make all the difference in the world.

Frankl goes on to share that this mindset wasn't just about the future but also about *"the past; all its joys, and how its light shone even in the present darkness."* To unlock this secret, he quotes another poet who wrote, *"What you have experienced, no power on earth can take from you."*

Frankl has stumbled onto something compelling regarding the importance of evaluated experience. He then adds a statement that gives a nod to your imagination.

> *"Not only our experiences, but all we have done, whatever great thoughts we may have had, and all we have suffered, all this is not lost, though it is past; we have brought it into being.*

'Having been' is also a kind of being, and perhaps the surest kind."

If necessary, go back and re-read that piece again. All that you've accomplished matters. It can't be erased. And the realization of *"having been"* offers you a sense of being that can carry you forward. That's a real hope that can be shared.

Again, I'd like to credit my son, who taught me a vital lesson. His mindset has been a lot like Frankl's. Hope is what fueled his imagination. Real hope is not limited by a deadline but is marked by desire matched with persistence. When you combine curious desire and persistence, it fosters a hope that can lift others.

Chapter Summary

This chapter has focused on the Power of Curiosity. Curiosity opens our imagination by asking, *"what's that?"*, *"what can be?"*, and *"why not?"*. Curiosity is how we *"learn, test assumptions, become open to new perspectives, and push"* the limits of our capability.[31] Curiosity is a desire to know. You can't invent the future without the Power of Curiosity.

If we are not careful, curiosity can sometimes take a back seat. As we grow older, we become less curious. We become cautious and fearful. Fear is what limits us. But **fear never has no power over hope.** Hope is vision and faith. Hope is what leads us back to curiosity.

The dark side of imagination becomes a real problem when we ignore our vision and faith. When we give in to fear and doubt and let it grow bigger, we tend to miss our shots, hit the wall, and put Force "choke holds" on others. That's when we quit being curious.

Imagine how Orville and Wilbur must have dealt with doubt every time they got in their glider, yet they had a curious hope. Hope got them through each phase of the OODA Loop. The question, though, is how can hope and fear co-exist? Do we need to be void of fear to have hope?

Experience teaches us that hope doesn't mean fearless. Hope means finding courage despite our fear. Hope gives us the initiative to leverage the Power of Curiosity in overcoming our myths and doubts.

The goal of this chapter has been to encourage you to rethink your thinking through the Power of Curiosity. Consider that a struggling imagination is what can keep you from making free throws, competing for medals, discovering flight, or pursuing the world. But curiosity will propel you to at least try. The goal is to keep moving. Keep paddling. Don't anchor. Stay hungry. Stay curious!

◆ ◆ ◆

Additional tools and resources focused on
Hunting Down Misconceptions are available at
theimaginebook.com/ch-4

---

[23] Malcolm Gladwell, Revisionist History, *Free Brian Williams*, https://www.pushkin.fm/episode/free-brian-williams/, last accessed June 28, 2022.

[24] This thought can be attributed to William Wordsworth, who said, *"Imagination, which in truth, is but another name for absolute power. And clearest insight, amplitude of mind, And Reason, in her most exalted mood."*

[25] Huey Lewis and the News, *The Power of Love*, Note: The actual line from the song is "The power of love is a curious thing. Make one man weep, and another man sing."

[26] P. R. Clance and S. A. Imes, "The Imposter Phenomenon in High Achieving Women: Dynamics and Therapeutic Intervention," Psychotherapy: Theory, Research and Practice 15, no. 3 (1978): 241–47.

[27] Cabane, Olivia Fox, *The Charisma Myth* (p. 249). Penguin Publishing Group.

[28] The Bible, Proverbs 23:7.

[29] Taylor Maness, *Why "It Is What It Is" Is A Toxic Saying*, https://www.ninertimes.com/opinion/why-it-is-what-it-is-is-a-toxic-saying/article_4de0b1cc-f00e-5124-8d6f-967fa7992f3a.html, last accessed June 28, 2022.

[30] Sean Stephenson, Anthony Robbins (Foreword), *Get Off Your "But"*, Wiley, March 2009.

[31] Kathy Taberner and Kirsten Taberner Siggins. *The Power of Curiosity: How to Have Real Conversations That Create Collaboration, Innovation and Understanding* (p. 3), Morgan James Publishing.

5 – Evaluate the Gains
Understanding the Power of Assessment

"Your problem is to bridge the gap
which exists between where you are now and
the goal you intend to reach."

–Earl Nightingale

Now that we have tackled some of the myths that can limit the imagination, it's time to rev up our curiosity and explore the capacity of what's possible when we are fueled by a clear imagination.

This chapter is about increasing your awareness. Specifically, it focuses on the practice of evaluating the gains over your gaps. This centers on the Power of Assessment, which is about looking at the gains of what you have achieved more than the gaps in what you are trying to pursue.

Regarding observation, the Power of Assessment is a behavior you don't want to miss. The earliest example of this for me was the day I learned to ride a bike, twenty-seven years before I would inspire my son to ride his. Only my story has a much different twist.

Bike Ride – Part 1

"Who says you can't?"

My dad offered those words of encouragement as I nervously straddled my bicycle, facing the descending hill in front of our house. He had just stripped off the training wheels, and I was utterly scared.

My brother and I were given shiny new bikes for Christmas four months earlier. It was now late April, and the weather was perfect. The bike I had been on a handful of times was adorned with handlebar streamers and a personalized license plate with my first name. But it now felt instantly different without the safety of the training wheels. Rather than seeing the gain of what I had accomplished to date, all I could think of was the gap in what I still had never done.

The question that I asked moments earlier was an honest one. *"Do you really think I can do this?"*

Clearly, I had my doubts, and I needed his assurance. That's when he looked at me confidently and responded with a question of his own, *"Who says you can't?"*

There is no one better to offer hope than a dad.

Mind over Matter

My imagination had been wrestling with two different images related to the gap. One was a vision of success – of me bridging the gap and riding the bike with style like Evil Knievel. The other was a vision of failure and disaster – of me crashing in the gap – also like Evil Knievel.

Despite my inner struggle, Dad was confident in me and pointed the bike down the street toward a slight hill where we lived. He continued to offer more encouragement on how he would help me fill the gap. *"I'll be right alongside you. I'm NOT going to let you out of my sight."* He tried to assure me. *"You've got this!"*

Now, picture the scene. Here I am, a six-year-old blond-headed kid without a helmet, nervous as heck with his dad and brother looking on. Meanwhile, mom is in the house, probably too scared to watch.

I tried to do everything possible to fight off the fear that I would utterly falter and fail. Meanwhile, my older brother was finding amusement in my nervousness, grinning from ear to ear, trying to hold back a laugh. Thankfully, he managed to wipe off his smirk and offered some encouragement. *"You can do this, Paul."* He added, *"Hey, once you learn to ride, we can ride together."*

That thought made me smile. I wanted that. I then took a deep breath and muttered four keywords as I glanced at my dad, *"Okay. I am ready!"*

Hearing that, Dad gave me the prompt. *"Okay. Get your feet on the pedals, and just pedal away."* I firmly put my white Converse sneakers on the pedals, gripped the handlebars, and faced forward. *"Here We Go!"* Dad bellowed.

I immediately started pedaling – gathering momentum as Dad held on fiercely to the back of the bike as he ran alongside me. *"I got you! I'm right here!"* He shouted, letting me know of his presence. Looking back, I realize he was standing in the gap for me.

Moment of Impact

We started picking up more speed. I was amazed that my dad could run as fast as I pedaled. But that's when I realized he was no longer there. I was pedaling alone, even though I could still hear him behind me. *"You got this. You're doing great. Keep going!"*

I kept pedaling – and picking up speed. But remember, I was pointed downhill. The fear monster popped up again, and I instantly got scared. I realized I was going faster than my training wheels had ever taken me before. I began to doubt myself and my bike began to wobble. Suddenly it took a different vector – a path toward the curb.

At that moment, my short life flashed before my eyes, and all courage vanquished my body. Somehow, I managed to narrowly avert the lip of the curb, finding instead an entry to a driveway four houses down.

Despite the avoidance of the curb, I stilled flamed out in a mini disaster, plowing straight into a small bush in a neighbor's yard. The next thing I knew, I was on the ground, bike on top, with the back wheel still spinning. Did I mention I wasn't wearing a helmet?

It's hard for me not to laugh about that memory now. I survived, but I remember wishing I never even tried. I was embarrassed. I just wanted to go home and pretend it never happened. At that moment, I only saw the gap in what I still couldn't do. What I was missing was seeing my gains.

The Power of Assessment

Let's pause for a moment. Can you think back to your first bike ride? How about that first time you made something new in the kitchen or your father's garage? Did you get it right the first time? My guess is probably not.

In your initial assessment, did you have the urge to quit?

Any successful endeavor starts with a bit of apprehension. But **every next step starts with imagination.** Imagination lets you see what's on the other side of your apprehension.

Think back to the Wright Trio and the number of failed attempts. Even through failure, one can learn to rise. The challenge is to revisit what you desire – your curiosity – and identify what you've attained along the way. Look at the parts you've already conquered. This is what helps diminish the urge you might have to quit.

Imagination is measured not by the gaps of what you have yet to achieve but by the gains of what you have already accomplished. The clearer the gains, the stronger the imagination.

Measure the Gains

What you measure matters. If you count only the gaps, it will forever feel like you are never getting there. But if you count the gains, you see the progress.

Imagine an extended family car trip with the Griswolds. The *"are we there yet?"* question is bound to be asked. For a child, the long car trip can feel like an eternity. But if you start to take notice of the gains along the way, the car trip takes on a different perspective. Instead of harping on the gap, you take pleasure in seeing the gains.

When I was a kid, my family used to play the license plate game on our long road trips on our way from Virginia to Colorado. We'd look for a plate from every state and make it a competition. Whoever tallied the most plates each day was that day's winner. They got to pick where to eat. Each new license plate I spotted was a gain for me. It was like scoring a goal. Even my dad got into it, which was cool because he'd drive faster to catch up to new cars, and still make occasional stops at McDonald's, allowing us to case for new plates in the parking lot.

Dr. Don Wood shares, *"The things you measure have a funny way of improving. It almost looks like magic."* He adds, *"Measuring those things in your life that matter is a powerful way of emphasizing and improving them."* What he's talking about is tracking your results. Tracking the gains allows you to recognize that you are making progress.

Think of the perspective gained. However, when you track the gaps, you begin to focus on fear, doubt, or dread, and the gap never seems to close. For example, for me, I crashed into a bush. As I processed my fear on that bike and my "crash and burn" fall on the ground, all I saw was the gap.

Gaps, by themselves, create disillusionment. However, when you focus on a hope or a desire and learn to keep track of your gains, there's a high probability of seeing the vision realized. Gains create confidence. The key is the Power of Assessment.

Questions to Help you Measure

To get you going in the right direction, the questions to help you measure are simple:

- *"What is that you want or desire?"* = THE GAP
- *"What have you achieved so far?"* = THE GAIN

That last question may be the most important. Recognize the gains you are making to bridge the gap and prepare you. Think of how Mr. Miyagi trained Danielson in the *Karate Kid*. He was building up gains that gave him the confidence to face his fear. Bridge the gap by measuring your gains.

Think also about Thomas Edison. Despite experiencing frequent disappointment in pursuing his goal, he never considered a failed experiment a failure. He was able to look at his gains instead. He was all about the Power of Assessment. His famous quote in a 1910 interview looking back at his journey, is telling, *"I have not failed, not once. I just found 10,000 ways that don't work."* Edison adds, *"Many of life's failures are people who do not realize how close they were to success when they gave up."* He's talking about recognizing the gains.

Astrocytes – Why We Want to Quit

Let's not dismiss what story an uncontrolled imagination might tell us when we experience failure. Even the Wright Trio without their sister's encouragement almost packed it up a few times. It turns out that the *want* to quit is a function of how our brain responds to challenges.

How it works is fascinating. Your brain is fueled by something called neurons. They are like agents that deserve credit for our "behavior functions." But research shows that there is also another type of cell that's not a neuron called a neuroglia. So, swimming in your head are these things called neurons and neuroglia. To keep it simple, let's call these last fuel cells *Glia* for short.

At one time Glia was thought to be a kind of super fuel that supported the central nervous system. But recent studies have shown that these Glia cells are made up of different kinds of elements and one of them is called an Astrocyte. Elements like Astrocytes perform different functions within the brain responding to various signals. The research suggests that these *"Astrocytes may be playing the crucial role of gathering information and controlling the part of the brain that decides to give up."*[32] It turns out that when your brain detects failure and sees nothing but the gap, a signal is sent to these Astrocytes prompting it to send out the "give up" command. Further studies show that Astrocytes also control *"avoidance behaviors and sleep."*

Choose New Soundtracks

What we need are some other ways to rewire our brain to persevere despite the challenges. One technique is to have some internal *soundtracks* that we can play that encourage us to persevere and counterbalance the Astrocytes; soundtracks that increase our awareness.

This idea of soundtracks comes from best-selling author Jon Acuff who wrote a terrific book with the same title. His book *Soundtracks* focuses on the common problem we have in overthinking. He shares *"your thoughts are the internal soundtracks you listen to"* and encourages us to change out those soundtracks if our inner voice might be a bully.[33]

Use helpful soundtracks and other tools and symbols to remind yourself of the gains you've made along the way. It will help encourage you on this journey – especially when you face the ANTs.

Watch out for the ANTs

When it comes to pursuing what we imagine, sometimes the critic enters the arena and tries to throw us off.[34] The critic spews disparaging remarks telling us our shortfalls. Often that critic is us. Involuntarily, we choose to be our own worst critic. When the negative self-talk happens, ask yourself:

How does my self-criticism serve me?

Part of the OODA Loop is being aware of self-talk. World renown psychologist Dr. Daniel Amen, and his team, have identified seven types of critical thoughts that he calls ANTs. ANTs stand for Automatic Negative Thoughts. Here's the list:[35]

1. **All-or-Nothing ANTs**
   This happens when you think that things are either all good or all bad.

2. **Just the Bad ANTs**
   This happens when you see only the bad in a situation. Think of how this might trigger when you turn on the news, or track trends on Twitter.

3. **Guilt-Beating ANTs**
   This can happen when we reflect on words like *should, must, ought to,* or *have to.*

4. **Labeling ANTs**
   This happens when we attach a negative label to ourselves or someone else.

5. **Fortune-Teller ANTs**
   This happens when we predict the worst possible outcome for a situation with little or no evidence for it.

6. **Mind Reader ANTs**
   This happens when we believe we know what other people are thinking even though they haven't told us.

7. **Blaming ANTs**
   This happens when we blame someone else for our problems.

ANTs are the bad soundtracks that atomically play in your head that make you feel unqualified or unworthy. As you look through that list, *what ANTs do you tend to struggle with the most?*

For me, my two ANTs have been #3 and #6. I need to work hard to settle my imagination so that I'm not putting absolutes on the choices that are in front of me and I'm not trying to misread a person's intent. But on that bike that day as a kid the ANT that was kicking me was #4, the Labeling ANT. The inner critic in me was one bad bully giving me a label of defeat called "Loser".

Author John Townsend shares that *"We all struggle with those self-discouraging messages we listen to in our heads."* Those are certainly reflective of ANTs. One choice to make in the Decide Phase of the OODA Loop is to eliminate the ANTs, yet it's in this Observe Phase that you can first notice the invading ANTs. By recognizing the ANTs early on, you can identify the real gap that might be holding you back.

Eliminate the ANTs

Recognize that ANTs are often gaps, they tell you what you don't have. Most of the time these bad soundtracks are 100% false. Throughout this book, I'll try to share several soundtracks that you can leverage and use as substitutes to improve your playlist. Good soundtracks are statements of affirmation that can offer you courage, clarity, and confidence.

What I want to focus on specifically right now is eliminating the bad soundtracks. **What ANTs do you struggle with?**

Take a moment to evaluate the different types of ANTs you deal with. Here are some common ANT statements we tell ourselves:

- *"I never have time for myself."*
- *"No one seems to have an interest in what I offer."*
- *"If I can't do it perfectly, why should I even try."*
- *"She's upset, I wonder what I did?"*
- *"Why am I always the last to know?"*
- *"It's clear they don't like me, otherwise they would have said something."*

To eliminate the ANTs on your list, think through these questions:

1. What external event or internal message incites the ANTs?

2. How do I feel when I have this thought, and how do these ANT affect me?

3. Is the ANT really true 100% of the time, really?

4. What would I feel if I didn't have this thought, and how would I be different?

5. What is a turnaround statement that I can play in its place?

This idea of soundtracks is thought provoking and offers a fresh new look at dealing with the person you lead the most, which is YOU! It offers a way to minimize the ANTs. The bonus is if you are a parent or a leader, it provides some practical insights to shape those in your care too. Shifting your imagination can create a new awareness and better vision for yourself and your team.

Chapter Summary

This chapter has focused on the Power of Assessment. Assessment is about valuation. It's about measuring the progress you've made. The Power of Assessment is crucial for those who invent the future, otherwise, how do you know if you are getting there?

Recognizing where you are and where you want to go is essential, but if all you see are the gaps, it can leave you feeling defeated. To stay encouraged, evaluate the gains of what you have already accomplished.

The secret to inventing the future is measuring the gains while you step into the gaps. Measuring the gains creates a sense of achievement, propelling you to continue. It keeps the hope alive and your imagination active.

Seeing your gains in pursuing a dream, can often make all the difference. In their groundbreaking book, *The Gap and The Gain*, authors Benjamin Hardy and Dan Sullivan ask a fundamental question. *"Look at your life right now—what are all the GAINS you can think of?"*[36] When we look at the gains it gives us gratitude.

There's always something to be thankful for, but sometimes we just need to be reminded of them. I recommend capturing your list of accomplishments and blessings in a journal.

Start each day by identifying what you are grateful for. By taking inventory of the blessings in your life, you can more easily see the gains you already made.

Gains give you momentum; they embolden you to keep moving forward and leverage your imagination no matter what the challenge. That's the Power of Assessment.

◆ ◆ ◆

Additional tools and resources focused on
Evaluating the Gains are available at
theimaginebook.com/ch-5

---

[32] Jennifer Fabiano, *According To Science, Your Desire To Quit Is Not Your Fault*, https://www.theladders.com/career-advice/your-desire-to-quit-is-not-your-fault, published June 9, 2020, last accessed June 28, 2022.

[33] Jon Acuff, *Soundtracks* (p. 19), Baker Publishing Group.

[34] Theodore Roosevelt, *Citizenship in a Republic*, aka *The Man in the Arena*, April 23, 1910.

[35] Daniel Amen, *Conquer Worry and Anxiety: The Secret to Mastering Your Mind* (p. 43), Tyndale House Publishers.

[36] Benjamin Hardy, Dan Sullivan, *The Gap and The Gain* (p. 25), Hay House.

PHASE TWO

ORIENT

Position to Possibilities

Phase Two – ORIENT

"We all have possibilities we don't know about.
We can do things we don't even dream we can do."

—Dale Carnegie

The second phase of the OODA Loop is to ORIENT. Orientation is about putting yourself in a posture and a position to decide and do something with the knowledge and information you have gathered. In the Orient Phase, you are adjusting for possibilities.

Orientation follows observation and precedes decision. Orientation is what points you in the right direction and gives you proper alignment and bearings.

Think of the game show *Who Wants to Be a Millionaire* and how it can best be played. At the beginning of the game, the host actually does the OBSERVATION for the contestant. The host highlights the rules and rewards of the game, including how a cool one million dollars can be at hand if all 14 questions are answered. But every question is worth a progressing amount of money, and each proper "right answer" inches you closer to the big one. There are "safety levels" and three lifelines that you can use as incentives.

Once the host sets up the Observe Phase, the game is ready to go, and everything from that point forward is contingent on how well the contestant Orients.

Let's say you are in the hot seat, and the question on the board could land you $20,000 and move you further up the ladder tree. In that magic moment, you still have all three lifelines left:

- Ask the Audience
- 50 x 50
- Phone a friend (now called the Plus 1)

Think about it. If a contestant answers the first question correctly, they can walk away with significant money. Not only that, but the answer to every question is also revealed in one of four choices. You just need to pick the right one! 25% odds are pretty good! You can also choose a lifeline to help you. But what shouldn't be forgotten is that you can also choose to walk away with the cash you've already gained.

The game isn't solely about your trivia knowledge. Although that's important, being aware of your choices before you Decide and Act is how the game is won!

If you watch the show, notice how the best contestants think through all the options. Many of them self-coach their way to the answer. When they do that, they are orienting before deciding. If you were playing, the ability to walk away with cash in hand is 100% dependent upon your ability to Orient. Orienting is about positioning yourself for possibilities.

In this section, we will explore three key behaviors that every Imagineer can use to Orient and position themselves for possibilities. They include the following behaviors:

- Imagine the Possible with the Power of Belief
- Minimize the Distractions with the Power of Boundaries
- Align Your Steering with the Power of Values

Let's dive in!

6 – IMAGINE THE POSSIBLE
Understanding the Power of Belief

*"The future belongs to those who believe
in the beauty of their dreams."*

—Eleanor Roosevelt

Imagination. It's where it begins. When you think about all the things required to step into the gap and build on your gains, the one thing you need is your imagination. For those who pioneer and persevere, imagination is where belief starts, sustains, and finishes.

Think about where you are in the process. You are now done with the Observe Phase. Now, consider how you can examine the data and get situational awareness. Before you Decide you must Orient.

One way to Orient is by imagining what can be. Start with an idea, a need, a favorable outcome, or a desire. Like Phil Mahre, imagine it possible. Once you imagine it, you'll naturally begin to seek it. Some call it the law of attraction; I call it the Power of Belief.

There's an idiom that says, *"Seeing is Believing."* But that's a status quo belief. That doesn't propel the use of your imagination. Perhaps a better phrase is *"Seeking is Believing."* It's a little twist that can make all the difference.

Seeking is seeing at a whole new level. Seeking is seeing not just the apparent or tangible things in the present but also what's not so obvious. The Power of Belief is about looking for what you see in your mind's eye. This might be a goal, a desire, a calling, or a vision.

Let's head back to the bike story to understand this principle further. We discover that imagining the possible is founded on the Power of Belief.

Bike Ride – Part 2

When we last left the scene, I was piled up on the ground after a crash landing in a neighbor's yard. Despite the flame out, it wasn't a complete disaster though. My dad and brother helped me back up and dusted me off. The soft landing of the bush and grass kept me from serious harm. Other than my dad having to straighten out my handlebars and realign them with the front wheel, the bike was still road worthy.

Truth be told, I was hoping my dad would just tell me, *"Let's try again another day."* I wanted to quit. Looking back now, it may have been the Astrocytes talking. But my dad and brother played a different soundtrack and encouraged me to try one more time. They were trying to help me re-orient.

I remember hiking the bike back up the hill and balking. I didn't want to give it another go. But then my brother said, *"Paul. You just rode your bike for like half a football field. You just rode!"*

"I did?" I asked with astonishment.

My dad smiled. *"Yup. You did pretty good. Proud of you. Now is NOT the time to give up! You got this."*

Those last three words echoed in my mind. *"You got this."* That was a soundtrack I was happy to replay then and still today. *"You got this"* is a trigger to activate the Power of Belief.

The Power of Belief

Have you ever played Hide and Seek? How about Capture the Flag in the middle of the night with a small army of friends? That game played at night, on the prowl, can be intense – scary even. But despite the apprehension, you play the game knowing there's a flag to be found. The Power of Belief is the same way. It requires a little bit of courage despite the fear.

Belief is having trust, faith, or confidence in someone or something internal or external. Putting trust in someone or something is an act of courage. Courage is a choice, not a feeling. Belief is its own soundtrack of courageous seeking. It whispers to you and your teammates, *"Yes! We can capture the flag."*

Incidentally, have you ever noticed that if you wait to feel courageous, you may never decide to go capture. However, if you choose to be bold despite feeling fear, you can do the extraordinary.

The Power of Belief is about seeking what you see when your eyes are closed. Seeking is what makes the difference between good and great. Those who seek are the ones who discover.

Think about how seeking and imagination are tied together. When you dare to imagine, it means you are putting yourself in a position of seeking something for your greater good. It propels you to be courageous.

American historian Daniel Boorstin shares it best, *"The courage to imagine the otherwise is our greatest resource, adding color and suspense to all our life."* The *otherwise* in this statement reflects the possibility that can be realized when you choose to seek and pursue what you imagine.

What are you imagining? Does it align with what you are seeking?

What do you really believe – or trust? If you are not seeking what you believe, then what are you imagining? When this happens, your belief is in something else. Maybe you believe you will fail, you don't have what it takes, or it's impossible. **The mind looks to validate what you imagine.**

The focus of what you seek often becomes a self-fulfilling prophecy. It can be either good or bad. For instance, when you focus on fear or doubt or a gap, you'll likely see that fear or doubt realized, and the gap may never seem to close. When the fear, doubt, or gap penetrates your thoughts, ask yourself:

What is it that I believe that I will continue to seek?

This question can help you stay focused on the endgame and increase your chance for success. This is what it means to imagine the possible.

Seeking Belief versus Curiosity

You might be wondering, at this point, *"What's the difference between the Power of Curiosity from Chapter 4 and the Power of Belief here in Chapter 6? They seem similar?"*

It's simple. Seeking belief follows exploring curiosity. One sets up the other.

Curiosity is the predecessor to Belief. With curiosity, you are in the Observe Phase, gathering insights and increasing awareness. You can't observe without the Power of Curiosity. It's about being open-minded. However, at some point, you need to step forward with your findings and move to the Orient Phase. Seeking Belief is validating the proof that your curiosity finds. Seeking is about exploring what could be true.

At this stage, you can't Orient without the Power of Belief. It requires greater courage than curiosity. Curiosity was wonder – the belief hadn't been fully established. The Power of Belief, on the other hand, centers on pursuing what you know now might be true, despite what others might think or not see. The Power of Belief requires courage.

My friend Dave Cornell, who travels the country and speaks on the topic of courage, shares a thought that hits the mark.

> *"Fear calls us to be spectators.*
> *Courage calls us to get in the game."*

Only when we acknowledge our fear can we put ourselves in a position to get in the game. Getting in the game is the crucial step of a leader.

The Three Stages of Seeking: Past, Present, and Future

The seeking that accompanies the Power of Belief requires you to explore three phases of the journey: *past, present,* and *future.*

If you ignore the feats and foils of your past, then you'll lose the foothold needed to pursue the future. Evaluated experience of the past also gives you context for the present. It creates greater awareness. Knowing how you got to this moment – right now – can build confidence. Seekers are internally confident – otherwise, they wouldn't seek.

Seeking requires attention. A lack of awareness keeps you from seeing the gains and only seeing the gaps. Author Neville Goddard shared it this way. *"You are limited only by your uncontrolled imagination and lack of attention to the feeling of your wish fulfilled."*[37]

Let's unpack Goddard's statement. Several phrases jump out:

- Uncontrolled imagination
- Lack of attention
- Wish fulfilled

Only one of those three things is good – the third bullet. This reinforces why it is critical to look beyond the gap and see the gains you have already made.

Why Courage of Belief Matters

If you can control your imagination and hold your attention, then the wish you imagine – *desire* – has a much better chance of being fulfilled. It comes down to the courageous choice of seeking what you believe.

In this instance, courage yields confidence and clarity. Both are critical components of a healthy imagination. Courage is also contagious.

Courage Creates Confidence

Minutes after my fall, my dad had me straddling the bike again and preparing me just as before with this thought. *"Just imagine riding to the bottom of the street and turning and riding back up."* Finally, he gave the prompt. *"Ready?"*

My hands were trembling worse than ever as they gripped the bar, but I swallowed hard and nodded with affirmation. Despite my fear, my hope was intact. I envisioned myself riding just like my brother. I decided to hold on to that belief.

"Let's go." He shouted as he started jogging, holding the back of the bike. This time he almost immediately let go. But I just kept pedaling. I used the foot brake a bit but then pedaled some more. I turned a little. And then straightened out the bike. It was just like riding with training wheels, but only better! I felt freer. I felt... alive!

My dad smiled as my brother cheered me on. Mom came out for my third ride down and watched me navigate our street up and down that hill. My confidence was growing by the minute. I was making turns and pedaling my bike as if I had been doing it for months.

Afterward, my brother and I rode our bikes on our street for nearly an hour. I felt free as a bird. It was like we were Orville and Wilbur; all we missed was our sister Katherine. She must have been working that day. (P.S. My sister's name really is Katherine – it's just spelled differently).

Courage Creates Clarity

With newfound confidence, I remember asking my brother the big question. *"Kurt, now that I can ride, what are the chances of us going around the block? Can we do that? What do you think?"*

I was expecting him to say NO, but instead, he smiled. *"Around the block, huh?"* He paused as I nodded with excitement. *"Well, if you promise not to wander off, why not? Let's do it!"*

This was a dream about to come true. Something I had envisioned for months, and today was the day. It was what I had longed for. In those next 20 minutes, my brother helped bring a dream to life.

When we returned to the house, I was on cloud nine, having achieved something I had only wildly imagined before. A small dream had come to fruition – a dream that started in my imagination.

Courage is Contagious

Since that first bike ride, an active imagination supported by the Power of Belief has given me confidence and clarity to pursue other dreams. It's become fuel for my imagination. What's great about this power is its influence on others.

The most decisive moments of influence are when we choose to be courageous in pursuing a vision despite the fear. **There is nothing more inspiring than a dream courageously pursued.**

According to Billy Graham, *"Courage is contagious. When a brave man takes a stand, the spines of others are often stiffened."*

When it comes to pursuing a belief, ask yourself:

How can I step forward with courage despite the fear?

A dream pursued in the past is never as powerful as a belief pursued in the present. Life is about believing in the future and doing something right now.

The Future Chaser – *The Story of Reeve*

If you could wake up every day believing in the future and thinking that the future will be better than the past, what kind of impact do you think that might have? It might be significant, don't you think?

But what if, despite being hopeful and having an active imagination, you repeatedly endured failure, ridicule, and rejection along the way – time after time? Do you think you'd continue believing in a better future, or would you eventually give up?

Would you fall prey to *"it is what it is"* thinking and subconsciously listen to the Astrocytes telling you to quit, or would you continue to have hope?

Would you be prone to see the gaps and miss the moments of gain? What soundtrack would play for you?

Our next story reflects the real-life account of Reeve, whose pursuit of the future has been his mantra. You could say he is a person who invents the future because he feeds off imagination, experimentation, and evaluation. Hope for him has been a force multiplier. But that's not to say it has been easy.

The Early Days

As a young boy growing up in South Africa, Reeve was bullied by other kids. He just didn't quite fit in. One time he was hospitalized after a group of boys pushed him down a set of stairs. Despite that, his mind was imagining the future. He couldn't stop thinking about it.

Later, Reeve moved to Canada and then attended college in the United States. His appetite was for learning, and then taking what he learned and applying it – experimenting. He wanted to see how he could shape the future.

Reeve became proficient on the computer, especially programming, bringing new ideas to life. It was clear he had a gift. But the question was, did he believe in himself? He still had some self-doubt. He needed encouragement.

The Turning Point

After college, Reeve grew frustrated with how online payments worked on the internet and united with a few friends to create an e-mail payment company – one of the first of its kind.

Before they knew it, Reeve and his friend's little enterprise had over 200,000 customers as part of their service. He was encouraged. Investors, however, saw Reeve as *"inexperienced"* and brought in someone more credentialed to run the business. Reeve sat in the wings yet was still involved in the technical creation of solutions and offerings.

As things progressed, a merger happened with another company with its own money transfer service. They had a capability known today as *PayPal* – yes, that *PayPal*. The two companies became one and, needlessly to say, changed the whole game. Reeve was given another shot to lead the new business as CEO, but it didn't last long. Within a short period, he was booted from his leadership role. He was discouraged.

Despite the leadership woes, Reeve stayed on to support the technical development, and, of course, he held onto his company shares. He didn't give up. Later *PayPal* was bought out by *eBay*. At that time, Reeve had 11.7% ownership of *PayPal*. As you can guess, he became an instant millionaire. His net worth after the sale was valued at 100 million dollars. The crazy thing was he was only 31 years old.

Most people with that amount of money would probably choose a life of rest and leisure. Think about it – they have it made. They are set for life. They can buy a condo on the coast and take a yearly trip to Cabo San Lucas in the summer. Other than real estate investments, why risk further pursuit?

But remember, Reeve was *"future-minded"*. He had big goals. He wasn't done. And he wasn't afraid to fail. He still envisioned a different future. He lived with hope, which was fueled by his imagination coupled with experimentation. Because of that, his self-doubt began to turn to self-confidence. It encouraged him.

The Next Journey

One of Reeve's dreams was space exploration. Since he was a kid, he had always been a science fiction fan. He also had a fascination with the planets. So, Reeve, now a multimillionaire, decided to double down on his understanding of how rockets and space exploration worked.

He even headed to Moscow to see if he could physically buy one or two refurbished Intercontinental Ballistic Missiles (ICBMs). But much like the kids in grade school, he was mocked and ridiculed by the Russian subject matter experts he met. One engineer even spat upon him in disgust – wondering how someone so naïve could even ponder such a thought of space exploration. He told Reeve to go away. Imagine how embarrassed Reeve must have felt. Old self-doubt began to creep back in.

Reeve was persistent – even emboldened. He just tried to learn more of what he did not know, and after a few years, he and his team went back to Moscow, looking to buy 3 ICBMs. This time he was a more educated man, plus he had the money in hand to buy a Russian Rocket. But instead of an impulse buy for $8 million, he chose to pass on it. Not because he was giving up on his dream, but because he realized he could build it independently – from scratch and maybe even better. Reeve was a dreamer and a learner. Even though he wasn't a rocket scientist, he was confident that if he could imagine it, he could create it. The key was to get the right people to help him.

Twenty years after that first trip to Moscow, Reeve's track record will show you that he was right. The relentless pursuit of his dream, despite experiencing multiple failures and rocket disasters, has proven to be a game-changer. For example, he and his team invented the first rocket that can land safely on the ground after use – a reusable rocket.

The Real Reeve

Today, Reeve's Space Exploration Technology Company, more commonly known as *SpaceX*, has single handily changed the landscape of the space program for *NASA* and the world. As an innovator, he has revolutionized space exploration, influencing the likes of other billionaires like Jeff Bezos, Richard Branson, and more.

Reeve is better known in public circles by his full name, Elon Reeve Musk, but I used his middle name to share this story. *Why?*

Because the name Reeve means overseer. That seems appropriate. Whether on or off his game, Elon Reeve Musk is an overseer of novel and innovative ideas. He can be good at that. He is a Dreamer Imagineer who has learned to design and implement.

Granted, he struggles at times as a leader and gets distracted. Maybe he could benefit from a mentor, accountability, or a better inner circle, but his contributions prior to his Twitter acquisition have been noteworthy. He is an Imagineer.

One thing to note: It's not uncommon to find disrupters like Elon exhibit curious personality quirks. Few Imagineers are without some type of oddities. They can be eccentric. The good news is that Imagineers can *"learn to peacefully co-exist"* and manage traits including Introversion, Neuroticism, Thinking Outside the Box, Questioning Themself, and Attention-deficit / Hyperactivity Disorder (ADHD).[38] Elon himself has admittedly suffered from Asperger's Syndrome.[39] Whether you are fan of Elon Musk or not, it's encouraging to know we can persevere through traits that others see as impediments.

Like many of us, Elon occasionally falls and falters, but what's interesting to watch is to how he gets back up and continues to find a way to imagine possibilities.

Belief – *How Your Brain is a Search Engine*

The name of this chapter could have been "Identify What You Seek." Seek means to search for, to try to find. The funny thing about seeking is that it works much better when we identify – or clarify – what we believe in. *What's the idea you want to bring to life?*

Think of it like a browser search window. *What are you searching for? What are you seeking?*

When you type in the desired keyword in an internet browser search engine, you get a list of options. Your brain works the same way. Good things can happen when you seek ways to pursue the idea of what you hope for. Despite any fear or apprehension, being growth-minded and willing to learn through your experience fosters a results-oriented environment.

Neuroimaging research has shown that the hippocampus is one part of the brain that lights up when imagining the future. The hippocampus is involved in the formation of new memories and is a critical component of learning and managing emotions. Of intrigue is that it *"plays a central role in enhancing reward anticipation after receiving information."*[40] In other words, it anticipates the future. But the key is to first identify the information – namely, what we want.

My bike story offers a simple example. If I hadn't identified my desire to ride around the block with my big brother as a BELIEF, I would have had to wait another day and missed the moment. A dream was fulfilled because I identified what I desired despite my fear, and I chased after it. By identifying my desire, I put my brain on the search to recognize the opportunity I had to fulfill it. Imagineers like Elon Musk live this way every day.

Let's face it, we all want things. We are wired this way. It's how we are created. Our passions express our areas of interest that move us forward. The interaction of these forces makes us unique. What's remarkable is how it all works via our RAS.

What You Seek is Seeking You

Hope captured as desire is what helps shape the future, and it paves the way for Imagineers. Elon Musk leverages his imagination by identifying what he seeks, but it has never been easy.

Another reason I didn't initially share Elon's first name with you is that, as a reader, you would have likely filled in the story with what you already perceived about him in the news and then missed understanding the challenges he had to endure as an Imagineer. The world's image of Elon is either that of superhero stature – like Tony Stark. Or that of – a ruthless villain – like Gordon "Greed is Good" Gekko. In 2022 alone, Elon was featured as Time Magazine's *Person of the Year*, but later found himself in the social media's crosshairs as it relates to Twitter-gate. Whichever way you lean, recognize that Elon's success is a result of overcoming failures, defeats, and struggles. There's something for us to learn from his resilience.

The 13th-century poet Rumi once wrote, *"What You Seek is Seeking You"*. It may take a minute to sort through what that means, but as you look back at the journey of Elon Musk or the Wright Trio and consider what they accomplished, you can see evidence of this mystery. The mystery is profound. Einstein spoke into this mystery, *"Imagination is more important than knowledge."* He added that imagination is a *"preview of life's coming attractions."* Through your imagination, you seek purpose and become purposeful. Seeking helps us cast vision – a vision meant to be shared. All of this is fueled by your RAS.

Remember that your RAS sets a trap that allows you to take notice of things that align with your goals, including one's prayers. Jesus himself said, *"All things you ask for in prayer, you will receive if you have faith."*[41] Therefore, if prayer reflects the desire of your heart, then whatever you ask for and imagine is like pressing the ENTER key. It activates the search.

Sharing the Vision

Whether you are a fan of Elon or not, it's undeniable that as an Imagineer, he is a game-changer. He has not only ushered in a new race for space but a race for e-vehicles and sustainable energy with his *Tesla* brand. In the process, he has activated our imagination too.

One of the things that Imagineers intentionally do is cast a purposeful vision. When their imagination is well communicated, it is embraced by others. Think of *Star Wars*, *The Hobbit*, *The Marvel Universe*, *The Matrix*, and *Apple Products,* to name a few. But let's unpack the idea of vision just a little bit more.

A vision identifies a long-range target you are aiming for. It describes WHAT you seek and has all the qualities of belief. A mission, on the other hand, identifies the qualities of behavior. It defines HOW you plan to show up daily in pursuing the vision. Both vision and mission go hand in hand. One is a belief you are pursuing– the other is the behavior you choose in that pursuit. Your RAS plays on both.

If you visit the *SpaceX* site, Elon's vision is clearly spelled out. His vision is written in a compelling format suitable for reuse if you substitute a few words.

> *"You want to wake up in the morning and think the future is going to be great – and that's what being a spacefaring civilization is all about. It's about believing in the future and thinking that the future will be better than the past. And I can't*

think of anything more exciting than going out there and being among the stars." – Elon Musk

What if you substitute *"spacefaring civilization"* and *"being among the stars"* with the things that you have a vision for?

Additionally, Elon has revolutionized the car industry with *Tesla Motors* too. Their mission posted on their website offers an equally compelling format for reuse too. It's nice and short.

"Accelerate the world's transition to sustainable energy."

What if you substitute *"sustainable energy"* with the hope and dream reflective of your mission?

I encourage you to take Elon's vision and mission and refactor it for yourself. It provides a perfect template for your vision and mission.

Your Turn – *Orient with Hope*

What do you hope for?

It's a broad question, perhaps, but if you were to narrow it down just a little, it would likely create a flood of ideas. Is there an aspiration or a desire for what's ahead?

- *What do you hope for as it relates to your job?*
- *What do you hope for as it relates to your family?*
- *What do you hope for as it relates to the day ahead?*
- *What do you hope for regarding the legacy you want to leave?*

With just one well-crafted question, the imagination can be triggered and activated. My favorite question is:

"What do you hope for as it relates to _____?"

What's filled in the blank is critical. It creates context and focus.

You can use this question in almost any setting, whether someone is experiencing a peak of life or the valley in between. This question of engagement activates the imagination.

We Are In The Hope Business

One thing Imagineers share is a desire for hope. Our brains are simply wired for it. What's more interesting is that those who succeed in life learn to tap into hope. Not just their hope but recognizing the hope of those around them.

A lightbulb moment for me was realizing that those who genuinely make a difference are in the hope business. The products that I buy, the message that I care about, and the services that matter most are compelling because they help fulfill a hope. The leaders and entrepreneurs behind the best brands and businesses are purveyors of hope. You can see this pattern in how they live and how they lead. Just look at the companies they captain and the messages they share. Hope is the differentiator.

Think about the top brands and businesses like Amazon, Apple, Costco, Mercedes-Benz, Tesla, USAA, the popular fitness center across town, or your favorite band or musician. Can you see the hope thread? Those that stay consistently at the top are all in the hope business. They sell, and they deliver it. The problem is that some businesses and leaders can lose sight that they're in the hope business.

Those in the hope business do two things well: (1) they practice empathy, and (2) they work to fulfill hope.

To practice empathy, start with engagement. Get to know those you are called to serve. To fulfill hope, stay integrous. Deliver on that product, service, or message that others need. Those two things create a culture that matters and customers that will return.

If it helps, go back and look at the equation shown earlier:

The Future =
Imagination x Experimentation x Evaluation x Integrity

Remember, *hope* is the multiplier in this equation. It's the "x-factor". **Imagination** in the equation means you're thinking about what's needed and how an idea might make a difference. That's empathy.

Those who stand out and truly add value, **experiment** with what they can do to pursue and realize that hope, and then they continually **evaluate** to see how that hope is making a difference.

What's also important is to demonstrate **integrity** with sound moral and ethical principles throughout the process. This last element is likely where Elizabeth Holmes, the CEO of *Theranos*, went awry. She had a genius of an idea that offered the world hope, but she didn't stay integrous in her pursuit and was eventually convicted of fraud.[42]

Never let the pursuit of an idea eclipse the importance of integrity. As soon as you slip on integrity, you'll fold up quicker than a cheap umbrella in a windstorm.

Napoleon Bonaparte had a simple philosophy that is profound for today, *"A leader is a dealer in hope."* When it comes to being a person of influence, ask yourself:

What are some ways I can encourage hope in others?

Being a dealer of hope might be the untold secret to success, whether you are Mother Theresa, Walt Disney, Billy Graham, Oprah Winfrey, or Richard Branson. Deliver hope by helping people realize hope with integrity. As Branson shares, *"inspire a state of hope."*

Chapter Summary

This chapter has focused on the Power of Belief. Belief is having trust, faith, or confidence in what you see in your mind's eye – it's about seeking what you know when your eyes are closed. Belief is conviction and exploring what you know could be true. The Power of Belief is what gives you the desire and confidence you need to invent the future.

As humans, our *"wants"* can create a more motivating drive than our *needs*. The reason why is that it's how our brain is wired. We are motivated by desire fueled by hope. This is the Power of Belief.

Think of your Reticular Activating System (RAS). It's like a search engine subconsciously on the hunt for things that appeal to you. The computer programmer for this powerful search engine is none other than YOU. The question, therefore, is what do you hope for?

What we discover is that the most influential leaders and businesses are dealers in hope. Every successful entrepreneur is ultimately in the hope business. The reason why is that they likely started with needing hope themselves. Hope is the standard driver for every great achievement.

Hope feeds hope. But not just any kind of hope. It needs to be a hope that shapes the future and makes others hopeful. Hope is belief.

Think about how Phil Mahre, the Wright Trio, or Elon Musk changed their world by pursuing something they imagined. Their example of belief and inventing the future offers us a framework we can borrow. The Power of Belief is a value multiplier.

Additional tools and resources focused on
Imagining the Possible are available at
theimaginebook.com/ch-6

---

[37] Neville Goddard, Tweet Aug 24, 2021,
https://twitter.com/GoddardNeville/status/1430061778063429637, last accessed June 28, 2022.

[38] Alice G. Walton, 6 Quirky Personality Traits That Are Actually Linked To Success,
https://www.forbes.com/sites/alicegwalton/2017/08/09/6–bad–psychological–traits–that–can–actually–be–great–benefits, last accessed July 10, 2022.

[39] Hope King, *Elon Musk Opens Up On How Asperger's Has Impacted His Life*, published Apr 15, 202,
https://www.axios.com/2022/04/15/elon–musk–aspergers–syndrome, last accessed July 10, 2022.

[40] Helen, *The Honey Effect*, February 21, 2021, https://www.agelesspossibilities.org/blog–1/the–honey–effect, last accessed June 28,2022.

[41] English Standard Version Bible, 2001, Matthew 21:12 (ESV), https://biblehub.com/matthew/21–22.htm, last accessed May 28,2022.

[42] John Carreyrou, *Bad Blood* (pp. 52–53). Knopf Doubleday Publishing Group.

7 – MINIMIZE THE DISTRACTIONS
Understanding the Power of Boundaries

"You will never reach your destination if you stop and
throw stones at every dog that barks."

– Winston S. Churchill

The struggle is never coming up with an idea; it's staying focused on a thought long enough before getting distracted by a bunch of other ones. Distraction has been and will be the number one challenge that Imagineers face. Distraction has plagued even the great ones.

The irony is that what we call a distraction comes disguised as an attraction. They look the same. It feels like an attraction because it captures our interest and attention. When something pulls us away from the vision or mission, the culprit is *distraction*. We just might not realize it until too late.

Attraction Distraction

Years after my childhood bike riding adventures, I found myself imagining a different future lost in my own multiverse. I was in my last year of college, daydreaming about what life would be like once it was over. This fascination wasn't a healthy state of imagination; it was imagination without experimentation and without seeking out encouragement or even staying integrous with my real-world commitments. It triggered a rush of wonderment and fresh new ideas, followed by an avalanche of fear and anxiety.

I thought about my future job, where I might live, the girlfriend I might marry, the car I might own, the places I might travel, the family I might have, and the business I might create. Each of those thoughts triggered a flood of other ideas, and I started to get ahead of myself. As critical as it was, my imagination was taking my eyes off the ball. You could say I was distracted.

Distraction means the *"drawing away of the mind"*[43] There's a pull on our imagination. The distractions that affect us the most are often internal, not external. They come from within us. Whether the initial stimuli started as an external or internal trigger, the distraction takes up residence in the imagination. That's what was happening with me.

Responsibility Avoidance

As excited as I was about the future, my present circumstances were less than ideal. As I was nearing the end of my college run, the world around me felt heavy. School had only gotten harder. In what was supposed to be my final semester, I found myself overwhelmed and in over my head.

Honestly, I didn't want to think about school. I was tired of it. As anxious as I was for the future, there were other things in the present; distractions that helped numb my pain, which I became more interested in.

For me, it was playing pickup basketball, fiddling with my computer, spending time with my girlfriend, working part-time for tips at a local Pizza Hut, helping a youth group, making mixed tapes, and even dreaming up a band.

Yes, you heard right. Some friends and I formed a band my final year of college, even though I couldn't play a single instrument. We called ourselves *Boundless,* and somehow, we managed to book one gig. It was for a youth group event after a local high school basketball game. We had the whole gym for a post-game celebration. It was a good thing they won – or maybe not.

My forte was picking the songs and pulling in the other people to play and perform. We may have only played one gig, but it was a blast. Oh, I should mention that my résumé wasn't totally musically void. While I couldn't play an instrument, I occasionally wrote lyrics or laid down a melodic rap song with my friend Larry. We called ourselves *Toast, Jam, and the Raisin Bran Band*. I was Toast, and he was Jam. The Raisin Bran Band part was just instrumental tracks of popular songs that we reworked with some melodic tones and lyrics. Everything was done with reverb effects and a little echo to make us sound better.

Hopefully, any of those tapes that were made are now burnt or properly disposed of. The last thing I want anyone to hear is us singing a rendition of Kenny Loggins' *Playing with the Boys*. Our cover reworked the lyrics and title a bit. Our tune was retitled *Playing with the Brain*! ☺

Facing Failure

Hopefully, you can get a sense of my distractibility back then. It was bad.

Because of my distractions, my grades started slipping, and before I knew it. I found myself behind in almost every class. I'll never forget that sense of fear that I might fail – that I might not make it. The only thing is, I never told anyone.

Rather than trying to get help, I just kept busy with other things that pleasantly distracted me. I just wanted to create mixed tapes, pen out wrap songs with Larry, or hang out with my girlfriend Barb.

One day between classes, Barb and I found some time to chat for a few minutes. We grabbed a quiet corner in the student union to sip on a Coke. She was relaxed, but I was a mess.

Usually, I was upbeat, but lately, I had been kind of gloomy. I remember glancing at her while I took a sip of my drink. Despite my poor spirits, I was thankful for her. She caught my gaze and flashed a smile as she sipped her Coke. That caught my attention. She was a looker. Easy on the eyes, her smile was a welcome distraction. What followed next would change my life.

"Paul, I want to talk about what's going on." She said with a concerning yet comforting look. Internally, I braced myself for what I thought might be coming.

She continued. *"I've noticed you haven't been yourself lately. What's going on? Is everything okay?"*

I shook my head to wave off her worry. *"Oh. Nothing,"* I nervously laughed. *"It's just classes. I'm good. We're good."* I tried to smile as I swallowed.

"No, what is it?" she pleaded, not letting me skirt the question.

I took a deep breath and slowly let out what I had kept bottled up inside.

"All right," I muttered. *"I feel like I am under a rock and can't move. I've got something due in every class. Homework. Projects. Reports. Upcoming tests. And my teachers are relentless. They aren't giving us any slack!"*

She looked at me calmly and asked, *"So, is that all there is?"*

I then buried my head into my hands and just stared at the table. Her question echoed in my mind. *"Is that all there is?"* Inside, I just wanted to quit school. It was a battle of the Astrocytes. The work seemed too hard. Life seemed too hard. It wasn't supposed to be this way.

Finally, I responded, *"I'm just overwhelmed. I'll be honest with you; I'm not sure I'm going to make it. I don't know how I am going to finish, much less graduate."* Then after a long pause, I added, *"I just want it to be over."*

We sat there for a moment before I added. *"And I'm so sorry for being so distant lately. I'm sorry for not being there for you like you are for me."*

Internally I was a mess, and I felt lost. Not only that, but I also quietly feared I might lose her too. The whole world felt like it was about to implode.

Then she asked me a life-changing question I'll never forget.

"But you still have hope, don't you?" she gently probed.

Those seven words resonated in a way that I didn't expect. Her question stirred something in me. It wakened me. I realized that despite my gloom and doom, I still had hope. I'll never forget that moment.

"Yeah, I still have hope," I answered. *"I do."* She was the first person that ever asked me that question.

She then offered a smile and grabbed my hand. *"I believe in you. I know you can do it. Just remember that hope inside you. It's gotten you this far, hasn't it?"*

It was another great question. *"Yeah, it has,"* I responded as I returned the smile. The Astrocytes were losing their grip on me.

Two months after sipping that Coke with my girl, I found myself walking with the rest of my class to receive my engineering diploma. Less than five months later, I would ask that girl to marry me.

She would say, *"Yes!"*

The Power of Boundaries

In moments of desperation, I often think back to the question. *"But you still have hope, don't you?"* The answer every time is, *"Yes!"*

Sometimes the *yes* is more potent than other times, but a yes is still a yes. Hope can awaken you. It can change your awareness and your outlook. That question often allows me to see the path through the chaos.

The hope question also puts "me" back into the front seat. It makes me realize that I have control. I have a choice. I have the Power of Boundaries to help shape the future.

Boundaries help clarify our work zone and our no-fly zones – not just for ourselves but for others. Boundaries *"define us"* by clarifying what's acceptable and not acceptable, and what should be you and not be you.

With boundaries, you have better clarity on what should be the attractions that deserve your attention – otherwise, everything will seem important. The question is, how can you define these boundaries?

The key to minimizing distractions is to shift perspective and maintain priorities. It can be as simple as asking:

What do I hope to accomplish?

Prioritizing using the hope question takes the guesswork out of what needs to be done. It forces you to think ahead and identify what's important over what's urgent.

The follow-on question is asking:

What sacrifices do I need to make to achieve my desired outcome?

Asking these two questions focuses our imagination – our mind – on what matters and away from those unrestrained thoughts that divert us, including the Astrocytes that try to influence us to quit. The specific part of our mind where the Power of Boundaries is leveraged is through the Executive Function of the brain.

Executive Function – *How to Improve Your Focus*

The frontal lobe of your brain is where control for the Executive Function exists. Like a conductor in an orchestra, the Executive Function is what leads you. You use the Executive Function every day. It's essentially on the clock 24x7, but it needs to be especially attentive during your working hours. It's what's in charge, and is responsible for focusing and decision–making, and dealing with distractions.

In her 2018 TED Talk, Sabine Doebel, a cognitive scientist shares, *"If you want to improve your Executive Function in some aspect of your life, don't look for quick fixes. Think about the context and how you can make your goals matter more to you."*[44]

In his revolutionary book *Boundaries for Leaders*, Dr. Henry Cloud shares more of what is happening when we have the right focus – the right context. He describes how your Executive Function relies on three internal processes to drive a vision forward and conquer an objective. These processes include subsystems for Attention, Inhibition, and Working Memory.[45]

We need to have all three of these components working together. They complement and work in conjunction with our RAS.

Attend to What Matters

What are you paying attention to? Cal Newport, the author of the best-selling book Deep Work, shares *"We often tell ourselves a story that we're observing the whole world around us. But really the world around us is shaped by what we're paying attention to."*[46]

Attention is the ability to focus on relevant stimuli and the right priorities. For this subsystem of our Executive Function to properly work, find and use tools to attend to what truly matters. While the RAS might help us keep our antennae up regarding the awareness of external opportunities, we need internal tools to help us make the right choices. The tool I recommend is a simple question that you should use daily.

When it comes to staying focused, ask yourself:

What one thing do I hope to accomplish?

This question gives you focused attention and creates boundaries. It's a question to ask throughout the day.

What is essential for this to work right is to make sure the hope you identify is measurable and attainable. Sometimes this means dividing the big goals into smaller pieces. Hope represented in smaller, achievable chunks elevates your attention and ability to focus.

Inhibit What Does Not Matter

Inhibition is the ability to say no and "not do" specific actions that might be irrelevant or destructive. This is the part of our imagination that often needs the most help. We are easily distracted – at least I am.

For this subsystem to work right, find ways to block out what is irrelevant to our hope or goal.

How?

One way is by asking a simple question when something is competing for your attention:

Can it wait?

There are two answers to this question: Yes or No. But if you don't ask the question *"Can it wait?"* then the answer will likely be *"NO; it can't wait,"* and your mind ends up straddling two activities. The one you were trying to work on and the new task.

But by asking this simple question, you can maintain control when something is competing for your attention. If the answer to the question is *"no, it can't wait,"* then bookmark what you are currently doing so that you can pick it up later. Then block a limited window of time to respond fully to the interrupt. This permits you to handle the interrupt.

If the answer is *"yes, it can wait"*, then "pocket" the request quickly by acknowledging it and putting it on your TO DO list for later, and then carry on with your original work.

Here's a simple flow chart that can help guide you in blocking and tackling the interrupts.

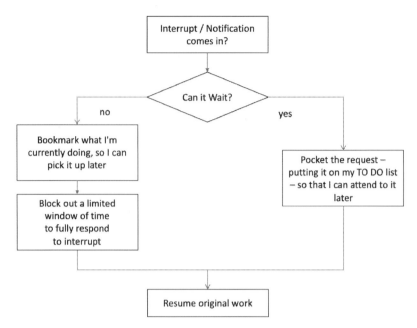

Figure 2 – Blocking and Tackling Interrupts

The internal question on *"Can it Wait?"* comes down to also asking, *"Will it help me achieve what I seek?"* This is where the next component comes into play – Working Memory.

Maintain a Working Memory

Working Memory is the ability to *"retain and access"* relevant information needed for reasoning, decision making, or taking next step actions. Being aware of your present state and having situational awareness is the key. The Working Memory and RAS in this capacity need to work together. But we set our RAS through our internal dialog using our Attentive processor and Inhibition processor. Namely, *what's important, and what's not essential?* We need Working Memory for the conversations we have, the tasks we do, and the experiences we are taking in. Working Memory is focused on the ongoing journey – of where we are. It requires being fully present.

Working Memory is considered part of our conscious system that taps us into our physical world, but it can also access the imaginative world. Think of how you conjure images when you listen to stories. Some of these stories may be fictional. They are not real. But your brain emotionally experiences it as if it is real.

Working Memory can be activated when you sleep too. Your dreams are vibrant and seen in your Working Memory. (Remember that RAS is playing a part in your dreams). The only problem with dreams when we sleep is that retaining those dreams requires another part of the brain to engage quickly: our long-term memory.

When awake, the key is keeping our Working Memory optimal. We need our Working Memory to be at its best for the Attentive processor and our Inhibitor processor to work right. Keeping the "hopes" you have front and center – supported by the RAS – can help immensely. Other tricks, like having a notepad next to you or your computer to jot down insights as they occur, can help immensely. I keep a notebook next to my keyboard to capture ideas during a Zoom or WebEx call.

To understand the notepad trick as it relates to Working Memory, think of how a server often takes an order. The server writes it down. As impressive as it might be if a server seems to have the ability to take an order without jotting it down, you'd probably be more satisfied if it were captured.

Why?

Because, if you are like, you know the likelihood of the server remembering your exact order is limited. You want your food right.

In the same way, we need good working memory to function at our best, so it's okay to use tools to help you. For me, I keep a Kanban board that captures my "TO DO", "DOING" and "DONE" list. I share more about this in the free bonus resources available on the web at TheImagineBook.com.

Also, what can help is good sleep, thorough exercise, and healthy eating habits – they are critical. Declutter your environment too. Clean space gives you a clean mind to think; it helps the Inhibition processor, whereas the symbols you place in your environment might support the Attentive processor.

One question you can use to keep your Working Memory focused is to ask:

What do I hope to accomplish in this moment?

This resets your RAS and allows you to minimize distractions and focus on the possible.

The Builder – *The Story of Emmitt*

By minimizing distractions using the Power of Boundaries, your attitude can shift to see greater hope. This makes it easier to take responsibility for your actions despite the circumstances. As for me, being reminded of my hope is what encourages me to break average and persevere, but I'm not the only one.

One of my favorite examples of this power of imagination is the story of Emmitt Perry. Emmitt is a well-regarded American actor, director, producer, and screenwriter.

Growing up, though, the odds were heavily against him. Things weren't so rosy. Emmitt grew up outside New Orleans, and the daily adversity he experienced was beyond comprehension. As a young child, Perry suffered multiple instances of physical, sexual, and emotional abuse. His father would often beat him. Perry even contemplated suicide at an early age. However, deep inside him was a small flame of hope that would eventually light a fire and change his world and those around him. He somehow found a way to minimize the distractions.

When Emmitt was 16 years old, he changed his name. Today, you know him as Tyler Perry, the actor and movie mogul who starred as Medea and built his own movie production business in Georgia. As of 2020, he was the highest revenue-producing entertainer in the industry.

The Past is Not Your Future

Despite a rough upbringing, Tyler Perry has become an encouraging voice to millions of people. He is a transformational leader that figured out how to minimize the greatest distraction of all – our past. He changed his name to Tyler to separate himself from his abusive dad. Tyler, by the way, means Builder. Seeing what he has imagined and built, I can't think of a more meaningful name than that.

In his early 20s, Perry was watching an episode of The Oprah Winfrey Show while trying to find his place in the world. One of the guests shared with Oprah the therapeutic effect that writing can have in helping people work out problems, including dealing with past trauma.

Perry had indeed experienced a lot of that. The idea of writing triggered something for him, propelling him to give it a shot. It's what launched his career.

Writing gave him focus, and it allowed him to minimize the distractions. The first step was writing letters to himself. This activated his imagination in a powerful way.

The Influence of a Letter

A few years ago, on CBS's Morning Show, Perry shared excerpts from one of those letters while clasping an early childhood photo of himself. Here's some of what he shared.[47]

> *"Dear child of God, in this picture, I see you trying to smile, but that smirk is all you can muster. I know that you are having it really hard right now. And you spend a lot of time using your imagination seeing yourself running free in the park, away from all the pain.*
>
> *In the reflection of your very sad eyes, I see the hurt of watching your mother be belittled and beaten. I see the pain of your own beatings and the barrage of insults that you suffer and endure every day. I feel the horror of the hands of the molesters who are trying to rob you of who you are.*
>
> *As I search your young face for any sign of myself, believe it or not, I'm able to smile.*
>
> *Because just behind all of that darkness, **I see hope.**"*

There's even more from Tyler's letter, and I'll share just an excerpt or two, but before I do, I want to pause on that last thought. He said, *"Behind all of the darkness, I see hope."* Did that catch your attention? It's a powerful thought, isn't it?

You and I can have a fire inside us despite what's happening to the world around us. With just a little bit of hope, we can fan the flame, and we can cast some light. The faith that Perry is talking about is what casts a vision.

Here's what Perry shares next,

> *I know you don't know this right now, but who you become is being shaped inside of every one of those experiences. Every one of them. The good. The bad. And yes, even the really ugly ones.*

I want to encourage you to reflect on this thought at the end of each day,

How have today's experiences shaped me for tomorrow?

Perry's letter begs us to explore *"every"* experience. *"The Good. The Bad. And yes, even the ugly ones."* How have they prepared you for something significant in your life?

Imagine the impact that you can still make. Your past doesn't define you, but it can remind you of how far you've come.

There's much more in Perry's letter, where he talks about caring for his mom and making her proud. And he alludes to having a clear vision of his desired future despite the negative voices in his life.

Let's pick it up in the middle of the letter.

> *...you don't think you're going to live to see 30 years old. But there's a still small voice inside of you that says you are going to be okay.*
>
> *Looking back on it, I know now that that is and was the voice of God. That is the only way to explain how you knew how to navigate your way through turbulent times, and how you instinctively know how to bob and weave and survive. How you knew that when you had nobody to protect you, you heard something inside of you protecting yourself.*
>
> *Like when you were told that you're nothing and something says DON'T BELIEVE THAT. And when your teacher sits you down and tells you that you'll never be successful because you're poor because you were black because you were from the*

ghetto. There's something inside of you that says SHE'S WRONG. THAT'S NOT TRUE.

Perry is setting the table for you and me. As a child, he initially lacked confidence; he had doubts, and he was distracted. Yet, he found a way to regain his focus and minimize the negative voices and distractions; the ones that said he couldn't, he can't, and he won't.

One of the characters that he plays, Madea, once quipped, *"It ain't what people call you, it's what YOU answer to."* Perry is talking about the importance of minimizing the things distracting you so that you can stay focused on hope. In his letter, he shares the value of that focus and hope.

> *That will light a fire under you ... You will become better. You will become tougher. And when you get older, you will use it in your work to uplift and encourage and inspire millions of people.*

The key is minimizing distractions by calling out the doubt and living with hope.

Chapter Summary

This chapter has focused on the Power of Boundaries. Boundaries clarify your work zone and no-fly zones – not just for yourself but for others. With the Power of Boundaries, you have the focus on priorities you need to invent the future.

Our imagination needs to have boundaries to color between the lines. We need to minimize the things that can distract us so that our Executive Function is clear-minded and fully engaged. Boundaries help us prioritize and lead us to a *"sense of ownership."* It offers us focus on where our responsibilities start and end, and where someone else's responsibilities begin.[48]

Solidify yourself with the Power of Boundaries. With boundaries, you have better clarity on the attractions that deserve your attention – otherwise, everything might seem important. The question is, how can you define these boundaries?

Here are a few questions to guide you:

1. *What matters?*
2. *What am I responsible for, and why is this important?*
3. *What are others gifted at? How can they contribute?*
4. *What are the things that distract me/us that doesn't matter?*

If we can improve our working memory, attend to what matters, and inhibit what distracts, then we can lead ourselves and those around us more effectively.

Additionally, part of minimizing the distraction is to re-focus on the hope. In the 16th century, Martin Luther shared, *"Everything that is done in this world, is done by hope."* Hope is the fuel to fire up your imagination. Hope is what drives our boundaries.

Three centuries later, another Martin – Martin Luther King Jr. – stated something equally as profound,

> **"Life's most persistent and urgent question is,**
> **'What are you doing for others?'"**

Great leaders who change the status quo ask this question. It helps clarify the boundaries.

Think about what Rockefeller, Carnegie, Edison, Ford, and the Wright Trio accomplished after the Civil War and at the turn of the twentieth century. They forged new industries using their imagination, armed with clear boundaries – oil, steel, electricity, automobiles, and airplanes. They changed the status quo. Movie mogul Tyler Perry's own life exemplifies an Imagineer who has been working to make a difference.

If MLK could have gone back and asked these Imagineers, *"What are you doing for others?"* They would each have an answer reflective of someone who leads with boundaries.

From an organization's viewpoint, King's question can vary slightly. We might ask:

- *What are we doing for our customers?*
- *What are we doing for our employees?*
- *What are we doing for our community?*
- *What are we doing to make a difference?*

Good questions are what probe the imagination. They compel us to stay focused using the Power of Boundaries, giving us an even greater opportunity to change the world.

The Power of Boundaries helps you minimize the distractions so that you stay focused on the hope that's inside you.

◆ ◆ ◆

Additional tools and resources focused on
Minimizing the Distractions are available at
theimaginebook.com/ch-7

---

[43] Nir Eyal, *Indistractable*. BenBella Books, Inc.

[44] Sabine Doebel, *How Your Brain's Executive Function Works – And How To Improve It*, TEDx Mile High, 2018,
https://www.ted.com/talks/sabine_doebel_how_your_brain_s_executive_function_works_and_how_to_improve_it, last accessed June 28, 2022.

[45] Henry Cloud, *Boundaries for Leaders*, Harper Business.

[46] Netflix, *The Mind Explained Series*, "How to Focus", Season 2, Episode 1,
"https://www.netflix.com/watch/81273771, last accessed June 28, 2022.

[47] *Tyler Perry Shares Note To His Younger Self,* https://www.youtube.com/watch?v=HMNiPj8o6RU, last accessed June 28, 2022.

[48] Henry Cloud and John Townsend, *Boundaries: When To Say Yes, How to Say No* (p. 29), Zondervan.

8 – ALIGN YOUR STEERING
Understanding the Power of Values

"Keep your mind off the things you don't want
by keeping it on the things you do want."

– W. Clement Stone

Earlier I shared that a dream I had in college was to one day start a business. After graduating, that dream simmered on the back burner for years. I was afraid of the risk, so I stayed focused on more conventional patterns of living and making an earning. I never forgot my dream, but I became more afraid to pursue it.

It wasn't until nearly eleven years later that I officially did something with it. Looking back, I can see signs of me subconsciously pushing on the door on several occasions. I call it *"my season of exploration as a wanna-preneur."*

Seasons of Exploration

In the mid-90s, I chased website development during nights and weekends by building personal HTML pages on the side. A few years later, I added a second phone line to the house and had my computer connected to the internet via a modem 24 x 7.

After a few months, my Internet Service Provider (ISP), Monumental Network Systems of Chantilly, put me in "internet jail", not because of my overuse of connection time, which was probably true, but because they thought the home page that I submitted for a personal webpage contest was *"too professional"* – that it reflected a *business*, not a *hobbyist*. Yet, I had been paying only for a "personal" account.

Not to brag, but I thought the web page I designed was kind of cool. I had created a dark-mode web page featuring a virtual refrigerator that allowed me (and others) to post digital images on a photorealistic fridge door. Think Pinterest before there was Pinterest. I also had a blog on the page contributing new ideas about technology, programming, and the future of simulation every week. All of this was created in pure raw, beautiful HTML. It was something I did on the side.

I loved to code and create. I also loved the idea of being an author. I contributed to several programming books and wrote multiple white papers focused on advancing technology. Several of my early pieces were on the concept of delivering packet burst data to support simulation, which we know today as streaming.

Another idea was for a virtual whiteboard allowing multiple people to collaborate simultaneously from the comfort of their computers. The papers I wrote gave me opportunities to speak at technical conferences and trade shows. I learned to love the stage, but back in college that had been a place I was not fond of.

Things didn't get focused for me in launching a business until just before 2000 when Microsoft announced their idea for the Xbox. That lit a fire. I knew it was time. But I knew I couldn't do it alone.

Two of my co-workers, Larry and Steve, also had a long-standing dream stewing on the back burner. Like me, none of us had chased it. But here we were – three of us who shared common values with a mutual dream to start a business. It didn't take long to realize that maybe it was time to join forces.

In early 2000, Larry, Steve, and I became business partners, working nights and weekends in pursuit of the American dream. Our focus was on building a startup company called SimVentions. I'll never forget that initial collaboration and excitement.

In those early months, as we chased our dream, pursuing Microsoft, Kodak, and others, we also shaped a mantra: "*Imagine. Create. Explore. Discover.*"[49] We believed that what we could *Imagine* could be made real; with hard work, it could be *Created*. We had faith to believe in what we could not see, which propelled us to *Explore*. And because of that exploration, we were able to *Discover* the impact of hard work, perseverance, and faith. However, it wasn't easy. And there were a ton of pivots that we had to make.

Almost Quitting

After the euphoric start that most entrepreneurs have, a funny thing happened. Doubt knocked on our door. Much of the work that we had pursued failed to materialize. Soon months turned to years, and by the middle of 2002, we began to wonder if we had chosen the right path. The battle was more difficult than we expected. We started contemplating common questions of defeat that inevitably circle when doubt comes knocking:

- *"Maybe we can't?"*
- *"Maybe we shouldn't?"*
- *"Maybe we just don't have what it takes?"*

Our imagination started to take us off the rails.

Leveraging a new Playlist

Doubt almost stopped us from moving forward. It was ready to rob us of our future. It would have been easy to settle for the status quo and give up on the dream. But instead of declaring defeat, we chose a different path. We asked a different question that radically changed our perspective.

- *"Who says we can't?"*

The Power of Values

"Who says we can't" was essentially the same question that my dad seeded in me back when I was learning to ride a bike. I can still think back and remember my dad saying, *"Who says you can't?"* as I straddled the bike, ready to ride without training wheels. He seeded a soundtrack that still plays in my mind today.

The other soundtrack seeded was from my girlfriend – now wife – back in college. *"But you still have hope, don't you?"* These soundtracks, which are both in the form of a question, help challenge my doubt and trigger my values.

The Power of Values reinvigorates our imagination. It creates alignment from the inside out.

One of the best definitions for values I have found is from Dr. Russ Harris, the best-selling author of the *Happiness Trap*. He defines values in three components:

- *"Desired qualities of action"*
- *"How you want to behave"*
- *"How you want to treat yourself, others, and the world around you."*

Values are powerful because they set the course for both vision and mission. You really can't have a clear vision or mission without values. Values identify not just what you care about but why you care. Think about how it matches with the vision and mission.

A vision represents a desired dream or long-range goal. Think of vision as a target in archery. It's in the distance and something that you want to hit. The arrow that you use to hit that target portrays your mission. A mission represents the actions and behavior you'll exhibit in pursuing a goal. Think of how the arrow flies toward a target. If the mission is right, there's a good chance you'll hit the mark. But before the arrow ever flies, the archer with the bow needs to aim. This is where values come into play. The importance of the archer holding the bow and setting the course makes all the difference. The better the values the better the aim!

If vision describes what you want, and mission describes how you will execute, then values represent why it matters. **At the end of the day, YOU are your values personified.** What you do, why you did it, what choices you made, what reactions you had all reflect your values. Values give you focus and shape your future.

Your imagination, therefore, needs to be clear on those values ahead of time. People don't follow a leader's vision until they first buy into their values. ***What are your values?*** Be clear on what they are.

As for me, there are two soundtracks that I try to play: *"What do I hope for?"* and, *"Who says I can't?"* These two questions help me gather my focus, clarify my values, and unlock my imagination.

My values today are five-fold:

1. Keep growing
2. Connect with others

3. Live courageously
4. Break average
5. Be grateful

Notice how these five core values are action-oriented; they are values with verbs. They keep me fired up. I want to help people not quit. I want to help people become bulletproof, knowing there's always hope – real hope.

Why?

Because I need it myself.

We may not choose the cards we are dealt, but we do choose how we play the game. It comes down to alignment. When we align ourselves with healthy values, it propels us to move forward no matter what the challenge. Values shape our behaviors and build our habits. Alignment allows us to pull back on the bow and let the arrow fly toward the target.

Ready. Aim. Fire!

Oxytocin – *How Values Get Wired*

Inside your brain, over a hundred types of neurotransmitters are itching to arc from one nerve cell to another. While they all have different roles, their job is to keep you fired up and the mind properly functioning. One of those powerful neurotransmitters is something called Oxytocin.

Oxytocin is what builds trust and cooperation. This neurotransmitter creates in us the feeling of friendship, love, and deep trust. For example, it develops the parent-child bond – especially for mothers. But it works for dads, uncles, and grandparents too.

Another way to think of Oxytocin is that it *"acts like a volume dial, turning up and amplifying brain activity related to whatever someone is already experiencing."*[50]

Our conscious brain, called our moral brain, is networked like a computer integrating various brain components, including our frontal lobe. Our mind's operating system for the conscious brain supports our rational thinking and promotes empathy. And it helps evaluate threats, validate beliefs, and regulate behavior. Its guiding directive is driven by our values. But for this operating system to properly function and work, it needs a little help from the magical elixir Oxytocin.

Oxytocin is a chemical messenger – a hormone of signals – driven ultimately by what we value. Think of it as your operating system's command line prompt that provides instructions that affect your mental and physical behavior.

Having the right balance of Oxytocin in our system is critical. Too little, and we might experience a touch of depression. Too much, and we might exhibit a touch of oversensitivity. In other words, it can affect our emotional intelligence.

Hope creates alignment and fires up our Oxytocin. Hope is what resets our sails.

Finding Alignment

When it comes to alignment, we have two choices. We can either be driven by extrinsic motivations or led by intrinsic ones.

Extrinsic desires come from the outside – they are external. They are often pushed upon us by others. Many cultures, like the United States, are extrinsically influenced. We are bombarded with the push. You can see it in advertising, governance, media, work environments, school environments, calendar invites, and even in our smartphone notifications. Many of these external pushes include well-intended thoughts and prompts from loved ones. But the reality is they are not necessarily "our" motivations; they are someone else's.

A more powerful source to tap into is our intrinsic motivations, which come from our internal desires – our values. A typical example for many is personal prayer. Again, prayer is simply expressing the desires of your heart. When you express a heart desire, you are pulling on intrinsic motivation and not relying exclusively on external sources. These are prayers that are more meaningful and more likely to be pursued. They activate your RAS.

If you are a person who values prayer, perhaps it's time to do a status check. Take inventory of your recent prayers. Are they from "your" heart? Or are they a reflection of someone else's desires placed upon you? The ones from the heart align with the values that you keep. These prayers are more likely to be realized than prayers based on extrinsic motivation.

How Are You Motivated?

What energizes you? What gets you up in the morning and propels you through the day? Does it come from the inside of you or the outside?

When it comes to motivation, it turns out there are two types of people. Type X people who are eXtrinsically motivated by outside influence, and Type I people who are Intrinsically motivated.

In the bestselling book *Drive*, author Daniel Pink explores these two types further. We learn that the primary motivator for Type X is *"external rewards"*. Whereas the primary motivator for Type I is *"the freedom, challenge and the undertaking itself."* For Type I, it comes from their heart.[51]

Pink encourages us to look at how others are motivated too including our spouse, our children, and those we work with. Understanding what motivates us and where it comes from allows us to better lead.

Pink's research reveals four findings:

- Type I's consistently outperform Type X's in the long run.
- Type I behavior is natural and nurtured – *"born and made"*.
- Type I behavior is a *"renewable resource"*.
- Type I behavior promotes physical and mental well-being.

I don't know about you, but as I look at this list, my desire is to be sure I am part of the Type I team. Type I behavior is internally controlled and *"self-directed"*. It's fueled by a desire and dedication to personal growth and becoming *"better at something"* that makes a difference.

Type I behavior connects a quest for self-improvement to a significant purpose. Intrinsic alignment requires three things: Our Values. Our Hope. Our Imagination. We need all three. This can be represented by another simple formula:

Alignment = Values x Imagination

If you notice in this equation, the "x-factor" again is hope. Our imagination can lead us to some dark and disturbing places. The safeguard is to anchor your imagination with values. Values coupled with hope and imagination help create balanced alignment.

When it comes to evaluating your motivation, ask yourself:

Does what I pursue reflect
my values, hopes, and imagination,
or does it represent someone else's?

When what you are pursuing is Intrinsic (your own), you should feel a sense of alignment. It will offer a deep source to pull from that can keep you going.

However, if what you are pursuing is eXtrinsic, you may feel out of alignment, and it will feel more like a push that's been stacked upon you. Unless you are entirely sold on what's been pushed, the best it might offer you is temporary motivation. It's kind of like a new year's resolution.

The ability to realize a goal or a dream and live a life that impacts others – is dependent upon the values we hold dearly – whether those values are Intrinsic or eXtrinsic. Make sure the values are something YOU believe in. When it is, then your hope and imagination can follow. With alignment you are better equipped to face almost any challenge.

The Watchmaker – *The Story of Corrie*

Imagine waking up one morning and finding your whole world has shifted overnight. Imagine everything you cherished and knew is threatened to be gone.

That's precisely what happened in the spring of 1940 after the German Nazi forces invaded the country of Holland. That following day, millions of Dutch citizens tuned their radio to a BBC-sponsored broadcast to hear from their Queen. In that moment, Queen Wilhelmina of the Netherlands confirmed the grave news – their country had been overtaken and was now in the hands of the German forces.[52]

> *"Fellow Hollanders, the lights have gone out over free Holland. Where only two weeks ago there was a free nation of men and women brought up in the cherished tradition of Christian civilization.*

There is now the stillness of death. Oppressed ... Threatened ...
Watched on every side by a power that would tear out all hope
from the soul of man.

The unhappy people of Holland can only pray in silence. For
those who have lost their voice but not their hope or their vision
in the struggle against the onslaught of barbarism.

Long live the Netherlands!"

Sure enough, within days, Holland was officially overtaken. One family, the Ten Booms, well-respected watchmakers in the small town of Haarlem, decided to do what they could to help those in need. In particular, the two sisters, Corrie and Betsie Ten Boom, and their aging father worked together to create a haven and hiding place for any Jewish refugee or Nazi resistance worker.

The hiding place that they created was quite impressive. The foundation for their sanctuary was two apartments that had been attached years prior. On one side was their watch shop connected to the back of an apartment, which offered stair access to three upper levels. This provided living quarters for the family and their special guests. The top floor, which initially had been Corrie's room, was converted to create a hidden compartment behind the wall that could hide a small family. That hidden room was covertly built in those early days of Nazi occupation.

For several years, they risked their safety to protect any person who knocked on their door needing help or wanting hope. Corrie was resourceful, finding unique ways to obtain extra ration cards required for food distribution. This allowed them to feed those in need. One time, she was able to get a hold of 100 ration cards by boldly asking in a way that compelled compassion.

Intrinsic alignment does that for you. It creates the power to overcome just about any challenge. Corrie's mindset was unique. She was a Type I, fueled with intrinsic alignment. She lived with hope each day. She and her family intrinsically believed that the resources would be provided. Her RAS, therefore, was wired to receive. She was unshaken.

Imagine how it would be to have that kind of hope and trust during a holocaust – or any challenge!

The Ten Booms lived as prepared as anyone could. They remained hopeful. Ready to respond to life's challenges and prepared others by offering hope. A family of four under their care was able to evacuate to the secret hidden place in Corrie's room in just over a minute. This required traveling three flights of stairs and not leaving a trace as to their prior presence when the alert buzzer was triggered. They practiced evacuation multiple times to make sure guests were prepared. This is one of the many lessons we can learn from Corrie's example regarding hope.

Preparation empowers hope – it gives clarity of a *just cause*. Hope coupled with preparation creates a state of readiness. However, hope without preparation creates disillusion and confusion.

Corrie and her family were instrumental in helping the Dutch underground resistance. All told, they helped save at least 800 Jews and Dutch citizens. Having a sense of purpose creates meaning – and meaning is the foundation for hope.

About four years after the Nazi occupation of the Netherlands, the Ten Booms were eventually arrested after being snitched upon by a Dutch informant. At the time of their arrest, they were harboring six guests. But the Nazi soldiers never found the hidden guests despite extensively searching the house. Those six refugees remained undiscovered and safe the entire time behind a secret wall in Corrie's bedroom. They were protected.

As for the Ten Booms, after their arrest, they were placed in concentration camps for harboring Jews and supporting the Dutch underground resistance. Their father would die only a few days after his arrest but died knowing he lived to make a difference.

Corrie Ten Boom herself was later sent to the notorious Ravensbrück concentration camp, which was a hard labor camp for women in northern Germany. A week before she was scheduled to be put to death, she was miraculously released. Her sister, unfortunately, never made it out.

As a free citizen, Corrie did what her father and sister would have wanted her to do – to live with courage and offer hope. That was her *just cause*. She spent the rest of her days sharing this message of hope for the world to hear. Even in her death, her impact continues.

For Corrie, her inspiration came from the Bible. One verse became her life song. *"You are my hiding place and my shield; I hope in your word."*[53]

Hope was everything to her; she found alignment by being clear on her values. It protected her. It encouraged her and others.

I could not write a book on the powers of imagination and not include Corrie's story. By the time she was 80 years old, Corrie had traveled to over 60 countries and had written multiple books sharing this message of hope centered on being clear on your values. If Corrie were alive today, she would want you and me to share this message with others. She would encourage us to continuously align with our values.

Top Six Corrie Quotes

To get a taste of Corrie's encouragement, here are just a few thoughts in her own words, which have motivated thousands to persevere.

1. *"Worry is like a rocking chair: it keeps you moving but doesn't get you anywhere."*
2. *"Faith sees the invisible, believes the unbelievable, and receives the impossible."*
3. *"When a train goes through a tunnel and it gets dark, you don't throw away the ticket and jump off. You sit still and trust the engineer."*
4. *"Never be afraid to trust an unknown future to a known God."*

Chapter Summary

This chapter has focused on the Power of Values. Values are the qualities and standards of living you choose that matter most to you. They shape you and become what you are known for. **Values are vital for vision.** Don't try to invent the future without the Power of Values.

Have you ever noticed that *"you are happiest and most motivated when the admiration you seek is for something that matters"*?[54] This reflects the importance of being clear on your values. The key is alignment. Align your steering. This is about getting clear on your vision and what matters most. What often draws us to our values is our hope.

What is your hope?

My girlfriend's hope question all those years ago still creates alignment for me when life hits me hard. When I ask myself, *"But you still have hope, don't you?"* It forces me to think about what I want and care about; it brings me back to my values.

Your imagination is a proving ground for what's to come. That's why alignment is so important. Alignment creates traction.

When your alignment feels off, ask yourself:

What matters most?

Taking time to think through this question will help you align your steering. The Power of Alignment supported by your values and what you hope for will direct you to the future.

Additional tools and resources focused on
Aligning Your Steering are available at
theimaginebook.com/ch-8

---

49 *"Imagine. Create. Explore. Discover.™"* is a trademark of *SimVentions, Inc.,* first used January 2000.

50 Owens, Alexandra, *Tell Me All I Need to Know About Oxytocin,* https://www.psycom.net/oxytocin, published Sep 23, 2021, last accessed June 28, 2022.

51 Daniel Pink, *Drive* (pp. 78–82), Penguin Publishing Group.

52 *The Hiding Place,* 1975, Directed by James F. Collier, Note: This movie depicts the real–life account of a Dutch family that risked their lives by offering a safe haven for Jews during World War II. It is based on the autobiographical book with the same name, written by Corrie Ten Boom. It's presently available on Amazon Prime.

53 The Bible, "You are my hiding place and my shield; I hope in your word." – Psalm 119:114.

54 Mark Thompson and Bonita S. Thompson. *Admired: 21 Ways to Double Your Value,* Evolve Publishing.

DECIDE

Choose the Courage

Phase Three – DECIDE

The third phase of the OODA Loop is to DECIDE. This is about finding courage despite the fear.

Your choices determine your character. Think about how your life has been shaped more by your choices than by your circumstances. **Your future is a product of the choices you make** regardless of your prior circumstances. Choose well by recognizing who you are called to be. Then seek to identify what course of action might be best.

Think back to the epic *Star Wars* series and the choices Anakin, Luke, Leia, Han Solo, or any of the characters made. The story that unfolds is directly correlated to the choices that they make. You and I are no different. We can Observe and Orient – and get ourselves ready, but if we don't Decide to do something, then something else will Decide for us.

Think about how a professional football team drafts players coming out of college. We think the best teams are good at Observing and Orienting, and they should be. But the truth is, leaders of the best teams are excellent at Deciding. They are looking at players from three lenses:

- Deciding the best player for the long-term based on *vision*.
- Deciding the best player for their short-term based on *needs*.
- Deciding the best player that fits the system based on *culture*.

If a player on the draft board matches those three criteria, the decision should be easy. But let's say the owner injects his thought and desire at the last minute without looking at these three criteria. Maybe they are caught up in the hype of a player. When that happens, then the team at the leadership level is fractured. They are not on the same page.

When you make a choice – especially with a team that you are accountable to – it's essential to be on your "A" game when making decisions. Decision-making is where buy-in happens.

In this section, we explore three behaviors of an imagineer that are imperative for making sound, solid decisions:

- Get Bulletproof with the Power of Resilience
- Increase the Amplitude with the Power of Today
- Notice the Opportunities with the Power of Discipline

9 – GET BULLETPROOF
Understanding the Power of Resilience

"For there is always light.
if only we're brave enough to see it,
if only we're brave enough to be it."

– Amanda Gorman

Life is a series of choices. The choices we make, considering our circumstances, are not easy. Nonetheless, the choices we make shape our tomorrows.

My mantra these days is *"lead bulletproof"*. It's a choice centered on a need to pursue life with clarity of hope, the conviction of truth, and connection with others. Getting bulletproof is about *"finding the strength to bear the unbearable."*[55]

I wish I could say I have always had this mindset. The truth is, I continually go through multiple seasons that test me yet teach me the importance of leading bulletproof. One of those seasons stands out more than any other. It was an experience that I waited seven years to share.

The Unexpected

It had been a long week and a stressful day. I was traveling through Washington D.C., driving south on Interstate 95, finding myself stuck in Thursday afternoon traffic. With about 30 miles left on my commute, I noticed I was struggling to see out my left eye. I dismissed it, thinking it was just road fatigue and thought nothing more of it.

The following day, when I woke up, it was even worse. I could hardly see. Eventually, I went to the ER, and they sent me to a specialist. As he looked in my eye, he told me calmly, almost like a robot, *"Paul, you have Optic Neuritis. And that's a sure tell sign of MS."*

I couldn't believe what I was hearing. *"MS? Multiple Sclerosis?"*

More tests – including an MRI – confirmed the MS.

The Choice

A few days after my diagnosis, I was getting a steroid infusion to see if they could get my left eye going again, and the attending Nurse, after hearing my diagnosis, told me of another patient with a similar dilemma.

"Paul, we had a young mom that came in a while back. She had Optic Neuritis and MS just like you. When she got word of her MS, it devasted her, and she lost hope. She quit and sheltered at home. Now she can no longer walk."

Honestly, I'm not sure I wanted to hear that. I could feel the fear rising inside of me.

Then she said, *"But hang on. There's another story. Two other men had come in here too. They both had optic neuritis and MS, like you."*

Once again, she had my attention.

"Paul, they didn't know each other. But they became fast friends. Despite having MS, they now race competitively in 5Ks, 10Ks, and Half Marathons."

She then looked at me and added, *"Paul, they never lost hope!"*

Now, that was a story I needed to hear. I remember looking up at her and responding, *"Thank you for sharing that."* I swallowed hard, recognizing the choice in front of me, and then added, *"I still have hope too."*

The Clarity

Six months later, I was in Orlando at a Leadership conference, and somehow, John Maxwell, a mentor in my life, got word about the MS.

In a quiet little corner – with no one around – he pulls me aside, *"Paul, I just found out that you have MS."*

I nodded and confirmed the news. We chatted a bit, and then he asked if he could pray for me. He called it a prayer of provision. Of course, I said, *"yes"*.

Then right there, in the middle of a hotel hallway, this legend of a leader prays that God will order my steps. That I will be given strength that sustains me and my family. That God will turn my challenges into opportunities. And that I will live the rest of my days as a catalyst leader.

Do you have any idea what that prayer did for me?

It was like a battery recharge. It refueled my hope and changed my fear into faith!

Honestly, it restored the vision for my life. I felt free to IMAGINE again!

Looking back, John's prayer wasn't just a prayer for me. It was a prayer for all of us. You see, no matter what challenge you are facing. No matter what left hook you didn't see coming. There's still hope.

With hope, imagination offers you courage. It makes you resilient. It might even restore your vision. But without hope, your imagination will take you to some dark places. It can leave you depleted and discouraged.

The good news is you have a choice. It turns out that it's never over when you receive bad news, or when you stumble and fall. It's only over when you choose to quit.

Look for the hope. **Hope won't let you quit!**

The Power of Resilience

What has life thrown your way? Are there challenges and moments of crisis that have tested you? What if you could just be 10% more resilient? What would that look like? How might you handle things differently?

Resilience is the process of *"adapting well in the face of adversity."*[56] It's about standing strong during a challenge and bouncing back after you face defeat or discouragement. The Power of Resilience is not easy to attain. It's a mindset that takes some work, but once you develop it, it will take you far. It's one of the greatest strengths that can be nurtured.

Imagine losing sight in one eye or receiving the news you never want to hear. *How would you respond? Do you think you'd be resilient?*

I want to explore how you can develop a resilient mindset. A mindset where you instinctively know how to bounce back no matter what life throws your way. I call this *Lead Bulletproof.*

Lead Bulletproof is about being resilient and facing the bullets that inevitably will come. This Power of Resilience not only offers you the ability to be elastic and bounce back, but it can also influence and calm others around you.

As powers go, this is one you want to have. Like the American Express Commercial from years ago, you don't want to leave home without it. The Lead Bulletproof Mindset can result in profound personal growth, and it will help you be the leader you want to be.

Nurturing this resilience comes down to building healthy habits and learning how to use your mental simulation. Complementing both these habits and the mental simulation is something that fuels your drive called Dopamine.

Dopamine – *How the Brain Rewards Progress*

Dopamine is referred to as the *"motivation molecule."* It's how the brain stays motivated. Specifically, Dopamine is what creates feelings of pleasure and reward. On a good day, its primary job is to provide the information and clarity you need to be focused and to stay productive. It's the hormone associated with happiness in both men and women.

Like fast-moving cars on a network of highways, neurotransmitters carry different payloads to support brain activity. We've already talked about Oxytocin, but Dopamine is another powerful neurotransmitter worthy of understanding. Your imagination can't live without Dopamine.

We need Dopamine at the proper levels and in the right doses. Some of the responsibilities of Dopamine include supporting executive thinking and cognition, triggering feelings of reward and pleasure, and managing our voluntary motor movements. These are all super important.

The release of Dopamine can occur for each task you achieve. That's why lists and prayer items can be extremely stimulating. Checking something off, and seeing something accomplished or realized, gives you a hit of Dopamine. It makes you feel good. It is hope realized.

But Dopamine has its bad side too. It can trip you up.

As leaders, we should look for ways to keep our Dopamine tanks filled at the right level and for the right cause. This will allow you to run at your optimal best. It will prolong your health both physically, mentally, and spiritually. It can also help restore you to a better state of health if you have fallen.

To lead others better, we should understand how Dopamine triggers and travels in the brain. *Why?* Because the leader who can best manage their Dopamine levels is better at guiding others through a struggle, challenge, or pursuit.

What that nurse did for me, sharing the story of the two runners with MS, affected my Dopamine more than the IV of steroids being dripped into my blood. That was leadership.

What John Maxwell did for me, grabbing me in the hall of the hotel, and praying for me, did more for my Dopamine than any pill I could take. That was leadership too.

Both opened my imagination by reinvigorating my hope.

Hope shared can be a powerful Dopamine booster. Like a doctor that dispenses medication, a leader should be about dispensing healthy doses of hope to those around them. It's a game-changer.

The Four Highways

I live in one of the ten most congested cities in the United States. Knowing what highways and routes to take and understanding the flow of traffic can make all the difference.[57]

Your brain gets clogged up with traffic too. When it comes to Dopamine, there are four significant pathways. Knowing a little bit about them can help fuel your hope and others too.

THE "ML" HIGHWAY

The first highway is the Mesolimbic Dopamine Pathway – or the "ML". The ML highway is about transporting pleasure and reward to the to the Limbic System. Whenever you experience something satisfying, the brain releases Dopamine on this highway. The ML creates positive feelings reinforcing the behavior.

Like any other highway, we need to regulate the traffic on the ML. Too much overstimulation can lead to a dangerous path – addiction, obsessions, and compulsion. At the same time, not enough traffic can lead down a path of dejection and depression. We need just the right amount of Dopamine flowing. Hope can be an effective stimulant to trigger Dopamine. But it needs to be the right hope.

THE "MC" HIGHWAY

The second highway is the Mesocortical Dopamine Pathway – or the "MC". The MC highway is for transporting thoughts that turn to reason in the Prefrontal Cortex.

You need the MC working and flowing with minimal obstacles and traffic. This is where your working memory, cognition, and decision-making happen. You want this super sharp. Dopamine is critical. But the wrong elixirs can throw this one off. Working in isolation can also be dangerous.

Be careful of the sources of Dopamine you seek because this is where addiction, obsessions, and compulsions can also happen. The best thing for the MC is to get near the right people – the accountability they offer can help regulate the MC.

THE "NS" HIGHWAY

The third highway is the Nigro-Striatal Dopamine Pathway – or the "NS". The NS highway carries Dopamine to spur your motor control.

You and I need this pathway to work as smoothly as possible, but the work and life stress we put on ourselves can wreak havoc. Struggles on this highway can be manifested in potential things like spasms, contractions, tremors, motor restlessness, and more. A person with MS or Parkinson's may often have some challenges on this highway. The right amount of Dopamine can help regulate this.

Studies suggest that an improperly managed NS highway is what can lead to non-genetic autoimmune disorders like MS and Parkinson's. For me, I can look back and see my habits and health choices, specifically how I ate, worked, and slept, and my almost overnight addiction to caffeinated coffee. That may have led me down the road to MS. I can't help but think that if I had been more proactive in managing my

Dopamine early on by changing my behavior to reflect a Lead Bulletproof Mindset, I could have avoided these health challenges.

THE "T" HIGHWAY

The fourth highway is called the Tuberoinfundibular Dopamine Pathway – or the T. The T highway affects your libido and helps regulate your immune system. Dopamine released through this path is what can inhibit the secretion of something called prolactin. Prolactin is a protein hormone that plays a crucial role in your metabolism, regulating your immune system.

Why You Need to Get This Right

There seems to be no shortage of medication that promises to manage or increase the brain's Dopamine for any of your four highways. But, before you pop the pill, down the shot, or reach for another late-day cup of coffee, ask yourself:

What's the best way for me to be fully charged?

Looking back, I can't help but think I could have averted the MS diagnosis and the hypothyroidism diagnosed five years prior. All this could have been avoided.

How?

By changing my thinking, building better habits, and knowing how to leverage my imagination. Better choices lead to better living.

The best way to manage Dopamine is with drips, not hits. For example, a shot of *5-Hour Energy* may give you a jolt of alertness and affects another neurotransmitter called Cortisol, the primary stress hormone. But this isn't the long-term solution to regulate the MC or other Dopamine highways. My fix on caffeinated coffee in the form of triple shot Americanos and Caramel Macchiatos for ten years created hits, not drips.

The better way is to change your thinking – your mindset – and your behavior will follow. You can get all the benefits of Dopamine without the Cortisol overload.

As for me, while I can't change my past and go back and re-earn all the sleep I was missing, I have choices for my future. There is still a set of highways ahead to navigate. The same is true for you too.

When you choose to see hope, you change how you see the world. With hope you shape the future.

Going back to what the nurse shared with me, as I tried to get my eyesight back after my diagnosis of MS, were two choices: give up hope, or seize hope. I choose the latter. But this is a decision I must make every day!

There will be times you face the same predicament. It comes down to this one question:

What future do you imagine?

The future you imagine is going to be the one you pursue.

The Time Traveler – *The Story of Marty McFly*

Michael J. Fox and I share something in common. Our birthdays are on the same day. He is five years older than me, but the day itself, June 9th, is our day.

In the 80s, I grew up watching Michael J. Fox on the hit show *Family Ties* and in movies like *Back to the Future*. His humor and confidence on the screen as an actor have been a delight.

In 1991, at 29 years old, Michael J. Fox's world would come crashing down on him. That's when he was diagnosed with Parkinson's Disease (PD). It was devastating. But the news of his Parkinson's diagnosis wasn't made public until seven years later.

I also waited about seven years to share my autoimmune disease diagnosis of MS. I'm not sure about Michael but sharing publicly about a health challenge is not high on my list of messages to communicate. I just didn't want the stereotype of what people perceived. I still had a life to live. I'm sure Michael felt the same way regarding his PD diagnosis.

Head Down Living

I like to think of Michael J. Fox as a Time Traveler. This is not only to offer tribute to his role as Marty McFly in the iconic movie series *Back to the Future*, where he sped back and forth through time in a tricked-out DeLorean, but also to his writings. He is a great storyteller and has a knack for taking you back in time to various events and experiences. I encourage you to read one of his three books and enjoy the stories.

Here are a few things about Michael J. Fox that you may not know. After his birth in Alberta, Canada, Michael moved around as an Army brat before settling in British Columba outside Vancouver. When he was 15, he began acting, staring in a Canadian TV series called *Leo and Me*. By the time he was 18, he had moved to Los Angeles to further his acting career. It wasn't long until everything took off.

For the next ten years, Fox lived his life with a *"keep-your-head-down-and-keep-moving mentality."*[58] At his peak, he worked eight hours on the TV show *Family Ties* set and then rushed over to the *Back to the Future* movie set at night, working until 2:30 in the morning. That jaunt lasted for two months. But he'd often continue this cycle for other films. To get a quick taste of his success (and drive), Michael J. Fox completed ten movies in a six-year period starting in 1985.

We learn by going back in time with Michael J. Fox that before the diagnosis of Parkinson's – and even for a year after that – he struggled not only with overworking but with the consumption of alcohol. Now, I'm not presuming hard work or alcohol were the cause of his autoimmune disease. Not in the least. But I know that burning the candle on both ends dramatically affects our health. I can see that now in my own life. It impacted my Dopamine.

Unfortunately, none of us have a DeLorean to go back in the past and change things. *But what if we could?* What if we could learn from our past and change our future?

The goal is to get control of the life still in front of us. We can also encourage others to live their life in a way that optimizes what they have in front of them too. That's the life of an Imagineer.

Dopamine Havoc

Before we return to Michael J. Fox's story, let's take a moment to explore the impact of Dopamine Havoc that's so prevalent today. The thing about alcohol, caffeine addiction, workaholic tendencies, or any compulsive disorder is that it yearns for that Dopamine drip from our brain. Dopamine is the brain's pleasure chemical. It feeds temptation and can lead to addiction. Too much of a draw and it will deplete your Dopamine levels. Consequently, it can compromise your health, including your immune system.

Regarding the four major pathways, the best behavioral approach for managing Dopamine is limiting your exposure to unhealthy habits and adverse external stimuli, like alcohol, gambling, pornography, opioids, caffeine, nicotine, and sugary foods. Build good habits instead.

Think of your Dopamine levels as the fuel levels for the brain. You never want to let it run empty. You want enough Dopamine to keep you motivated. When the Dopamine is at the proper levels, you function better. It's one of the brain's primary fuels that drives you. Studies show that when Dopamine is at the right mix – and the right octane – *"performing a demanding task is elevated."*[59]

The key with Dopamine is not too much or too little. Too much, and it depletes fast. It burns up, and you burn out. Too little, and it leaves you feeling defeated and lifeless, barely able to get out of your bed. And, unless it's for medical reasons, medication is rarely the answer.

The healthy choice is to fuel Dopamine levels by pursuing hope. Dopamine feeds on hope. It thrives on hope pursued and hope realized. It's as if the two are designed to work together. **Imagination plays a crucial role in priming hope.** Hope triggers Dopamine.

They say when you are low on hope, you are low on Dopamine. Dopamine fueled by imagination can provide the motivation and focus you need to be productive. It is associated with *"attention span, focus, follow-through, motivation, and the ability to experience pleasure."*[60]

As you might have guessed, people who succumb to addiction often do it to seek pleasure or find relief in the absence of a natural way to obtain it. They may be low on hope. The good news is that we can change our behavior by getting clear on what excites us through our imagination and by also changing our environment and the response to the triggers and prompts.

The Lead Bulletproof Mindset

The Lead Bulletproof Mindset is centered on awareness both around you (externally) and inside you (internally). When you mentally see the environment differently inside and out, you see yourself differently too. See yourself for who you can be. See yourself for what impact you can make.

By seeing things with hope, you change the temperature in the room. You learn to be a thermostat instead of a thermometer.

Understanding Behavior

What are your habits? A habit is a pattern that is repeated regularly. Patterns become part of your subconscious behavior – both good ones and bad ones. Over time habits become a conditioned response to familiar stimuli and adverse challenges. These patterns either help you or hurt you. The primary person who shapes these patterns is none other than you! They are made by YOUR choices.

B. J. Fogg, a leading authority on habits, offers a simple formula to understand human behavior.

$$\textbf{Behavior =}$$
$$\textbf{Motivation x Ability x Prompt}$$

Fogg simplifies this formula using the initial letters for the equation: B = MAP, which makes it memorable. It all starts with **motivation**. I used to think **behavior** started with a **prompt** – some sort of trigger. But now that I understand the RAS, I know that we don't see the *prompts* until the *motivation* has been rooted in us.

Ability is secondary to motivation. I might argue that *availability* is more important than *ability*. *Why?* Because *ability* is nurtured more than natured. You're not born with ability; you grew into it.

Availability is the prerequisite for ability. When we are *available*, then *ability* can be developed. However, for the *behavior* to reveal itself, we still need a *prompt*; something that triggers our *motivation*.

The **prompt** is often external. Think of it as an *interrupt* like a notification, warning, or surprise. It's what life unexpectedly throws your way – good or bad. It might be a notification from a digital device, a traffic delay, a power outage, an unscheduled meeting, a flat tire, a lost credit card, a slow elevator, a delayed flight, or even a compliment or surprise gift that comes your way – maybe like a plate of delicious chocolate chip cookies, or a dark blue pickup truck. By using our imagination, we can also fire off internal prompts. These prompts can be good or sometimes bad. ANTs are an example of the latter.

When a *prompt* appears – even in the form of a suggestion – notice how your imagination kicks into gear based on how you are already *motivated.* I like to think of it as a simulation that pre-plays the expected *behavior.* It reveals your *motivation* – what you hope for. It can also reveal your fears and doubts.

On this last point, *have you had a call come in on your smartphone from a number you knew but rarely got?* What flashed through your mind before you picked it up? Recognize there's a simulation that plays that triggers the ANTs. But the same simulation can trigger your resilience.

Understanding Your Onboard Simulation

A simulation is a virtual representation of one or more models executed over time. A model might be a concept, a structure, a system, or an image that represents something we want, wonder, or worry about.

Your imagination plays this simulation giving you a limitless realm to explore the possibilities. Your imagination is a multiverse. It can create a narrative of the past and a preview of the future. As a simulation, it can train, prepare, and position you for what's to come. In this way, it changes your *ability.*

Your Simulation is Powered by Motivation

Your onboard simulation is fueled by your motivation, and it's always running. But like a computer, it's only as good as the hardware and software that runs it. Therefore, loading your working memory with a Lead Bulletproof Mindset is vital. You want a secure, robust system that can handle any kind of stimuli. Most likely, you want your onboard simulation to help you with decisions. Therefore, make sure the mental models you load are healthy ones that represent a Lead Bulletproof Mindset.

For a Lead Bulletproof Mindset, *motivation* is an emotional urge to do something that moves you forward through a challenge or an opportunity with a goal of a rewarding conclusion. Otherwise, if the motivation is holding you back – and making you withdraw, then the fear and doubt may be greater than the hope and the courage. The only way to get to a Lead Bulletproof Mindset is to modify the motivation.

Your Simulation Is Always On

Before we dive deeper into motivation modification, let's understand how our internal simulation works.

Picture yourself entering a movie theater. The first thing you notice is the beautiful aroma of freshly popped popcorn. The scent of the popcorn, coupled with the sound of it being made, is a *prompt*. But the prompt is not the threat. It triggers your internal motivation.

At the sight or sound of a prompt – in this case, popcorn, your imagination might instantly play a mental simulation of "what could be" based on your *motivation*. A voice in your head quietly whispers, *don't you want some popcorn?* The same voice might add, *"And maybe a nice cold Coke to go with it?"* Notice how motivations can stack on each other. Habits are the same way.

Your imagination reveals your *motivation*. In this case, you think about the reward and sensation you're going to experience if you consume the popcorn – and maybe even the Coke. This simulation plays faster than real-time, and it's planting (or pulling) seeds of thought in your RAS. It's previewing the potential reward. It's preparing for the behavior that follows.

What you might not know is that your RAS is nudging you to get in the concession line. *Why?* Because you are motivated by the idea of consuming popcorn – and a cold refreshing Coke.

Understand what's happening here. The emotional part of the brain does not know the difference between real and imagined. Motivation is executed as a simulation first. Whether it's *real* or *imagined*, your brain triggers the release of Dopamine through the ML and MC pathways. As a result, your brain reacts and craves the reward.

Advertisers have already figured this out. They know the trick is getting you to think about enjoying popcorn. They want you to play the simulation. It's the greatest sales trick in the book. It's why, before a movie starts, the local theater often shows visual images of popcorn and a cold icy refreshment.

Can you see how your imagination influences your decision-making in this example? Your brain, through your own RAS, wants to next play out the *motivation* in real life. There may be an external trigger, but all it takes is a complying internal motivation. **Motivation is like an itch that you want to scratch.** Before you know it, you're in line buying popcorn.

Recognize what's happening here. For the onboard simulation to run, which is part of your imagination, it needs motivation. Yet, it's the prompt that awakens the motivation. The prompt might be a word, phrase, color, smell, song, visual image, or more. Prompts trigger *motivation* through our imagination by releasing a drip of Dopamine. The Dopamine enters our Prefrontal Cortex through the MC where we process the choice in front of us. The decision tree is simple. *What is it that I want? Do I want the popcorn?*

Our motivation is revealed by our *behavior* that follows. But our imagination gives us a sneak preview before anyone else sees it. Because behavior can be played out in the imagination before it's played out for real – using the OODA loop – we can course correct before taking action.

Your imagination can protect you if it's tuned right. Its onboard simulation plays the future that you can control. This is where the Lead Bulletproof Mindset comes into play.

Your Simulation Rebooted

When we can see the impact of our choices, then we can alter our motivation and change the simulation. Again, your imagination is the original multiverse, it's that powerful. We can see multiple scenarios.

If you look back at the B. J. Fogg behavior equation, you'll see an *x* in the formula. The x-factor for this equation, like the others, represents *hope*. Hope is a multiplier that gives you direction, starting with your motivation. The beautiful thing about hope is that it's a lever that you use to reset the simulation.

For every *prompt or trigger,* you want your brain to evaluate your *motivation* with one simple question:

What do I really hope for?

What you hope for drives your *motivation* – even when an unwelcomed or unexpected *prompt* appears.

Motivation is fulfilled by your *ability* – or in some cases availability. Behavioral science shows us that if you can check your *motivation* when an unwelcomed *prompt* appears, you can alter your *ability* (or change your availability) and become more resilient. Resilient Behavior is the goal. This allows your Dopamine to fire at the optimal levels.

Recognize the three components of behavior: *motivation, ability,* and a *prompt.* Presumably, if you change one of those three components, you change the entire simulation and your potential response. But think about which of these components you have the most influence. It's not the *prompt* – that might be external. It may not even be *ability* – at least initially. It's the *motivation.*

What drives *motivation* is the reward or satisfaction you seek. Motivation is the catalyst for imagination. If we change our motive, we change our behavior. **Motivation compels us to invent the future.**

Motivation Modification – Becoming Bulletproof

So, what motivation should we have? Well, motivation is a personal thing, of course, but there are several common commitments we can make that will positively impact our motivation and our simulation. I call them **The Four CORE Commitments**. They will improve your motivation no matter who you are or where you are at. These commitments help condition you to be resilient.

1. **Stay Calm**
2. **Be Open**
3. **Get Ready**
4. **Engage**

Just one of these commitments alone won't cut it. You need all four, and they build on each other. These commitments can be pre-established attitudes that help shape a Lead Bulletproof Mindset.

Let's walk through each of these.

Stay Calm

This first commitment is critical. When the unexpected happens remain calm. Recognize that adversity doesn't just build character; it reveals it. Let calm be your default.

When things don't go according to plan, it might trigger disappointment or frustration. In this state, it can be hard to make "on-the-fly" choices that steer you in the right direction. The reason is because we tend to react emotionally instead of responding logically. But understand what's happening inside the brain.

When a bad prompt happens, it can trigger in us an undesired emotional reaction. The reason why is that there is an incongruent match between what we originally wanted and what we're getting.

Your imagination – as a multiverse – will want to compare how things should have gone to how things now seem to be going. The two worlds are quite opposite. This is when the ANTs might invade. The four most prominent ANTs of the seven that might take up residence are:

- Fortune-Teller ANTs
- Blaming ANTs
- Labeling ANTs
- Just the Bad ANTs

Any of the ANTs tend to fire up our emotional – reptilian brain. If we're not careful, we might lash out, quickly move from hope to doubt, or develop some unhealthy patterns that lead to bad habits.

But there's some good news. Circumstances don't define who we are; our choices do. **Calm is always choice.**

Despite the disappointment, the unexpected challenge, or even the invasion march of ANTs, the brain is elastic, and it can be resilient. It is designed and more than capable of helping you rebound. The same imagination that might take you off the rails can be used to help you improvise, adapt, and overcome.

There's a two-step **strategy** that can help create calm:

1. ***Pause*** - When bad news happens, recognize it's a trigger that wants to open the door to the ANTs. But I like to think of ANTs more like Wolves. Wolves want to invade out of nowhere. They will attack your character, your confidence, and your commitment. They will devour you. When you feel the emotion starting to rise – and the invasion of an automatic negative thought (aka Wolf) – give yourself five seconds where you don't react or respond at all. Just be aware of the Wolves. Awareness helps keep them back. Pausing can help you diffuse the situation quickly and slow it down. Recognize that these Wolves may be more disruptive than the bad news itself. Keep the Wolves away from your fire by letting calm be your default.

2. ***Pivot*** - Remember, your imagination is there to help. Now that you've noticed the ANTs (aka the Wolves), start to look for the blessings and gains that can protect you. Look around. You are not hopeless. My friend, Richard, calls these Sheepdogs. Sheepdogs are first responders. They are ready to take a stand against the evils of this world – the Wolves. When you Pivot, you're activating the Sheepdogs to protect your values and vision. **Pivot to find a new path.**

The whole goal of *pause* and *pivot* mirrors the Observe and Orient phases of the OODA loop. When you pause and pivot it calms you and prepares you for the opportunities that lie ahead.

Be Open

The second commitment is about being open to new possibilities after you pivot. My friend, Jesse Smith, succinctly puts it this way. *"It might not look how you thought it was going to look, but that doesn't mean it won't look the way God designed it to look."*

I love that thought. When we are open to new possibilities, new paths become available. For millions of people, this is where faith plays a part in concert with their imagination.

Faith is the assurance of things hoped for and the conviction of things not seen. That conviction is a reliance and trust in something greater than yourself. It's in those difficult moments that we might find ourselves not alone. Some call this a peace that passes all understanding. It's a peace that must be present in your imagination for it to be real.

One trick is to leverage peace in your imagination is to focus on the bigger picture that yields a successful outcome. When you use your imagination in this way, it's as if you've been there before. By being curious and open you can prepare yourself. Like Michael Jordan, you can *"go into situations"* and already *"know the outcome."* Why? Because you've already *"experienced them"* in your mind and trained yourself using mental simulation and thinking big picture. It's about knowing your *why*, which is your purpose.

Lead Bulletproof is about choosing the new path in front of you. This path is not the one of least resistance but the one of greater resilience. Therefore, be open! Recognize the possibilities.

Get Ready

Now that you are *calm* and *open* to new possibilities, it's time to *get ready*. This is where you need your imagination the most. Your imagination is ready to lead you onward. To *get ready*, leverage your hope, but still, be aware of the doubts. Here's why.

Hope and doubt both play a mental simulation. The hope is important, but the doubts might tell you where things may go off the rails – don't discount them. Daniel Pink calls this a premortem. A premortem is like a postmortem, but only in reverse. If you consider everything that can go wrong ahead of time – you can course correct – and maintain your hope. In fact, you'll increase your hope because you've already evaluated the experience. This hope will help show you how you can adjust and determine a path to success.

Always remind yourself of what you hope for. Remember your mind is a multiverse showing you a variety of choices. Play enough scenarios, and you'll find a way to persevere.

Be sure your hope is fueled by a strong *why* aligned with your *values*. When you face the doubt in your mind, imagine a different path around the doubt that satisfies your hope. This is what constitutes a Lead Bulletproof Mindset.

If you can see yourself preserving, that's a healthy sign of hope. Hope aligns with your values, whereas doubt aligns with your fears. Both can be powerful models for your simulation. If your simulation is value-driven, you can overcome any fear. *Why?* Because you still have hope.

Hope fuels Dopamine. Fear fuels Cortisol. One is intended to create pleasure, the other creates stress. Healthy hope is the kindling you need to keep your fire lit. The fuel for this fire – what loads your simulation multiverse – is Dopamine. Dopamine will work for you or against you. While it might make you crave popcorn, it can also motivate you to live and Lead Bulletproof. It will help you choose to be resilient.[61]

Questions to help you get ready.

- *What influences you most: your values or your fears?*
- *What values matter most to you?*

Engage

To Lead Bulletproof means you know your mission. I call it your *why*. **The *why* represents your purpose and passion.**

If you ever watched an episode of *Star Trek: The Next Generation,* you might have observed Captain Picard giving his second-in-command, Lieutenant Will Riker, orders to *engage*. Picard has already walked through the first three steps of the Lead Bulletproof Mindset. He's *calm*, he's *open*, and his *ready*. After all the preparation, the next step is to engage and go forward. The same is true for you.

What inspires you and influences those around you? Think about Michael Jordan again; His passion and *"love for the game"* activated his RAS every night before stepping onto the court. He didn't make every shot, but he seized every opportunity to create a shot.

What shots are you creating? Are you highly motivated? Recognize **you can't get to high performance without high motivation.** Each shot starts in the imagination before it's ever put into action.

When your *why* is clear, you are more confident in your ability to engage. Ability isn't only about aptitude or skill, it's also about beliefs. Beliefs drive behavior. When you believe you can, you are more willing to try. That results in engagement.

What Happens If You Don't Have the Right Mindset?

Think of the alternative of not staying calm, not being open, not getting ready, and not engaging. Let's say a threatening prompt tries to make a play – a tornado warning. In this scenario, *how would you react?*

A prompt, like a tornado warning, wants to trigger a reaction in you. This is when your reptilian brain is ready to kick into gear. It's responsible, whether good or bad, for self-preservation. Think Sheepdogs.

In the case of the tornado threat, rather than staying calm, let's say you freak out. You let the Wolves parading as ANTs paralyze you. In this situation, you are likely spinning up the emotions and reactions of those around you.

But what if you choose to stay calm? It's not that you are ignoring the prompt; you are simply *"going around the leaf."*[62] You're taking an alternative action – rather than flight, fight, or freeze, you choose to be calm, open, and ready. And you engage! That's resilience.

Remember your imagination wants to run a simulation all the time.[63] For this simulation to be efficient and effective, your imagination must go through a progression. **The Four CORE Attitudes** help prepare you by decentralizing yourself from the situation. When you are calm and open, you can see things more objectively.

When you are not calm or open, the mental simulation might run a narrative driven by doubt or emotion instead of the ground truth data. This is when your reptilian brain will take over. Your faster-than-real-time simulation wants to pull on your emotion. Often, your emotional intelligence (EQ) will be reduced in this state. However, if you go through the progression to get calm and open, you raise your EQ, and you are more apt to operate at your non-stressed IQ.

The whole point of mental simulation is to help you be a better Decision Maker. Mental simulation guides you through the decision making process.

One more note on *motivation*. This is where Dopamine is clearly in play, thereby influencing you. This is also where you want to be "on point" to steer the ship. You want your *motivation* to be emotionally balanced. Otherwise, your motivation might lead you to do something regrettable.

Check your motives. The motivation you choose ahead of time is what sets the Power of Resilience.

Back to the Future

If you ever encounter a high-driven "go-getter" or someone who may be a little intense, recognize that they may be burning Dopamine faster than they ought to. The result could be dangerous.

Michael J. Fox was admittedly high driven from his account, and it affected him. Again, I'm not saying it was the cause of his PD, but for me, I can't help but think that my Dopamine burning habit of late nights, little sleep, and high caffeine ultimately affected my health.

The concern with most autoimmune diseases like PD is that nerve cells that produce Dopamine can gradually die. Dopamine is what helps control our muscles. Without Dopamine, a person with PD will likely experience muscle stiffness and have problems with movement.

But let's take PD or MS off the table and look at what happens naturally when Dopamine gets dangerously low. Here's just a tiny sampling of the long laundry list of conditions.

- Fatigue
- Apathy
- Lack of focus
- Forgetfulness
- Moodiness
- Difficulty concentrating
- Insomnia
- Sugar cravings
- Lower motivation

The point is simple. Short of doctor-prescribed medication, we must do what we can naturally to keep the Dopamine at the right levels. That might mean changing our habits and staying fueled with hope.

Reading Michael J. Fox's books, you will quickly get the sense that he is making the most of his life despite the PD. He stays optimistic. And clearly, he believes and loves those around him. Sure, he may be taking prescribed medication to control the effects of PD, but he's also keeping his mind sharp and imagination fresh, which keeps his hope alive.

I can't help but think of time traveling in *Back to the Future*. If Fox could go back in time, maybe he could avert the PD, just like I think I could prevent the MS. While we can't physically go back in time – we do have some options. **Imagination can take you anywhere.**

Just for fun, pretend you have a DeLorean equipped with a Flux capacitor. It represents your imagination. Set your intent on where you want to go in the future and then rev that baby up to 88 miles an hour. Go shape the future! A Lead Bulletproof Mindset can give you the edge you need. It's not about looking back. It's about going forward!

Incidentally, I love what the number 88 represents. In some cultures, it represents fortune. In music, it represents the keys of a full-size piano and all the notes. In amateur radio, it represents "love and kisses" when someone signs off. Finally, in science, it represents the atomic number of radium, which contains 88 protons.

Radium is one of the most significant discoveries in chemistry. It showed us how an element can be transmuted into another element. Think transporter. That's what imagination does for us too.

Marie Currie and her husband discovered radium. She was the first woman to win a Nobel Prize, not just once but twice. One of my favorite quotes is this thought from her:

"Nothing in life is to be feared. It is only to be understood.
Now is the time to understand more. So that we fear less."

Take a moment to think that through. Nothing in life is to be feared – including the future you imagine.

- Stay Calm
- Be Open
- Get Ready
- Engage

Chapter Summary

In the final scene of the third installment of *Back to the Future*, Doc Brown offers Fox's character, Marty McFly, a piece of wisdom for all of us.

"Your future is whatever you make it, so make it a good one."

Doc's directive sets the stage for what you and I need: a Lead Bulletproof Mindset.

This chapter has focused on the Power of Resilience. Resilience is the process of *"adapting well in the face of adversity."*[64] The Power of Resilience gives us the fortitude we need to invent the future.

Let's face it, we ALL face challenges. The bullets will fly your way. The question is, ***are you ready for the battle?***

We explored an underlying chemical in our brain that affects our resilience. It's a powerful neurotransmitter called Dopamine. The right hope and habits can help keep the brain motivated with just the right amount of Dopamine. Dopamine fuels our imagination. Likewise, our imagination triggers Dopamine. They both help us be more resilient and lead us through fears and challenges when they are at the right levels.

One way to keep Dopamine fueled and ready is to be decisive and celebrate wins. Start with structured goal setting, clear lists, or prayer; this can boost your Dopamine and increase your blood flow. Blood flow is critical for your brain. I recommend that you measure goal achievement and answered prayers. Also, incorporate things like exercise, healthy water consumption, and good protein and nutrients like Omega-3.

The Power of Resilience also focuses on tweaking your underlying hope so that when an unexpected challenge comes your way, you are called to lead despite the fear and apprehension. We call this pattern a Lead Bulletproof Mindset. Set your motives ahead of time.

When a prompt might lead to a negative response, ask yourself a turnaround question:

What options reflect my hope?

To formulate a Lead Bulletproof Mindset, leverage your imagination as a simulation. It's a tool to improvise, adapt an overcome. Think of your imagination as the multiverse – a place where you can see the various possibilities that will lead you through a challenge and on to success. Look for the paths that will take you around the leaf.

When you do this, you can cultivate a newly learned pattern that forms in the Conscious Mind. Over time, this pattern will take up residence as one of your nurtured leadership habits in your Subconscious Mind. It's how Imagineers like Michael Jordan became the world's best.

A healthy supply of Dopamine, a Lead Bulletproof Mindset coupled with a mental simulation of your multiverse empowers you with a decision-making toolset that offers you clarity, courage, and confidence. This enables you to be resilient leading you "Back to the Future."

◆ ◆ ◆

Additional tools and resources focused on
Getting Bulletproof are available at
theimaginebook.com/ch-9

---

[55] Evy Poumpouras, *Becoming Bulletproof: Protect Yourself, Read People, Influence Situations, and Live Fearlessly* (p. 297), Atria Books.

[56] APA Dictionary of Psychology, *Resilience,* American Psychological Association, https://www.apa.org/topics/resilience, last accessed June 28, 2022.

[57] Jordan Friedman, *The U.S. Cities With the Worst Traffic*, U.S. News, https://www.usnews.com/news/cities/articles/10–cities–with–the–worst–traffic–in–the–us, Oct. 13, 2020, last accessed June 28, 2022.

[58] Michael J. Fox, *Lucky Man* (p. 17), Hachette Books.

[59] Radboud University, *Ritalin Enhances Your Ability To Do Tasks By Making You More Motivated*, https://www.radboudumc.nl/en/news/2020/ritalin–enhances–your–ability–to–do–tasks–by–making–you–more–motivated, published March 26, 2020, last accessed June 28, 2022.

[60] *How to Raise Your Dopamine Level Without Drugs*, https://www.thedistrictrecovery.com/addiction–blog/how–to–raise–your–dopamine–levels–without–drugs/, published July 19, 2018, last accessed June 28, 2022.

[61] *Do This When Cravings Hit*, https://healthtalk.unchealthcare.org/do–this–when–cravings–hit/, published January 28, 2021, last accessed June 28, 2022.

[62] Pixar, *A Bugs Life*, Note: "Go around the Leaf" is a phrase cited in one of the scenes in the movie when a leaf falls from onto the ground disrupting an army of ants carrying food to storage. The ants

are initially less than resilient; however, a leader ant comes in and redirects them with the instructions, *"Do not panic. Do not panic. Go around the leaf."*

[63] Amishi P. Jha, Peak Mind (p. 194). HarperCollins. Amishi shares *"We are simulating all the time."*

[64] The American Psychological Association, *The Road to Resilience*, https://advising.unc.edu/wp-content/uploads/sites/341/2020/07/The-Road-to-Resiliency.pdf, last accessed June 28, 2022.

10 – INCREASE THE AMPLITUDE
Understanding the Power of Today

"Never leave that till tomorrow
which you can do today."

– Benjamin Franklin

If habits help shape results, then how do you keep the fire going when life comes fast and hard?

It turns out that part of leveraging your imagination – and playing your onboard simulation – is about continually stepping forward with hope despite the setbacks. It's about leveraging the Power of Today.

Finding the Power of Today requires real–time situational awareness. Like Jack Bauer in an episode of *24*, work to figure out the next step despite the turmoil around you.

Being diagnosed with an autoimmune disease has somehow served to heighten my situational awareness; it's made me more alert. I'd like to think that maybe it sharpened my imagination by making me more aware of the special moments we are given each day. But I'm still a work in progress.

Michael J. Fox also discovered something very similar. He shared, *"I have no choice about whether or not I have Parkinson's. But I have nothing but choices – a million other choices – about how I react to it."* He added, *"In those choices, there's freedom to do a lot of things in areas that I wouldn't have otherwise found myself in."*[65] He's talking about greater situational awareness and the Power of Today.

A humorous example that comes to mind is a cruise ship voyage my wife and I took a few years back to celebrate our wedding anniversary. Despite our well-laid plans, we had to learn to adjust our sails and make the most of our journey with a limited set of items.

Who Says You Need Your Bags?

We originally had hoped to celebrate our 25th wedding anniversary on a cruise to Alaska two years earlier, but that got derailed. Now, we were set to sail to the Bahamas to celebrate our 27th wedding anniversary.

This cruise was billed as a reunion tour for the iconic band *DC Talk*. They hadn't played together to a live audience in 15 years, so it was a big deal in the music biz. Barb was first introduced to them in their early days when she was a freshman at Liberty University. As one of their classmates, she witnessed the humble beginnings of the trio and had sent me one of their early tapes. The cruise was something we were looking forward to too.

The Flight Down

We had scheduled an early morning flight from Washington, DC, to Miami on the day our cruise was to depart. It was going to get us there with plenty of time to be on the ship by the three o'clock "all-aboard" call. However, something was amiss when we arrived at Reagan National Airport just before 6 am. The airport was packed with travelers, news reporters, camera crews, and lights that morning. I remember wondering, *"what's going on?"*

As I was trying to figure it out, my phone chirped, alerting me of a crucial notification. I glanced at it to read that the flight we were booked for had been scrubbed. It then instructed me of new flight plans, indicating that we would now be arriving in Miami until 11:30 pm that night.

I couldn't believe it. I remember thinking, *"No way. Not again! No, we've already missed our 25th. I am not going to miss our 27th!"*

At that point, I'm trying everything to find a new flight down to Miami. I'm even calling charter flights, you know, the private, VIP kind that $60,000 might have gotten you. But I didn't have that kind of money to spend. So, we just kept trying. We searched, prayed, and hoped. Just as I nearly scored a flight out of the neighboring airport in Baltimore an hour away, my wife happened to be at the front of the line at the right time when the United Airlines worker whispered these magical words. *"Hey, I have just been alerted that the Miami flight canceled last night is now opening back up. There are two vacant seats left on the next flight to Miami. Do you want those?"*

My wife looked at me as I smiled. We both responded in unison. *"Heck yeah!"*

We were able to get new ticket issues on a direct flight to Miami that left 3 hours later than our original plane. In our mind's eye, we still had plenty of time. Our vacation anniversary get-away was back on!

By the time we arrived in Miami, it was close to noon. We had three hours to get on the boat. We headed over to get our bags, but they never showed.

After standing in line at the baggage claim office for nearly an hour, we were informed that our bags would not arrive until 11:30 that night. I looked at the agent and told him, *"That's not going to work. We've got to catch a cruise that shuts its door at 3 pm."*

I looked at my watch and realized we had about 90 minutes to make it on the ship. I then told the attendant. *"We'll just get our bags when we come back."* He took down some information regarding our trip, and we scrambled to find an Uber ride.

The Uber Ride

The lady who picked us up, Maria, was a friendly yet novice Uber driver. She had lived in Miami most of her life but didn't know the intricacies of the Miami roadways and exits. As we got closer to the boat terminal, we could see our ship looming on the horizon. We are almost within reach. However, for whatever reason, Maria couldn't make the turn to take us there. As she continued driving on the highway, the image of the ship started getting smaller and smaller out the back window.

"Ma'am, the ship's back over there." I hollered. She then said something in Spanish before finally saying something in English that we could understand. *"I'm so sorry; I don't know the turn."* She was frantic. At that moment, my wife pulled out her iPhone, opened the Google Maps app, and helped guide Maria back in the ship's direction. By the time we pulled up in front of the terminal where the ship was docked, we had just 10 minutes to board.

We jumped out of her Toyota Prius with all we had – just two carry-on bags – and dashed in. At the security checkpoint, they looked at us cautiously bewildered, before commenting, *"Folks. This ship is only for passengers. We can't let you board."*

I smiled with a laugh, *"We are passengers. We should be on the ship's manifest."*

"Where then are your bags?" The security guard asked.

"They didn't make it, but we are here," I responded.

He smiled, checked our passports against the manifest, and waved us through. *"Have a great cruise."*

The Check-In

Once we were safely on the ship, we were genuinely relieved. We then headed down to the check-in counter to get our room. At the front desk, we were asked, *"Where are your bags?"* It became a broken recording, but we didn't let it get us down.

"Um. They didn't make it." I responded. *"But we're here."* I smiled. I was honestly just happy to be there.

Feeling sympathetic, they instantly offered to "comp" our laundry service for the trip since we had no luggage.

I looked at her and chuckled, *"Well, thank you, but I'm not sure how much we need that."* I gestured to what I was wearing. *"What you see is what we've got. At least for me, I'm only one layer deep."* Barb added, *"we don't have many clothes to launder."*

The clerk grinned in response with an *"oh dear"* look, but I swear she also chuckled to herself. She then offered some encouragement. *"Well, we do have some shops with clothing. If you find something, you can charge it to the room. But in the meantime, we have some complimentary crew t-shirts we can offer you."* She then disappeared for a moment and returned with several undersized white t-shirts wrapped in a clear bag. Each shirt was adorned with the cruise line logo printed on the front in dark blue.

"Thank you," I responded. I was more than happy to receive the shirts. She then handed us our key and directions to our cabin. We headed up to the room to check out our quarters. The cabin porter was

there to immediately greet us, wondering the location of our bags again. I smiled and offered a similar line. *"No bags. This is all we have."* I then asked, *"Can you tell me where the stores are?"* After we checked out the room, I went on the hunt to add new pieces to our wardrobe for the next few days.

The Swim Trunks

Now, keep in mind that this was an Italian cruise ship. There was no JC Penney's or Kohls. I am six foot four and weigh over 220 pounds. The choices are minimal. But what I wanted more than anything was some swim trunks. I wanted to take a dip in the pool and just hang out and read the John Grisham book I had brought on the plane.

I remember walking into one of the small clothing boutiques, asking, *"Do you have any swim trunks"* and the lady smiled with almost a snicker as she pointed to one corner of the small store. I walked over to find a half dozen various-sized Speedos. I looked at my wife, and she just laughed. I remember telling her, *"Nope!"* Next thing I knew, I was asking if any other shops had swim TRUNKS.

Fortunately, they sent me to another small ship store that was more of a souvenir shop. Sure enough, they had some swim trunks that looked like boxers more than briefs. But they were more 70's style shorts. You know, the kind that shows a little more thigh than you want.

To make matters worse – the sizing was way off. Usually, for shorts, I'm an XL kind of guy. But these were Italian fit and sized. The Double XLs in the Italian ship store were more like Mediums in an American store. Fortunately, they had some 4XLs in a red Italian cut style. It was better than nothing, so I bought them.

We headed back to the cabin so that I could change into my new trunks, and I grabbed my book to read. We went straight to the pool. I realized I was probably exposing more leg than I had in quite some time, revealing a tan line three inches below the hem of my shorts. Barb tried very hard to hide her expression. But clearly, she was amused. By the way, she was smarter than me. She had packed her swimsuit in her carry-on.

The Rest of the Cruise

By late afternoon I had gotten too much sun on the old thighs, so I needed to go inside. It was also "White Night" that first evening. Everyone was supposed to wear white. The complementary white t-shirts they gave us at check-in were thinner than a sheet of paper – and kind of tight – so we decided to wear the same solid dark attire from earlier in the day. With our black tops and jeans, we stood out like a sore thumb but managed to make a few new friends.

That essentially was our wardrobe for the week. In the morning, it was the Italian red swim shorts; in the evening, it was the same pair of jeans I wore on the flight. Fortunately, we picked up a couple of concert shirts on the cruise, giving us a slight change of wardrobe above the waist.

Truthfully, not having bags turned out to be a blessing. It made our choices super easy. We just rolled with it. And the people we met on the cruise were super kind, gracious, and empathetic. The key was to make sure I lathered up with deodorant a few times each day. And, yes, I did shower.

The big thing I learned from that trip is that there's more to life than what we see or have. That lesson became even more apparent on the very last day of the cruise.

United Airlines somehow coordinated with the MSC Cruise line and delivered our bags on the final day in the Bahamas. I remember being called down to the registration desk on the ship, and the same lady that checked us in was beaming with a smile. *"Good news Mr. Paul. Your bags arrived!"* We were beside ourselves. Onlookers gazed bewildered as we wheeled our tall suitcases to the ship elevator. *"Are you guys just arriving?"* Someone asked. We smiled and simply shared our story.

When we got to our ship wing, the cabin porter immediately greeted us and saw the bags. *"I can put those in your room for you."* We watched him lug our bags half his size into our tiny cabin, and I knew instantly that we had brought too much. The cabin porter then offered to launder any clothes that we had. I laughed. *"For sure. I'll have something for you in a moment."* I responded. My wife and I then disappeared into our room and changed into different threads. At first, we were excited, but then we realized we didn't need but just a few things out of our bags.

We tried to style out that final day by changing into a fresh but wrinkled outfit throughout the day, but it was overwhelming. We had too many choices. Finally, we returned to the room, and I put on the black t-shirt and jeans that I had worn all week. Fortunately, it was now laundered courtesy of the cruise line.

Looking at our bags that last night – trying to maneuver through our tiny cabin, we realized we had overpacked. That brought us a moment of epiphany. *"We should never pack more than three days of clothes. Ever. What were we thinking?"*

Since then, our beliefs have changed in how we pack for travel. We don't need more; we usually need less. **Less things competing for your attention means you have more focus.**

The bottom line is this. I used to think it was smart to bring as much as possible to prepare for whatever might come. Now I think you should only bring what you need and just be present.

Fewer choices mean less stress. Less stress means better opportunities. The key to fulfillment is to see beyond your resources and the cards you have been dealt. You have more than you realize. Recognize the Power of Today.

The Power of Today

When you have greater situational awareness, you notice more opportunities each day. These aren't just present-day opportunities but opportunities that will shape your future. The important thing is to evaluate if the opportunities of today can advance you toward a greater vision than just yourself. Michael J. Fox shares that situational awareness allows him to *"see possibilities in everything."* He shares that, *"For everything that's taken away, something of greater value has been given."*

The Power of Today is perhaps one of the most important powers you can leverage. It's given to you every day. Every day is a reset. You get a new clock and a fresh set of downs. What you choose to do with each day is up to you.

You've heard the saying; there is no better time than the present; it's true. Today is not yesterday, and it's not yet tomorrow. **Today is one of a kind – it has something unique to offer.**

The Power of Today is about seizing the moment. Realize that there's a window of opportunity and a need to Increase the Amplitude.

What we do today makes an impact for tomorrow. Our focus will be greater if we live today as if it counts for tomorrow. But tomorrow starts right now in your imagination. When imagination casts a vision of something to look forward to, that offers a hope worth pursuing.

What will you do today? Are you being intentional? Are you thinking about yesterday? Are you worried about tomorrow? The wise mentor in Kung Fu Panda once said, *"Yesterday is history, tomorrow is a mystery, but today is a gift. That's why it's called the present."*

Think about one thing that you want to accomplish today. What one thing will make a difference for you today? What would make today successful?

As a Brain Thinketh – *What You See Is What You Get*

Have you ever heard the phrase *"what you see is what you get"*?

It's a widely used expression – an idiom – meant to trigger understanding. But does it?

A common use of *"what you see is what you get"* means that there's nothing more to what you see than what's right in front of you. It could be used to describe a person, a place, an object, or a season of life. In other words, what's on the table is all there is and nothing else.

If you've seen The Matrix, it's like what happens if you take the blue pill.

Looking back on that cruise trip, I remember using the idiom *"what you see is what you get"* more than once. I often used this when I joked that I was only *"one layer deep– and this is all I had."* But was it? Truth be told, I found a way to improvise and adapt the whole trip. Clothes don't make the man; attitude does. Phil Mahre, the Olympic skier, shared that *"the most vital aspect of winning is a mental attitude."* Attitude drives experience.

The problem with the idiom *"what you see is what you get"* is that it can limit the imagination and our ability to see the opportunities hiding in the shadows. It can keep us from realizing that there may be something more than all that the eye can see. When we use idioms like this or phrases like *"it is what it is,"* which we discussed earlier as one of the myths, it keeps us from asking the question, *"What if?"* In other words, it keeps us from growing and taking the red pill and activating our RAS.

We See The World As We Are

Let's take a moment to understand what's going on in your brain at this very moment. Your focus determines your reality. Mark Batterson shares it this way, *"We don't see the world AS IT IS. We see the world AS WE ARE."* That's the simulation that plays in our personal multiverse.

Not having our bags on the cruise trip may have been a downer, but it enabled us to see beyond our resources. *Why?* Because we had to! It opened our awareness of other things. It made me reflect more and appreciate what I did have – not what I didn't. After all, I was just happy to be aboard the ship. We had made it!

WYSIWYG Thinking

In the computing world, *"What You See Is What You Get"* is a phrase commonly abbreviated as WYSIWYG. It's used to describe or market an application that provides a user interface with an appearance that mirrors how it will look when it is printed (like a typed page) or presented (like a website). The intent is to signify that there is a creative workspace – like Microsoft Word – showing you the desired end state even though you in the design phase.

What I love about the computer use of this idiom is that it opens your mind for your imagination and growth. WYSIWYG thinking isn't just meant to describe what we physically see; it can also leverage what we mentally see with our imagination.

For example, as I'm typing this paragraph in real-time, I am formulating words down on a blank page – words that existed nowhere else other than in my mind. To use the Matrix analogy, it's like I took the red pill, and something new comes into my awareness.

163

Think back to the cruise ship story.

- Blue pill thinking sees the lack of bags, clothes, or resources (the gaps).

- Red Pill thinking sees something more that can be brought to life (the gains).

Life is a canvas inviting you to participate. Your job as an Imagineer is to see what can be filled on an empty canvas – or in my case, a blank page.

Using my imagination, words find a way to come to life on a blank page. What you see is the manifestation of that imagination. The page is not empty.

Our imagination is what gives us foresight. It's what we need to see the canvas. This opens our mind's eye.

Think Outside of the Box

Another common idiom is *"think outside of the box"*. Now, this may be overused a bit, but as an idiom, it's not bad. Most idioms contain a figurative meaning that is different from the phrase's literal meaning, like *"under the weather"* or *"bite the bullet." "Think outside the box"* basically says there's more to what you see, and it invites you to look deeper.

I want to challenge you to see beyond the physical too. Let your WYSIWG thinking be more aligned with *"think outside the box"* than *"it is what it is."* In other words, see the canvas and then go fill it.

The best example of someone who could think outside of the box is reflected in the life of Steve Jobs.

The Reality Distortionist – *The Story of Steve Jobs*

Legendary leader and pioneer Steve Jobs is one of the most intriguing Imagineers that comes to mind when it comes to someone who could see more than others could. Think of all the products and solutions that he helped bring to life.

His colleagues affectionally used a term for Jobs: his knack for creating a *"Reality Distortion Field."* It described a behavior pattern he used to promote and champion new ideas. This Reality Distortion Field was Job's way to *"convince himself and others around him to believe almost anything."* It was the way he challenged the status quo – for his team to think differently. This might have been what set him apart.

One of the engineers on the original Macintosh Team, Andy Hertzfield, shares this commentary. *"It was dangerous to get caught in Steve's distortion field, but it was what led him to actually be able to change reality."*[66]

Steve's tactic – his persuasive stance – was a mix of charisma, bravado, and persistence. Honestly, for many, it made them uncomfortable, especially those that didn't want to be stretched.

Based on first-hand accounts, when you were with Steve, you didn't want to cross him. And because of that, you might choose to *"go along to get along"*, which is the same thing as Social Desirability Bias. But if Jobs ever found out that you held back on sharing your real perspective, he'd get hot. He wanted honesty.

Jobs would challenge you, but he didn't mind being challenged back. Feedback for him was critical, even though it may have looked like he didn't want it.

In his biography of Steve Jobs, author Walter Isaacson shares, *"People who were not crushed ended up being stronger. They did better work."* In one interview with Joanna Hoffman, who was on the original Mac team, she shares, *"You could also push back – sometimes – and not only survive but thrive."* Isaacson adds, *"If Jobs sized you up and decided that you knew what you were doing, he would respect you."*

But employees who couldn't see what Steve could see were the ones who failed to make progress, and eventually, they disappeared.

What Jobs wanted and needed were true contributors. These were impact players who found a way to diminish their cognitive biases, overcome any initial doubt, and bring to life what Steve Jobs had imagined.

Jobs' Most Significant Innovations

A person might stand in wonder, watching how this Reality Distortion Field motivated change and created impact. Here's a partial list of the Apple team's significant and revolutionary products and solutions that started in the imagination of Steve Jobs.

- **The Macintosh (1984)** – this was the first consumer computer with a graphical user interface, which included typography on screen. Think WYSIWG.

- **iMac G3 (1998)** – in his second stint at Apple, he conceived the most iconic computer that perhaps had ever been created, proving that technology didn't need to be boring.

- **The Apple Store (2001)** – he revolutionized the shopping experience by creating spacious stories that offered consumers a compelling space to engage, experiment, and evaluate new tech. With their iconic glass, full-sized wall storefronts (and even glass staircases in some locations), these stores continue to invite and welcome consumers from all over.

- **The iPod (2001)** – he may not have been the first to create a portable music player, but he overcame the barriers by creating a simple and effective touch-based physical device that made it easy for you to put 1000 songs in your pocket. With the supporting iTunes Store, the iPod alone changed how music is distributed, licensed, and marketed. It also ushered in the era of podcasts.

- **The Apple TV (2006)** – he conceived a small computing device that could be attached to a Television using an intuitive remote comparable to the iPod. This was a device that could download, store and even steam television shows, movies, and music. This ultimately would revolutionize the entire consumer electronics industry, influencing other streaming devices, including Smart TVs, and would influence today's streaming network platforms.

- **iPhone (2007)** – he reinvented the phone from the ground up, bringing to life an easy-to-use device featuring an intuitive operating system that offered access to subcomponents like touchscreens, GPS, Wi-Fi, cellular, accelerometers, and more. Additionally, he conceived how to build and deliver an ecosystem through the App Store that would usher in a myriad of vetted applications to consumers. It indeed was and is revolutionary.

- **The Magic Mouse (2009)** – Even before the Magic Mouse, Jobs knew instinctively how to conceive a simple yet highly effective hand-held pointing device. The mouse, along with the equally effective trackpad with gesture support, created a means for consumers to easily maneuver and manipulate the controls and the data on a computer screen with the natural use of their hands.

- **The iPad (2010)** – he delivered what had only been previously envisioned and portrayed in science fiction movies, integrating a digital clipboard and display that could be easily carried around, allowing consumers to view, watch, read, and create simply with the touch of their fingers.

These technologies and more have revolutionized our world, and each of us, even if you don't have an Apple product in your arsenal, has been influenced by Steve Jobs' Reality Distortion Field. All told, Jobs is listed as a primary or co-inventor on 241 patents. He also influenced the entertainment industry helping put Pixar on the map. Think *Toy Story*, *Finding Nemo*, and *The Incredibles*.

One More Thing

Perhaps the best way to close on this topic on the Power of Today is to allow Steve Jobs himself to share. Of course, he's no longer alive today, but if you have studied his life, you know from what was captured that he would have some poignant thoughts to contribute.

Here are five perspectives that help increase the amplitude and leverage the Power of Today:

1. *"Your time is limited. Don't be trapped by dogma – which is living with the results of other people's thinking. Don't let the noise of others' opinions drown out your own inner voice. And most important, have the courage to follow your heart and intuition."*

2. *"Be a yardstick of quality. Some people aren't used to an environment where excellence is expected."*

3. *"Trust that the dots will somehow connect in your future. You have to trust in something – your gut, destiny, life, karma,*

whatever. This approach has never let me down, and it has made all the difference in my life."

4. *"Don't lose faith. If you haven't found it yet, keep looking. Don't settle. As with all matters of the heart, you'll know when you find it."*

5. *"One of my mantras [is] focus and simplicity. Simple can be harder than complex: You have to work hard to get your thinking clean to make it simple. But it's worth it in the end because once you get there, you can move mountains."*

Allow the wisdom from Steve Jobs to encourage you.

Chapter Summary

This chapter has been focused on the Power of Today. The Power of Today is about seizing the moment. It's about awareness of the unique windows of opportunity that come your way each day. The Power of Today creates the momentum we need to invent the future. What you do today makes an impact on tomorrow.

Additionally, the experience of others goes a long way. The best teams consist of individuals who are willing to work together and share their experiences. They challenge our thinking – and they shape our tomorrow.

As you learn to lead as an Imagineer, think of how you can empower others to help. Part of the secret is being crazy enough to believe you can change the world. Steve Jobs said it best:

"The people who are crazy enough to think they can change the world are the ones who do."

Look at the challenges that are in front of you. *What needs to be done?* Next, underneath the exterior of what seems impossible, identify the opportunities for others to step in and help. *Who can help you achieve the dream?* By asking this question, you can learn to increase the amplitude and make the most of the Power of Today.

❖ ❖ ❖

Additional tools and resources focused on
Increasing the Amplitude are available at
theimaginebook.com/ch-10

---

[65] Michael J. Fox, *10 Questions for Michael J. Fox*, Time, Apr. 27, 2009,
    https://content.time.com/time/subscriber/article/0,33009,1891739,00.html last accessed June 28,
    2022.

[66] Walter Isaacson, *Steve Jobs*, Simon & Schuster.

11 – NOTICE THE RESISTANCE
Understanding the Power of Discipline

"In the middle of difficulty lies opportunity."

– Albert Einstein

Have you ever experienced Murphy's Law?

Murphy's Law states that anything that can go wrong will go wrong. It seems to be an opposing force whenever we attempt to take meaningful action and is one of the common representations of resistance.

Resistance is what we often experience once we decide to move forward. Resistance, if we allow it, can stop us dead in our tracks.

If Murphy was cast in an epic movie, he might be personified as Agent Smith from the Matrix, Dr, Doom from the Marvel comics, or the Joker from the world of Batman. As our archenemy, Murphy might try to leverage the same tool that sparked your hope in the first place – it tries to tug and pull on your imagination through doubt, discouragement, and disillusionment.

With your imagination, Murphy can trick your mind, twist the truth, and trip the breaks. He is *"resistance to momentum,"* and feeds us with fear. But the antidote to Murphy is to recognize that momentum may still be on your side. The key is to understand the Power of Discipline. **With discipline, anything is possible.**

Riding with Murphy

As you can probably imagine launching a business – like SimVentions – brings forth a cadre of challenges. Challenges tend to come in batches, and we have been no exception. But the best example of dealing with Murphy and persevering with the Power of Discipline is a personal one.

A few years back, I was vacationing in Colorado with my family. On the day before we departed home, I suggested to everyone one more bike ride to cap off the trip, but there were no takers other than me. With their blessing, I loaded up a bike on a borrowed Nissan Pathfinder. I promised to return in a few hours and drove off to the trailhead. Little did I know that I would be facing Murphy head-on, and it would almost ruin our trip.

My ride plan was simple. At the edge of town, right next to the Arkansas River, was a 3.3-mile trail loop that would take me from a base elevation of 7900 feet to an apex of just under 9000 feet. The upper trail would give me a clear view of a breathtaking valley.

With my gear packed and my helmet on, I peddled off on my adventure, first crossing a footbridge over the roaring rapids of the Arkansas River. I traveled the first quarter-mile with ease, just a rolling trail along the side of the river's edge, offering the sight and sounds of its rapids. But then the real climb began as the path suddenly turned uphill with an endless series of switchbacks.

No Chain. No Gain.

As the trail steepened, I vaulted out of the saddle to push down on the pedals. I needed some momentum. But just as I did, the chain slipped – skipping several teeth on the sprocket. I quickly lost momentum and had to restart the climb. A minute later, it happened again. It was frustrating.

I compensated as best I could, determined to make the most of my last ride. My mind was set on reaching the top and taking in the view.

Finally, when I was just a few hundred yards away from the final ascent, I vaulted out of the saddle again to leverage more momentum. But as I did, the crank broke free as the chain snapped in two! The broken chain lay on the dirt like a dead snake. I was demoralized. Clearly, Murphy was kicking my butt. Imagine the Joker just laughing.

Test of Commitment

I thumbed through the saddlebag for a chain tool to replace a link, but as I began to use it, I discovered the tool was broken – it was useless.

My frustrations begin to build. At this point, I knew it would be a while, perhaps much longer than when I told my family that I would be back. So, I pulled out my cell phone to call them, but there was no signal. No bars.

I went back to try to use the chain tool – but to no avail. My options were limited. Then a rare thing happened, two other bikers on a seldom-used part of the trail suddenly came riding up and offered to help. With their tool, we got the chain relinked, and I was back in business.

But time was getting late. I had a tough decision with only two choices:

(1) Not see the summit – and turn around and return home.

(2) See the summit – but risk getting back a little late.

I thought for a moment, I knew that if I headed back down, I'd be riding the rest of the journey in defeat. I would have fallen short of my goal knowing I was just a few hundred yards away from the grand view I had imagined.

I didn't hesitate a second longer and I started pedaling forward – uphill. Little did I know my experience was just beginning.

Mountain Top Experience

This next portion of the trail carved across the side of the mountain at an altitude close to 9,000 feet in elevation. The view was spectacular. Below me was the small town of Buena Vista and the Arkansas River. Across the valley were the Collegiate peaks: Mount Princeton, Mount Harvard, Mount Yale, and Mount Columbia. These were all mountains over 14,000 feet in elevation. The shadows in the late day though were growing long, and the sky was turning dark blue as the sun prepared to set behind the "14ers".

Before heading downhill. I took in the view one last time. As I pulled out my water bottle, I noticed something very wrong. My saddlebag underneath the seat had ripped open and all the contents were missing.

My heart sank. I couldn't believe it! No phone, no keys, no ID, no emergency cash, and no broken chain tool. At that moment I realized I was screwed. Without the keys, we couldn't get back to the airport. Without my ID, I wouldn't be able to travel.

Frustrated, I went back and re-rode the top trail retracing my steps. I began hunting down everything I could find. The first thing I spotted was the tire patch kit and the broken chain tool. I grabbed them and rode further. Off the trail, I saw my emergency cash blowing down the rocky terrain. I scrambled to grab two $5 bills but would have gladly cashed them in for my keys and my ID.

Another 50 yards or so further I discovered my cell phone sitting right on the trail. Again, I tried to use it – but there was no signal. I rode further – looking and searching – but the keys and ID alluded me. I finally ditched the bike and just walked the trail – scanning the dry and dusty ground. The sun was near ready to set, and I was coming up empty.

I could just hear Murphy in my head whispering *"Ahh – you are screwed! Just ride to the bottom. They're worried about you. You don't need your ID. Just tell them you lost the keys. They'll understand. They'll forgive you. Maybe..."*

Honestly, I couldn't tell Murphy's law from the truth. I thought he might be right, and I almost rode back down empty handed. But then something grabbed a hold of me. They were my soundtracks.

- *Who says you can't find your keys?*
- *Who says you can't find your ID?*
- *You still have hope, don't you?*
- *You can do this!*

Despite the urge to ride down the mountain empty-handed, I kept walking the trail. Looking. Praying. Not ready to give up. I knew without my keys and ID, we'd be stranded. I knew they had to be here somewhere.

Mental Resistance

A while back, I noticed a *Reddit* post that caught my attention.

"I am noticing resistance (to thoughts, emotions, physical sensations etc.) in daily life. Can anyone offer any advice (or point me towards some good resources) on how to first know what resistance is, and then to recognize it in daily life?"[67]

One person replied saying, *"Resistance is a physical or mental tension."* They added that mental resistances can be noticed *"in places you try to deny, reject, or judge reality."* Some of the examples they highlighted included the discomfort you might feel when looking at the mirror, or the avoidance you have on a time sensitive project by choosing to watch TV instead.

The next comment grabbed my attention. *"Mental resistance is a defense mechanism the mind uses to avoid a painful emotional reaction."*

It reminded me that the resistance that we experience is not always external, many times its internal.

Our own internal struggles are the greatest resistance we battle – not the external ones. With internal struggles, our imagination and reality can be at war, and we become more distracted or apprehensive. The distraction and apprehension take our eyes off the ball, and it elevates our fear, so much so that we try to avoid what we should really do. The mental resistance often results in a negative emotional response.

What if we can flip the resistance and see the opportunities that lie before us? **What if the resistance wasn't there to stop you but there to guide you?**

The Power of Discipline

As I walked the trail on that mountain, my hope came back to life. I knew that in this situation I had to lead myself before I could lead my family. I couldn't give up. I still had hope. I realized that those keys had to be somewhere on that mountain. They simply couldn't be anywhere else. They were meant to be found by someone. It might as well be me.

A few minutes later, my eye latched onto an object that seemed out place. Partially masked in the dead center of a cactus plant were a set of keys. I couldn't believe it. As I reached down and grabbed the missing keys, I then saw my driver's license just a few feet way.

In that split moment, my grief turned to instant joy and relief. I took out Murphy and conquered that mountain. The rest of that journey was sweet and satisfying. I had NOT given up, and it felt good!

Like a scene in the classic Steve Martin movie *Planes, Trains and Automobiles*, I couldn't wait to see my family.

What I learned from that experience is that leaders (including parents and spouses) stay the course. Sure, they must pivot through the challenges, and possibly change their path, but they lead through adversity. They don't give up. They find victory. And, only by leading themselves with discipline, can a leader truly lead others.

For me, I was riding back down to lead my family, and I knew I had a story of victory to share that they needed to hear. The alternative would have been much starker, if I had not persevered, if I had given up hope, it would have been harder to lead them. It would have been harder to gain their trust. It would have been harder to go home.

Followers long to hear and need to hear stories of hope pursued. Hope pursued matters and can only be achieved by the Power of Discipline. Jim Rohn defined discipline as *"the bridge between goals and accomplishments."* Discipline is the consistency of action.

Endorphins – *How the Brain Relieves Stress*

The benefit of discipline and the drive that comes with it is that it triggers the release of Endorphins in your body. Endorphins interact with the receptors in your brain, and much like morphine, they can minimize and mask pain.[68] A little bit of Endorphin can be a good thing. Endorphins give you an edge. But too little, and it increases your risk of depression, mood swings, and compulsion. Too much, and it might spike your system. You need the right balance.

Your imagination can play a big role in triggering and managing these Endorphins. Remember your imagination functions like a simulator. A mental simulation in this capacity can stimulate your emotional response – it can prepare you. And the Endorphins themselves can stimulate your imagination even further.

Deep in the brain, there is a system called the hypothalamus. One of its responsibilities is stress control and emotional response. It works in conjunction with your pituitary gland to release these Endorphins.

With your imagination, you can affect what happens with your hypothalamus and can trigger the release of Endorphins. It's what allows you to prepare and take on challenges. In turn, these Endorphins can fire up your imagination even further.

The Kobayashi Maru

Think about James T. Kirk, the infamous captain of the Star Trek Enterprise played by William Shatner. In an almost impossible situation in the movie *Wrath of Kahn*, Kirk responds to the challenge with a famous line that reflects the influence of the imagination, *"I don't believe in the 'no win' scenario."*

With this mindset, Kirk has preempted his emotional response, and has trained his brain to look for successful outcomes. He knows how to pull on his Endorphins. Because of that, he navigates his team through the challenges, and they slay Murphy – or in this case Kahn. Endorphins are kind of like laser fire coming out of a photon gun; they help you blast through the threats and challenges. They feed on discipline.

Incidentally, Kirk's mindset *"to boldly go where no man had gone before"* was established as a cadet at Starfleet Academy. It was through a simulation, called the *Kobayashi Maru*, that presented the "No-Win" Scenario. It was meant to test the emotional response of how a promising Starfleet commander would handle Murphy. Kirk was the only one to beat the *Kobayashi Maru* – but it did take him three tries. I call that perseverance! That's what Imagineers do.

Simple Ways to Boost Endorphins

Here are a few simple ways to boost Endorphins:

- Exercise
- Listen to Music
- Laugh
- Eat dark chocolate
- Meditate
- Watch Top Gun Maverick

At least three of those ways reflect imagination: listen to music, meditate, and *Top Gun Maverick*. But if dark chocolate and laughter help, then leverage that too!

At some point or another, we all will face resistance and mythical foes like Murphy. Murphy is simply the experience of *"Momentum Under Resistance"*. He inevitably shows up when we are trying to move forward. When we face him, there are two options:

- Option A – we can quit
- Option B – we can keep going

The first option is easy, but the second is hard. This is when you need some Endorphins.

In one of the shortest speeches he ever made, Churchill shared what might be the secret for Imagineers who leverage the Power of Discipline.

"Never give in. Never give in. Never, never, never, never—in nothing, great or small, large or petty—never give in, except to convictions of honor and good sense."

If we are to heed Churchill's advice, the challenge for you and me is to go for Option B. I believe that when you act and persevere with hope, if you don't give up, that's when you'll see leadership at work.

One way to encourage yourself is through the acrostic found in the letters of Murphy's Law.

Momentum Under Resistance?
Persevere with Hope.
You'll See Leadership At Work

Work, valley or mountaintop, Murphy is an unwelcomed nemesis. You and I will face him – and face him often. I am sure of it. But when you do, try to remember you are in control! Like Kirk, think Kobayashi Maru. **Refuse to believe in the no-win scenario**. Leverage the Endorphins. Remember your stories of triumph – trace your path. Recall the times when you wielded the Power of Discipline and slayed Murphy. Those are GAINS to assess. Allow them to build up confidence in you.

Recognize that any worthy pursuit might bring out Murphy, but Murphy is no match against hope relentlessly pursued and those who don't believe in the no win scenario. Just ask the Wright Trio, Elon Musk, Tyler Perry, or other Imagineers like the former CEO of Intel.

The Momentum Builder – *The Story of Mr. Intel*

Overcoming resistance is the story of András Gróf. When he was 8 years old, the Nazi army invaded his hometown in Budapest, Hungry. He and his family were Jewish. So, the threat of being deported to a concentration camp was real. To avoid being arrested, Gróf and his mother took up false identities and were sheltered by friends. Perhaps people just like Corrie Ten Boom.

Unfortunately, András' father wasn't as lucky as the rest of the family, as he was sent to a Nazi hard labor camp. Years later his father, would survive, and the family would be reunited after the war. But like Murphy, a new threat came. This time, the USSR had taken occupation in Hungary and the communist began to control the country.

During the Hungarian Revolution of 1956, András escaped from this new threat – fleeing over the border into Austria. He was virtually penniless. Eventually, he moved to the United States even though he could not speak a word of English. Once he reached the States, he finished his education. Soon after, he changed his name from András Gróf to Andrew Grove.

He recounts the story, *"By the time I was twenty, I had lived through a Hungarian Fascist dictatorship, German military occupation, the Nazis' 'Final Solution', the siege of Budapest by the Soviet Red Army, a period of chaotic democracy in the years immediately after the war, a variety of repressive Communist regimes, and a popular uprising that was put down at gunpoint... [where] many young people were killed; countless others were interned."*[69]

He adds, that *"Some two hundred thousand Hungarians escaped to the West,"* and he was one of them. If that's not overcoming Murphy, I'm not sure what is.

Eventually, Grove took up residence in the Catskills of New York, where he would meet his future wife, who was also a Hungarian refugee.

Grove had a passion for learning; being growth-minded was his secret weapon to gathering momentum.[70]

Eventually, Grove earned a bachelor's degree in Chemical Engineering and then earned a Ph. D. from the University of California in Berkeley. In 1968, he became the third employee of Intel, helping make static memory chips.

Unfortunately, the memory chip market was barely keeping Intel alive. They had dabbled in the semiconductor business and knew that there was greater promise in that niche.

Grove is often credited for having transformed Intel from a manufacturer of memory chips into the world's dominant producer of microprocessors. It's a great lesson in leadership perseverance.

Momentum's Impact

During his tenure as CEO, Grove oversaw a 4,500% increase in Intel's market capitalization from $4 billion to just under $200 billion. This made Intel the 7th largest company in the world, with 64,000 employees.

Most of the company's profits were reinvested in research and development, along with building new facilities, to produce improved and faster microprocessors.

Why?

Because it's a formula for building momentum. **Invest in yourself – it creates value that can multiply.**

More importantly Grove and his team created a culture within Intel that allowed innovation to flourish. According to Grove, *"Business success contains the seeds of its own destruction."* His belief was that *"Success breeds complacency. Complacency breeds failure. And only the paranoid survive."*

According to biographer Jeremy Byman, Grove refused to let Intel *"rest on its laurels."* Grove urged executives to allow people to test new techniques, new products, new sales channels, and new customers, to be ready for unexpected shifts in business or technology.

Grove explains his reasoning: *"A corporation is a living organism; it has to continue to shed its skin. Methods have to change. Focus has to change. Values have to change. The sum total of those changes is transformation."*[71]

The proof of hope is found in the actions we take. Grove was driven by hope, and even came up with system for capturing hope called OKRs. OKR stands for Objectives and Key Results. An Objective is something you hope for that reflects a vision. Leadership is responsible for identifying the core objectives. A Key Result reflects what you hope to accomplish that can be measured against the Objective. Key results can be identified by the team responsible for the objective. Grove's OKR strategic tool transformed Intel and many other businesses since then.

Grove shares that *"The early movers [aka Imagineers] affect the structure of the industry and to define how the game is played by others. Only by such a strategy can you hope to compete for the future and shape your destiny to your advantage."*[72]

Perhaps the most practical advice from Grove is this thought. *"Seeing, imagining and sensing the new shape of things is the first step. Be clear in this but be realistic also. Don't compromise and don't kid yourself. If you are describing a purpose that deep down you know you can't achieve, you are dooming your chances of climbing out of the valley of death."*[73]

Momentum's Foe

In *The 21 Irrefutable Laws of Leadership,* John Maxwell shares about the Law of the Big Mo. Mo is short for Momentum, and Maxwell describes it as *a Leader's Best Friend."*[74]

Think of momentum as the wind in a sail. It can move you and it can move others. Like pistons that drive an engine, momentum gets you going and will help keep you going. It's what is needed to start and finish. It can be the difference between winning and losing.

As we've already stated, momentum doesn't come without an adversary, a foe called Murphy or Murphy's Law. Murphy's Law states that if *"Anything that can go wrong it usually will go wrong."*[75] It's observed when a succession of problems occurs one after the other.

If you've ever faced frustration, disappointment, or discouragement because of setbacks, then you have undoubtedly faced Murphy. But Murphy is the set up for a story of significance. Murphy is the adversary in every story of success.

Chapter Summary

This chapter has focused on the Power of Discipline. The Power of Discipline gives you the drive to "push through" and invent the future despite the resistance. Discipline represents the path between your goals and your accomplishments. It's reflected by the consistency of action.

Perhaps the best way to help summarize this principle is through a simple but powerful Cherokee Indian fable.[76]

The Two Wolves

One evening, an elderly Cherokee brave told his grandson about a battle that goes on inside people.

He said, *"my son, the battle is between two 'wolves' inside us all. One is evil. It is anger, envy, jealousy, sorrow, regret, greed, arrogance, self-pity, guilt, resentment, inferiority, lies, false pride, superiority, and ego."*

"The other is good. It is joy, peace love, hope serenity, humility, kindness, benevolence, empathy, generosity, truth, compassion and faith."

The grandson thought about it for a moment and then asked his grandfather, *"Which wolf wins?"*

The old Cherokee simply replied, *"The one that you feed."*

Feed the Beast

Endorphins are stress fighters. Putting them into play is vital. They help naturally mask the pain and keep you focused.

To feed the right wolf, look for opportunities in the challenge. Gather momentum with small wins. Create momentum by declaring intent. Be clear on your values and be willing to learn in the struggle.

Brené Brown offers an encouraging thought. *"There is no innovation and creativity without failure. Period."*

Riding with Murphy offered a personal story about setbacks and perseverance to overcome them. It was a story centered on a ride in the mountains of Colorado that started with a simple goal to experience one last amazing mountain view. Like most endeavors, the Endorphins were firing me up initially, but it soon became something much more than I bargained for.

Riding with Murphy isn't just a memorable journey on a mountain bike. It's a leadership lesson about the battle of two wills: one that says, *"you can't,"* and the other that says *"you have to."* Waiting to respond is the wolf inside each of us, and there are two.

One is evil; one is good. The evil one will tear you down. The good one, which I prefer to see as a Sheep Dog, will encourage you, protect you, and build you up. The beast that wins is the one you feed.

It's all about the Power of Discipline. Let self-discipline be a perennial strength of your imagination. That way, the next time you notice the resistance, you'll already have the edge to overcome. You'll know which beast will win!

Hint: it's the one that looks to find the keys; not burry them.

Additional tools and resources focused on
Noticing the Resistance are available at
theimaginebook.com/ch-11

---

[67] *How to Notice Resistance,* https://www.reddit.com/r/Mindfulness/comments/2yi2c5/how_to_notice_resistance/, last accessed June 28, 2022.

[68] Simon Sinek, *Leaders Eat Last: Why Some Teams Pull Together and Others Don't* (p. 39), Penguin Publishing Group.

[69] Andy Grove, *Swimming Across* (pp. 1 and 4), Plunkett Lake Press.

[70] For more on the Values Bucket, visit theimaginebook.com

[71] Mike Sager, *What I've Learned: Andy Grove,* Esquire, May 1, 2000, https://www.esquire.com/entertainment/interviews/a1449/learned–andy–grove–0500/, last accessed June 28, 2022.

[72] Andy Grove, *Only the Paranoid Survive: How to Exploit the Crisis Points That Challenge Every Company,* The Crown Publishing Group.

[73] *Ibid*

[74] John C. Maxwell, *The 21 Irrefutable Laws of Leadership.*

[75] *Murphy's Law,* Wikipedia.

[76] *The Tale of the Two Wolves,* https://www.nanticokeindians.org/page/tale–of–two–wolves, last accessed June 28, 2022.

PHASE FOUR

ACT

Move with Velocity

PHASE FOUR – ACT

"The most difficult thing is the decision to act,
the rest is merely tenacity.
The fears are paper tigers.
You can do anything you decide to do.
You can act to change and control your life;
and the procedure, the process is its own reward."

– Amelia Earhart

The fourth phase of the OODA Loop is to ACT, which is about moving forward with velocity. If *intent* is the resolve and determination to do something, then *velocity* is the measurable direction and speed towards that objective. We need velocity to get to vision.

In physics, velocity is defined by a formula:

Velocity = Distance x Time

If we decide and don't act, the distance we progress over time is disappointing at best. However, if we do decide and we do act, even if we stumble and fall, we will at least find ourselves falling forward. Any forward movement is good movement – it's progress.

If we decide, but never acted, then we deceived ourselves. We don't want that to ever happen. Velocity is about choosing a direction and to go with speed. It's about motion.

In this section we explore three behaviors that every Imagineer can practice, to act and move with velocity:

- Enter the Matrix, with the Power of Movement
- Engage with Others, with the Power of Encouragement
- Reinvent Continuously, with the Power of Growth

Tozer adds, *"Truth is creative, saving, transforming, and it always changes the one who receives it."* Clarity of truth comes with movement. Change comes with movement. Movement creates meaning.[80]

Mark Cole, one of my mentors, shared this observation, *"I have seen too many leaders get caught up in perfection over progress and never take a step. Leaders, hear me: you can't steer a ship that isn't moving. START MOVING!"*

He then added. *"We are to leave footprints in the sands of time, not butt prints!"*

It's easy to get caught up in the Observe, Orient, and Decide Phase and never Act. Leaders like Cole encourage us, *"Don't wait for perfect clarity before starting to move. Find your goal and start heading toward it. You will begin to see things more clearly with each step."*

The Only World That Matters?

In one of the most recent Matrix movie scenes, the antagonist, known as The Analyst, expresses an intriguing thought, *"The only world that matters is the one here!"* He shouts this as he physically jabs a finger at the temple of Neo. He's referring to the mind.[81]

He then continues by asking Neo a question, *"What validates and makes your fiction real?"* He pauses to let Neo think about it before answering for him. *"Feelings!"*

He then comments. *"Here's the thing about feelings: they're so much easier to control than facts."*

That line grabbed my attention. I couldn't help but wonder, *"How often do I choose what I feel over facts?"* Let's face it; our imagination is a powerful medium. We need to make sure we have it dialed in and then move. If we don't move, then we start to overthink, and that takes us in the direction never going.

Here's another statement worth reflecting on, *"People See Only What They Want to See."* Most people innocently subscribe to this expression. There's both truth and danger in it. It's comparable to the phrase *"perception is reality"* that I intentionally used earlier.

If we're not careful, we will fill the voids of what we don't know with a narrative of what we think we know (or feel) and call this the TRUTH. When this happens, we might be completely wrong and never know it. Our propensity is to either think the best or the worst and leave little room for the grey – but it's in the grey that may hold the truth – the grey of the unknown when we step forward and move out of our comfort zone! That's how we can see for ourselves the truth that's out there.

But if what we think is being driven by a prior experience, an impression, or a belief, then we might be stuck in The Matrix. Our self-judgment, past experiences, beliefs, and critical thoughts can lead us astray and keep us from moving forward.

Trapped Inside The Matrix

As I noted earlier, our tendency is to process what we see by looking for information that validates our feelings or expectations. This is called *confirmation bias*. Even writing a book like this, I had to be careful. If I wrote what I felt or believed initially, I knew I could miss something profound. Even with those careful steps, I'm sure I still have.

In his best-selling book *Think Again*, author and researcher Adam Grant defines confirmation bias as *"seeing what we expect to see."* There is also a related cognitive bias called *social desirability bias*. Social desirability bias is *"seeing what we want to see."*

Both biases can be dangerous, but confirmation bias is more so. It's how the Matrix Trap happens.

Confirmation Bias – *People Only See What They Expect to See*

With confirmation bias, you may see a tendency of individuals to interpret the conditions, attitudes, and reactions of others as confirmation of an existing belief, theory, or feeling. With confirmation bias, your imagination can trip you up by trying to validate what it feels.

Let's understand the battle with confirmation bias. My friend Mike Harbour posted this on the topic recently.[82]

> *"We all have confirmation biases and seek to affirm those based on what we look for. This makes us feel good about who we are, versus being open to exploring new perspectives. This*

is a huge challenge in our world today. People watch the news of choice to confirm their own beliefs not to get a new perspective. That's why I don't watch any news. This allows me to be open to other's perspectives and not try and just defend mine."

Harbour adds:

"Our programming from way back has a lot to do with this if we don't create an awareness and path change when needed."

He's right. Just 30 minutes of viewing mainstream news can sway me with information that feeds an unhealthy perception. As human beings, we are wired to either accept what's being told because it matches our preconceived beliefs, feelings, or myths or outright reject information that contradicts our views. In both cases, our perception becomes a reality.

What is happening under the hood is that our subconscious memory has stored up a bank of values and beliefs that might be biased, and it is darn near impossible to overwrite it. *"It's a bit like uploading an image onto the internet. Once it's out there, it's difficult to remove it."*[83]

Social Desirability Bias

With social desirability bias, you may see a tendency of individuals to answer questions that make them look good or favorable in the eyes of others. You frequently see this on social media posts, product reviews, or survey responses. People are mindful of how others might interpret what they post and share. As a result, they comment with socially acceptable answers, or politically correct responses, as compared to what they might feel, believe, or know. This plays havoc on our imagination, causing us to second guess our actions and responses. We confuse ourselves.

Grant shares that *"these biases don't just prevent us from applying our intelligence. They can contort our intelligence into a weapon against the truth."*[84] In other words, our biases get us trapped in The Matrix. Our imagination can miss seeing the truth.

The Impact of Cognitive Biases

As a very simple example, my wife and I experienced these cognitive biases the very first day on that cruise that I shared in Chapter 10. Again, it was at the White Night Party, and we were wearing black shirts. At first, we felt totally out of place. We felt hundreds of eyes on us, and we began to create a narrative that said we didn't belong based on how we felt. Confirmation Bias begin kicking at us.

The idea of White Night is to take advantage of the phosphates commonly used in laundry detergent. The right lighting at night will make white clothing stand out – glowing in the dark. It's quite a spectacle. The only thing I had going for me that night were my pair of white ankle socks.

Barb and I were trying to find ways to just style it out, and fit in. The *"fit-in"* part is what Social Desirability Bias is all about. We wanted to connect and be part of the fun, but our imagination was getting off track. Because we weren't aligned with everyone else, we became self-conscious. I felt like a freak.

Finally, my wife said, *"We just need to let it go. What else can we do?"* With that thought, we somehow stepped into the experience, realizing it wasn't about the phosphates, it was about just being present with some like-minded people. It's okay not being like everyone else. What made the difference that got us there was the Power of Movement.

Like I said earlier, few seemed bothered by our black shirts, we finally realized *"why should we?"* Truthfully, we probably fit in better with the black shirts than if we wore white shirts anyhow. *Why?* Because we chose to see more than what was on the surface. We chose to be ourselves, even though it looked like we missed the memo. We were no longer trying to just fit in like everyone else. We chose to be present by moving forward.

The Two Minds

Several things drive our cognitive biases. One is our upbringing. What we are taught to believe can become unquestioned knowledge that we store up. The other is our ego. We want to be liked. We don't want to be wrong or perceived to be weak.

We learn that the Conscious Mind and the Subconscious Mind might be at war. The Conscious Mind is like a scanner – active polling stimuli – trying to process the information weighing it against our RAS. It likes to chew on things. Meanwhile, our Subconscious Mind is quietly whispering to our Conscious Mind through impulses, feelings, and instincts. It's also pulling on the RAS but in a different manner. The warning system wants to tell us quickly, *"See. There's it is!"* Pointing out things that validate our misbelief. It's a battle of the minds.

The Battle

The knowledge captured in the Subconscious Mind was originally keyed in long ago by values, beliefs, and experiences. If we don't evaluate those values, beliefs, and experiences, biases start to form. It's like the formation of plaque or a cavity.

Let's take a moment to understand more about how these two parts of our mind work, and how we can tap into them. Author Daniel Kahneman calls our Conscious Mind our slow-thinking brain and our Subconscious Mind our fast-thinking brain. He describes them as two systems.[85]

The operations of your slow-thinking brain are NOT automatic. There is some heavy mental thinking that's going on. This is where we might say our *"wheels are turning."* In those moments, we are processing and reasoning about what to do and what choices to make. We're contemplating, even though we may have already decided. It's like a child inching to the edge of a diving board. They are already on the diving board, so the choice was made, but the jump – that's not so easy.

Some attention must be allocated for us to concentrate and make choices. For example, as you read or listen to this book, you are leveraging your Conscious Mind – your slow-thinking brain – to process what's being shared and offered to you. You are trying to make sense of this information – especially if the information is new to you.

But there's the potential for a little battle in your brain. The Subconscious Mind runs at a processing speed more like bullet time for those familiar with The Matrix.

Bullet Time

"Bullet Time" refers to the ability to process information and react to stimuli super-fast, thereby slowing down time. By thinking faster than real-time, we get a sense that we can freeze the world around us as we make intuitive, rapid-fire decisions.

The problem with bullet time is that is constrained by how good our programmed response is. This means that we must do some serious training to think faster than real-time and be good at it.

The bottom line is this. The Subconscious Mind is more involved in how you think, feel, and act than you realize. The Subconscious is more in the game than you think. For example, if I were to tell you that it takes seven years to digest chewing gum if you swallowed it, then your Subconscious Mind wants to immediately confirm or deny that bit of knowledge based on your prior coded beliefs.[86]

Our Subconscious Mind – which is our fast-thinking brain (remember it wants to run in Bullet Time) – operates automatically and quickly with little effort or conscious control. Yet, it continues whispering to our Conscious Mind through feelings and instincts.

The key is to find ways to get your fast-thinking brain – your Subconscious Mind – tuned and sharp and to be a help, not a hindrance.

It's this fast-thinking brain that allows you to orient yourself to sound, detect the distance of objects, answer to "2 + 2 = ?", complete phrases like "salt and ...", react with facial gestures when encountering a pungent odor, identify fear, distinguish frustration in someone's voice, or ride a bike.

And The Winner Is?

Which mind do you think is the difference-maker for those who succeed in life? Is it the Conscious Mind or the Subconscious Mind? If you could only pick one, which one would it be?

I want you to think about it. The Conscious Mind is the more accurate system, but it's not fast enough for the real world. The Conscious Mind is just too slow.

For example, if your Conscious and Subconscious were competing in a game of *Family of Feud* or *Jeopardy*, Subconscious would hit the buzzer faster than Conscious almost every time. This is true in the game of life too. *Subconscious seeks to hit the buzzer first. Doesn't it?*

While your Conscious Mind is ultra-important, your Subconscious Mind wants to be the dominating player. *Why?* Because it's faster on its feet. It wants to lead.

But the Subconscious needs some help. While super-quick, the Subconscious is neither as effective nor as smart as the Conscious. It can't go alone for long. It needs to be constantly tuned and trained; otherwise, it will get stuck in its ways or embarrass you. When it does get stuck or embarrass you, a call goes out to the Conscious Mind. *"Hey, can you come and rescue me?"* The Conscious Mind does what it can to save the day.

Subconscious, even though it was first on the buzzer, is frequently wrong. It often gets the buzz of rejection. That's when Conscious gets a chance to redeem the day. It's not as efficient, meaning it doesn't get things done as fast as the Subconscious, but it is super-effective. Like a slow cooker, it eventually gets it right.

Sometimes the Conscious Mind must do a little damage control in the wake of the Subconscious Mind's bullet-time reactions. That might be why we have phrases like *"think before you speak"*, *"be quick to listen, slow to speak, and slow to anger"*, or, my favorite, *"engage brain before putting mouth into gear."*

Confirmation bias rears its ugly head when our Subconscious Mind might already have a preconceived idea. If you are lucky enough to catch the bias as it happens, your Conscious Mind can work extra hard to overcome it. If you don't catch the bias, you will quickly lose your footing, become a victim of the bias, and react poorly. Either way, it's going to be a battle. The good news is that there are some success stories to overcome the bias.

Train Your Brain Like You're QB1

"Open Up Your Imagination." Those were the words that quarterback Russell Wilson heard from his dad years before he would be drafted into the NFL. Despite being one of the top prospects coming out

of college in 2012, Wilson would have to wait for 74 other names to be called before the Seattle Seahawks finally drafted him. In his first ten years as a pro, Wilson went to nine pro bowls and two Super Bowls. As of this writing, he now plays for the Denver Broncos.

When talking about his transition to finding success in those early years of playing in the NFL, he shares how he overcame the bias. *"An important element of who I am comes from my dad. My dad would always ask questions. He would say something and then ask me what it meant to me."*[87] Wilson adds that his dad would probe him. *"Tell me what you are going to be. Tell me what you are going to do. What does it look like?"*

Wilson would share his aspirations with his dad, but if his dad saw they were status quo answers, or there was a bias that kept him from his best, he would comment. *"Hey, that's not good enough. You could do better. **Open up your imagination.**"*

Think about what makes a quarterback like Wilson, Tom Brady, Aaron Rogers, Patrick Mahomes, or Jeff Allen stand out in the National Football League (NFL). It isn't just their cerebral fortitude and conscious thinking but also how they think subconsciously. Their Conscious Mind is way up there, no doubt, but the Subconscious Mind is what allows them to play almost instinctively. It turns out that the greater the Subconscious, the higher the confidence. But understand how they got there. They didn't learn to walk upright out of the womb. They learned just like the rest of us. Repeated training made the difference coupled with painting a picture of what they could be in their imagination.

The question for you and me is simple, *"What are you feeding your Subconscious Mind to improve it?"* In other words, what are you imagining that is training your brain?

That training starts with recognizing that your Subconscious Mind needs to continue to expand. Being growth-minded is the most important thing you can do.

Here's a short list of things to do: Seek knowledge and understanding. Learn from others. Read good books. Experiment. Share your experiences. Learn from other people's experiences too. Be open. Be aware. Look for patterns. Remember, the opportunities are out there. Move!

And when you move, allow your Conscious Mind to be aware, and your Subconscious will follow. This trick can turn a 6th-round draft pick in the NFL, like Tom Brady, into one of the greatest of all time.

We need to allocate attention to what's coming in, and the filter for that is our Conscious Mind. While the Conscious Mind gathers all the info, as the years go by, our Subconscious wants to refute the incoming data – fight it. It wants to take over. It challenges or even ignores our Conscious when new information isn't familiar. Stubborn in its ways. It doesn't like to learn like it used to. It can get biased. Remember, the Subconscious just wants to take over and do what it already knows to do. Therefore, how are you training it?

If you've ever watched a football game or any other sport, you'll see talented players come into the league who can play instinctively, but they never really advance.

What separates top QB1s from the rest is their ability to face fear and have a Lead Bulletproof Mindset. For a 2nd tier player, however, their Subconscious Mind is prone to reacting more to their fear and emotion, resulting in poor form and potentially harmful habits. Before long, they may find themselves out of the league. Whereas, for a QB1, they work to improve their awareness constantly. Rather than being reactive, they are proactive. They are always learning, constantly using their imagination. They are moving.

You can see how a top-rated QB1 might leverage their imagination right before a snap. As they look over the head of the center and scan the defense, they take in how everyone is positioned, and in their mind – their Conscious Mind – they are using their onboard simulation to explore the mental images of how they can make the most of the play.

Focused leaders operate with hope and a *just cause* fueled by their imagination. If necessary, they may even adjust to what they see. With imagination, the Conscious Mind prepares the Subconscious; they work together. Best of all, the hope and confidence of a leader can be transferred to those around them. **Hope is contagious.**

The Bridge

The bottom line is this; there needs to be a two-way bridge between our Conscious and Subconscious. They need to work together to be at their best. What makes us human are both these components. The Latin expression to describe us as human beings is the phrase *Homosapien*. Homo means human or man; that's the Subconscious part of us. Sapiens means wise or astute; that's the Conscious part.

There's no shortcut to the secret. No matter how young or old you are, keep seeking knowledge. Be open to new insights. Take it in and seek to understand. This is the Power of Movement.

The World Was Once Flat

Think of it this way. At one time, almost everyone on the planet thought the world was flat. You would have difficulty convincing anyone that the earth was round, even though logically, it should have made total sense that it's elliptical. The moon is round; the sun is round; all the other planets are round. How did this learning happen?

For thousands of years, people believed that the world was flat. It got programmed into our Subconscious and ingrained as a universal belief. It wasn't until a few knowledge-seeking people questioned this belief starting with the Power of Curiosity, and eventually proved that the world was elliptical. How did they prove it? It was through the Power of Movement. They sailed the seven seas. Once that happened, people's Subconscious beliefs changed too. Now we see the world as it is, it's round –at least kind of.

The Sub 4-Minute Mile

The sub four-minute mile in running is another excellent example. Until Roger Bannister bought into the idea that it could be broken in competition, nobody had achieved it or even thought it was possible. But, through his imagination and a coach who helped guide him using interval training, he found the belief he needed, and he did it!

Over 1400 athletes have broken the four-minute mile since he set the mark in 1954. The fastest time recorded to date is 3:43.13 by Hicham El

Guerrouj of Morocco. He did this in 1999 at the age of 24. That's over 23 years ago. Who will set the mark next?

Incidentally, the world is still waiting for the first woman to break the 4-minute mile. But who says that it can't be done? The only thing that might be limiting today's female athlete is the Subconscious Mind.

Imagine the possible using the Power of Movement.

Free Your Mind

Let's return to Neo's conversation with Morpheus for a moment in the Construct in the original movie. As Neo looks at the environment around him, he asks Morpheus a simple question *"Is this real?"*

Not surprisingly, Morpheus answers with a question of his own. *"What is real? How do you define real? If you're talking about what you can feel, what you can smell, what you can taste and see, then real is simply electrical signals interpreted by your brain. This is the world that you know."*

For all intense purposes, Morpheus is describing Neo's imagination. Our imagination is where our attention lives 100% of the time. Even what's happening in the real world is viewed through the lens of imagination.

As Morpheus shares with Neo more about the Matrix, a world built to control them – control their thoughts, feelings, perceptions, and awareness. And a world seeking attention. Neo is in disbelief. *"No. I don't believe it. It's not possible."* He argues as he struggles with different biases.

Morpheus calmly responds, *"I didn't say it would be easy, Neo. I just said it would be the truth."*

Morpheus' goal is simple; he wants Neo's Conscious Mind to awaken. You and I are positioned to do the same.

Like *The Construct*, your imagination is a place to evaluate and prepare yourself for the world around you – a world that requires action. The common thread between preparation and action is to be intentional.

Think about how the QB1s leveraged their imagination. The same is true for the Mahre Brothers, the Wright Trio, Tyler Perry, and more. The best Imagineers seem to be intentional. Even the Apostle Paul talks about the importance of taking every thought captive and pressing forward. Otherwise, your thoughts will take you captive if you sit too long.

Why is this important to understand? Because your imagination is where your attention lives.

Think about it – if someone has your attention, then they have your imagination. With attention, thoughts can be seeded, including images in your mind. An attempt for this happens every time you turn on the TV, watch a commercial, scroll through your social media feed, hear the ding on the phone, or smell that popcorn.

If something is trying to grab your attention, it's trying to take residence in your imagination.

So, what can you do about it? First off, there's nothing wrong with something seeking to grab your attention. It can be lifesaving. It can alert you to a real need or urgency. The question is, *how are you going to respond?* Will you take your thoughts captive, or will you let outside thoughts take you captive? Don't sit idle for long. Be intentional with action.

For the QB1s, they are intentional in using their imagination to prepare them for what's next. Like Jason Bourne in the movies, they take every thought captive so that they can have greater situational awareness and can act quickly.

What if you could use your imagination, in the same way, to help train you?

The good news is that it's possible.

If you could simply be more intentional with your imagination and the attention trying to seize it, you could change the game. Think about how that might look.

This idea of The Construct taken straight out of *The Matrix* offers you a metaphorical tool to reset your internal game board and clear out your cognitive biases. Keep in mind, your biases affect how you recall and process the world around you. A proper reset can help you with your decision-making and improve your behaviors. This allows you to achieve what you want and whom you desire to be.

The best part is that you don't need a computer program to load up to make this happen. You don't need to plug into the Matrix. All you need is to focus your imagination by using a single sheet of paper that explores five essential elements.

- How are you Reflecting?
- How are you Thinking?
- How are you Performing?
- How are you Learning?
- How are you Connecting?

Four of these elements are identified in the book *The Potential Principle* by Mark Sanborn, so full credit is due to him. The fifth element, *connecting*, is a vital principle of leadership. We need to explore each of these behavior elements so that we can be intentional in how we lead with the Power of Movement.

Step 1 – Reflect

Reflection is where you address who you are, where you are, and where you are going. According to Sanborn, *"good reflection leads to action, improving both your inner and outer life."*[88] Reflection offers fresh context, offering something to load before acting with the first step of the Power of Movement.

Starting early in life, reflection is how we contemplated life and moved from existing to persisting. It was part of our being. But over time, after so many familiar reflection "downloads" coupled with the busyness of life, we tend to neglect this area and put it on autopilot. Think back to how your Subconscious has been conditioned and prepared. Much of this work was done through reflection.

According to Sanborn, reflection is the *"aspect of leadership that is least often considered...but probably most important."* Maxwell adds that *"Reflective thinking is like the Crock-Pot of the mind. It encourages your thoughts to simmer until they're done."*[89] Both share how reflection gives you true perspective. Reflection allows you to gain a new appreciation for things that might have been unnoticed.

Reflecting is about introspection. The benefits of introspection are compelling. Here are just a few:

- It helps you provide more profound understanding.
- It gives you a greater perspective.
- It allows you to see yourself as you really are and who you will choose to be.

The struggle with introspection is that it is not a frequent practice. Typically, in the hustle and bustle of life, we are distracted and find ourselves with limited time. Avoiding introspection is not uncommon for individuals. The idea of facing fears and doubts can be unpleasant and hard. But if you can just block out some time to reflect and *"engage in contemplative thinking,"* you will find it can be highly productive.

Take time to reflect daily. When you do, be intentional, quiet the judge in your head, allow yourself to listen. This will set you up for the next element.

Note: to support this first step the Power of Movement, go back and review the powers of imagination used for the Observe Phase including the Power of Patterns, the Power of Curiosity, and the Power of Assessment.

Step 2 – Think

Thinking appears like reflection, but it's not. You are thinking about what information you already have in front of you before acting.

According to Sanborn, *"Thinking is about proactively contemplating the world around you."* He adds, *"It's the source of dreams, plans, and strategies"*. If we are not careful, this is where cognitive biases might start to congregate, and let our narrative stray. Thinking is how we evaluate needs, ideas, and opportunities. It's what births strategies and gives dreams a plan. This is the area where Designers shine.

Sanborn adds that *"the only thing that limits your thinking is your imagination."* He encourages you to think better, longer, and harder. It's what gives you an edge.

The other value of better thinking is that it helps you identify problems and solutions. It activates the Conscious Mind, and helps you eliminate errors and assumptions.

Question: *are you intentional with your thinking?* Look at your schedule each morning. *What's in front of you? What ideas do you want to bring to life that you've marked on your schedule? Do you have one or two?*

Note: to support this second step of the Power of Movement, go back and review the powers of imagination used for the Orient Phase. This includes the Power of Belief, Power of Boundaries and Power of Values.

Step 3– Perform

Sanborn likes to call the next behavior element *"performing"*, which is a good word, but I also refer to it as the "DOING" behavior because it maps with the responsibility that we should be actively taking daily. (See bonus materials for Chapter 7). According to Sanborn, this is where we spend most of our time. We are *"doing things"* and keeping busy.

Let's face it, you and I are seen for what we accomplish. The number of items on your "TO DO" list don't matter, what you are "DOING" and what gets "DONE" counts the most. This is what brings home the paycheck, triggers the promotion, and activates your Endorphins. But just because you are busy doing doesn't mean you are productive. The other four elements matter just as much, if not more. Perform, yes, but get ready to Learn.

Note: to support this third step of the Power of Movement, go back and review several of the other powers of imagination including the Power of Today and the Power of Discipline.

Step 4 – Learn

Learning might be the most measurable element of the bunch. Sure, we can measure what gets done – the GAINS, but what we learn might be even more encouraging and a greater measurement. According to Sanborn, learning is the *"precursor to performance"*. Learning is how we get better. He adds that *"ideas act on us if we seek them out and are receptive to them."* Learning builds new skills, new awareness, which leads to better thinking, and better performance.

John C. Maxwell, whom I consider a mentor, spends a few moments each morning thinking about the learning opportunities he sees for the day ahead based on the meetings, connections, and resources in front of him. He shares, *"I mentally cue myself to look attentively for something that will improve me in [each] situation."*[90]

As you contemplate what's ahead of you each day, ask yourself:

What opportunities do I have to learn and grow today?

If you keep seeking knowledge, you might surprise yourself no matter how old or young you are. Think again to Michael J. Fox. He has Parkinson's disease. He has physical limitations, but his Conscious Mind is now more aware. He is noticing the hidden choices he can now make. The trick is to keep learning, and to recognize that you're only as old as you feel.

When you get your mind to believe in new goals and ideals, then it will keep you sharp. It will keep you fresh. Otherwise, we become stuck in our old patterns and beliefs. Nothing brings on the feeling of *old* faster than a mind that has stopped wanting to learn. Therefore, keep learning.

Note: for additional tools to support this fourth step of the Power of Movement, look at one of the powers of imagination used for this Act Phase -the Power of Growth (Chapter 14), but also go back and look at the Power of Curiosity (Chapter 4).

Step 5 – Connect

A final important element central to our imagination is the behavior of connection. We are social beings. When we Reflect and Think, these begin as inner world activities. Those happen from within. When we Perform and Learn, those come from outer world activities. Those are behaviors that can occur with an external focus influenced by the world around us.

Our connecting behavior is the one element that combines both our inner world and outer world. We have ideas that need to be shared with the outer world that originated perhaps from within us, but we have needs that originated from the outer world needing to be understood within us. Connection is more about listening than talking. It's about finding common ground. An imagination pursued will need the assistance of others. That's why connecting is vital. Look to explore how your ideas can resonate with others.

Note: An additional tool to support this fifth step of the Power of Movement, leap forward and look at another one of the powers of imagination used for this Act Phase – the Power of Encouragement, which is in Chapter 13. Also, take time to explore the close-out chapter on Speaking Life, which is the Epilogue.

Chapter Summary

This chapter has focused on the Power of Movement. Movement is about acting, changing states, and advancing. It's what keeps you from falling trap to the status quo. The Power of Movement is the action necessary to invent the future.

Remember, *"we are to leave footprints in the sands of time, not butt prints!"* Therefore, get up and move!

Some of the traps that we might experience when we don't move include confirmation bias, and social desirability bias.

To avoid these traps, free your mind. Take time to reflect, think perform, learn, and connect daily. Consider masterminding with others. Lean into others who have the experience you don't. Find a mentor like real-life Morpheus, who can help you gain the experience you need, and fresh perspective that will take you further than you could alone. Push forward with the Power of Movement. Don't look back for long. *"Go!"*

As you act, NOTICE the opportunities and the growth. Opportunities are often disguised as challenges. Recognize that understanding truth is found out by the actions you take.

The Power of Movement expands your imagination. It makes it real, giving you new experiences. Like Neo in the Matrix, advance yourself by exploring the world you live and with this Power of Movement. Consider it as a requisite for inventing the future.

◆ ◆ ◆

Additional tools and resources focused on
Entering the Matrix are available at
theimaginebook.com/ch-12

---

[77] *The Matrix,* Warner Brothers, 1999.

[78] Galactic Archive, T*he Matrix (1999) – 'Construct' Scenes*, https://youtu.be/AGZiLMGdCE0, last accessed June 28, 2022.

[79] Charlie Peacock, *Experience*, from the album *The Secret of Time*, Track #10, 1990, It can be heard on https://youtu.be/voongSTDPOQ, last accessed June 28, 2022.

[80] A. W. Tozer, *To Be Understood, Truth Must Be Lived*, appeared as an editorial in "The Alliance Witness" between 1960–1963.

[81] *The Matrix Resurrections,* Warner Brothers, 2021.

[82] Mike Harbour, comment to my Facebook post titled, "People Only See What They Want to See", post January 1, 2022, https://www.facebook.com/groups/breakingaverage/permalink/881953039141082/, last accessed June 28, 2022.

[83] https://boycewire.com/confirmation–bias–definition–and–examples/, last accessed June 28, 2022.

[84] Adam Grant, *Think Again* (p. 25), Penguin Publishing Group.

[85] Daniel Kahneman, *Thinking, Fast and Slow* (p. 20). Farrar, Straus and Giroux.

[86] Growing up an aunt warned me it took seven years to digest chewing gum. I believed it for most of my life. Even today, I still catch myself thinking what would happen if I swallowed the gum. It's now an instinctive response.

[87] Uninterrupted, LLC, *Greatness Code*, Russell Wilson, Season 2 – Episode 2, aired May 12, 2022.

[88] Mark Sanborn, *The Potential Principle: A Proven System for Closing the Gap Between How Good You Are and How Good You Could Be* (p. 85). HarperCollins Leadership.

[89] John C. Maxwell, *How Successful People Think* (p. 71), Center Street.

[90] *ibid* (p. v).

13 – ENGAGE WITH OTHERS
Understanding the Power of Encouragement

"The most important thing is to try and inspire people so that they can be great in whatever they want to do."

– Kobe Bryant

Have you ever wondered why Morpheus and the gang chose to go back into the Matrix after being freed? That seems a little risky, doesn't it?

The answer, I think, is compelling. They went into the Matrix to free others. Think about how they rescued Neo, and then later even Morpheus himself. Trinity was rescued in the most recent movie. Let's face it; people need to be rescued.

One fan expressed it this way, *"the primary reason they plug back into the Matrix is to find more humans to unplug."*[91] In other words, they go into rescue them, to engage and equip them. Maybe we're called to do the same. People all around us are trapped and need to be freed. Their imagination might be limiting them. They need to be encouraged, and maybe you're called to do it.

More importantly, one person alone isn't called to save the world in the Matrix; it takes a team willing to collaborate. It was Neo, Trinity, Morpheus, Dozer, and more.

Imagination lights hope and fuels courage. Therefore, look for opportunities to unite with others on something you collectively imagine. Let imagination be powered by collaboration.

The best experience I had in seeing this was a trip I took to Guatemala a few years back. It demonstrated firsthand the Power of Encouragement.

Transformation in Guatemala

Like many Central American countries, Guatemala is a nation in dire need. Consider that 46% of the population lives in poverty.

In 2013, their government's leadership asked for outside help to share and teach leadership values to their people. *Why?* Because an image had been cast that gave them new hope for the future. The seed was planted to lead leadership values across multiple streams of influence. Guatemalans weren't content with where they were and believed in something greater for their nation.

Hearing the call, 150 coaches and leaders, including myself, converged in Guatemala City under the tutelage of John C. Maxwell. We teamed with a nationalized movement called *Guatemala Próspera*, who believed in the power of transformation for their people.

The mission was radical.

- What if we could mobilize coaches who are passionate about cultivating leadership and who are focused on personal growth and want to share it with others?

- What if we could go out into the marketplaces of Guatemala, across the city, and model and share laws of personal growth and desired leadership values?

- What if we showed them how to share it with others and resourced and empowered them to share and multiply a straightforward message of hope – *"Transformation Starts with Me"*?

Could we make that happen?

I'll never forget having a chance to visit unique places, including Guatemala's financial marketplace, high schools, churches, and more. I met with brokers, bank tellers, school bus drivers, college students, and a church congregation. I had a chance to talk and walk with real people who, despite the conditions of what appeared to be a depressed and deteriorating environment, had somehow never lost sight of the potential for something greater.

What I saw was a hunger for hope. I learned that pouring hope on top of hearts hungry for something more changes lives. It makes an impact on both the receiver and the messenger. And teaching leadership values influences people to grow and change and transform the world around them.

Imagine multiplying that experience with 150 other coaches and leaders sharing a common message of hope, and you get results that will blow you away. By the end of that week, we had trained and resourced over 18,000 Guatemalans across the city. That's 18,000 people who could then train, lead, and influence other Guatemalans across their country. Since then, other nations like Paraguay, Costa Rica, and the Dominican Republic have followed Guatemala's lead asking for similar help.

As for me, I have never seen HOPE more prominent than in the eyes of the Guatemalan people. That image of hope in their eyes will forever be etched in my mind. It is why I am passionate about sharing this message of hope and the powers of imagination. I want to pass it on.

The Power of Encouragement

We all have an opportunity to be dealers of hope. Hope is a message a leader shares with those they influence. It offers comfort for the tired, courage for the timid, and clarity for the team. With hope, a leader's influence is simply more effective. Yet, if our hope ever wanes, our leadership capacity becomes in jeopardy. We can lose out.

When you consider the greats in life – Abraham Lincoln, Martin Luther King, Jr., Mother Teressa, Winston Churchill, Ronald Reagan, Nelson Mandela, or Billy Graham – you'll find one thing in common. Each of them chose to inspire others with hope because they lived with hope – it was their most important message. Hope is how you shape the future.

Even Napoleon Bonaparte, one of the most influential military and political leaders in Europe in the late 18th and early 19th centuries, believed in the importance of hope. Reviews of Bonaparte today are mixed. I for one am not sure if I'd put him in the hall of fame of great leaders, but he's intriguing, nonetheless.

Despite all his conquests, he created hope for those he led. He is the one who said, *"A leader is a dealer in hope."* That's profound when you consider Bonaparte's accession as a leader.

Growing up, Bonaparte was bullied, and he became reserved – especially early on when he was an outsider. Yet he devoted himself to learning and trained to become a military officer. Eventually, he embraced hope and pursued it for his country. As a General, he became one of the most brilliant military strategists of his time. Soon after he became Emperor of France.

Historians say, *"He was fearless in battle and had enough charisma to draw people in with his words."*[92] How so? It's because he found a way to influence others with hope and encouragement. He was *for* them. And he was loyal to a *just cause* called France.

Each of us, no matter what our origin story or challenge around us, can influence others with hope and encouragement. We don't need to win wars; we just need to win hearts.

Serotonin – *How Our Hearts Want to be Led*

The impact of an encouraging leader is remarkable. Genuine encouragement physically affects those we lead by triggering a powerful neurotransmitter in our brain known as Serotonin. Serotonin fuels the imagination.[93]

Why Serotonin Works

When we genuinely share messages of hope, empathy, trust, and loyalty, those in our care become touched and moved. When that happens, the brain releases a hormone called Serotonin in both the giver and receiver.

Serotonin is what creates the feeling of respect, belonging, and self-confidence. It has the power to gently rewire the mind, reset the RAS, and change how people look at things.

Think of Serotonin as an anti-bully antidote. When Serotonin is released, it creates a feeling of safety. And when there's safety, there's an opportunity to encourage and empower others to open and adjust their sails. Hope - genuine hope - becomes the fuel to the fire. Serotonin is the chemical that is released when there is a renewing of the mind. It's how transformation starts.

According to medical professionals, Serotonin is a crucial hormone that stabilizes our mood, creates feelings of well-being, and promotes happiness. It impacts our mind and entire body. Mind-wise, it enables our brain cells and other nervous system cells to align and communicate, helping regulate things like anxiety. Body-wise, Serotonin helps us regulate our sleep, digestion, and bone health.[94]

Too little Serotonin often leads to depression, and too much Serotonin, however, may lead to excessive nerve cell activity. We need just the right amount. When they are at the right levels, you will feel more focused, emotionally stable, and simply calmer. Plain and simple, leaders need Serotonin to lead.

How Serotonin Works

While there is medication available for increasing Serotonin individually, this is a dangerous path. Common side effects to too much Serotonin includes shivering, sweating, confusion, high blood pressure, twitching, restlessness, or headaches. Even more extreme levels include seizures and irregular heart rates.

A more natural way to release Serotonin is through engagement, empathy, and encouragement. This requires leaders to get out of their comfort zone and spend quality time with others. This is sometimes called walk around leadership or *"management by walking around."*

Let's face it, it's easy to get hunkered down at our desk in our home office, or at work, and try to lead from there, especially in this new Covid-impacted world. Even in the days prior to Covid, most leaders and managers gravitated to their desk and led from afar. But eagles never stay all day in their nest. They get out and wander. Making connections with others is the best way as leaders we can naturally release Serotonin in others. A benefit is it also releases Serotonin in us.

Transformation Starts with Me

As I look back on that trip to Guatemala, I can see clearly how Serotonin washed over others. How the sharing of values by simply taking a position of attunement and connection created transformation. But not just in them, in me as well.

Transformation in the Financial Market

On one of the early days on that trip I had a chance to visit a business that offers financial planning service to Guatemalans. On the drive over, Cecilia, the officer manager, shared her excitement, but wasn't sure how many would show up to the training. I assured her that the numbers didn't matter; that Denny (my translator) and I would share with whomever would come.

Her English was respectable, and she replied with a smile, *"Oh, that is good, I know those who come will benefit greatly."*

I smiled back, and simply replied, *"Thank you for allowing us the opportunity to visit your workplace and share these values. I can't wait to meet your team."*

Cecilia smiled and passionately gripped the steering wheel tightly and pressed down on the gas. Denny and I could tell she was anxious and excited to get started.

Once we arrived, Denny pulled me aside and quietly whispered to me, *"Mr. Paul. Cecilia's English is very good. It is better than mine. And I feel that she hoped to translate for you. That I might not get the right words."*

Denny was a burly Guatemalan. He stood about 5' 6", but his shoulders were wide, and his legs, if firmly planted, were immovable. I looked over at Denny's bearded face. If I wanted a bodyguard, he would be the one. I knew that he had traveled by bus a long way to be with us and to translate for whoever needed it. He was a gregarious man, full of life, but it was the first time, in the short time that I had known him, that I noticed he wasn't smiling.

I realized he was with me for a reason, and I couldn't do this without him. So, I looked straight into his eyes and shared my conviction.

"Denny, my friend. Today, we are a team. I need you to work with me. You have charisma, you have energy, and you love people. I need that. Just

be you today as we work together. Let's mirror each other's energy. If we do that, I can assure you today is going to be great."

Quickly Denny's smile returned. *"You are right Mr. Paul"* As I looked into his eyes, I saw something I had seen a few times that week; his eyes reflected the image of hope. By the end of that week, I would observe that image of hope in almost every Guatemalan I'd meet. It's an image I'll never forget.

After setting up shop in the room that Cecilia reserved, I watched as pockets of individuals began to pour into the room. Most were wearing the business casual corporate ware of the company. A few with suits arrived – including Cecilia's boss. The room began to fill. Soon – we were asking for more chairs. Cecilia was relieved.

As I looked across the room, and greeted everyone, I could sense people were intrigued, yet skeptical of what they thought, *"I had to sell."* But I wasn't there to sell, I was there to give and encourage. I knew I'd have only a few seconds to capture their attention – at least initially – so I asked them a question.

"Before we get started sharing leadership values, I have a question for you. Outside of your jobs, what are you most thankful for?"

I gave them a moment to reflect and then shared with them that I was thankful for my family back home, and for Denny and Cecilia. Now, they didn't know much about Denny, but they knew Cecilia. And then I told them why. *"Denny traveled a long way to help me translate. I appreciate that. He's a good man. And we are both here for you today. Cecilia brought us here and invited you here too. And I can't wait to share with you. I want to know, what are you thankful for?"*

As Denny was translating my words, I could see the posture of those sitting in the room began to shift. They became more comfortable. With Denny's help we quickly found things in common with those in the room by letting them share what they were thankful for.

Looking back know, I recognize that was the start of trust that begin to fuel their Serotonin. Their interest for being there became even stronger. They were there to connect with one another. And to learn.

All told, Denny and I connected with thirty-five Guatemalans who became equipped to lead others with some new tools and values. They were supercharged. Looking back now, I can see how even more Serotonin was released through our round table discussion and breakouts.

One participant came up to me afterwards, a gentleman named Romero who was about thirty-five years old. I had noticed him earlier, and his posture at the beginning seemed to indicate that he did not want to be there. But he said something to me that I'll never forget. He leaned toward me, and in his best English, he whispered candidly just loud enough for me to hear.

"Paul, I want to thank you for the hope you and Denny have shared today." He paused for a moment. *"Today I will take home the lesson on 'el valor de escuchar' - the value of listening. I have not done well in this area."* He paused again and swallowed hard. *"Today, my wife will discover a new husband. Today, I go home as a new man for my wife and my family. I want to thank you."*

Romero's story boosted my own hope and courage – and Denny's too. I realize now that was Serotonin in play. It's a memory I will never forget. Serotonin heightens our memory.[95]

The Transformation of "Pilots"

The very next day, I was part of a larger group of coaches that headed to the other side of the city to a private school. In our van were eight coaches.

As we piled out of the van and walked through a covered outdoor basketball court onto the campus of a beautiful high school. The principal was eagerly awaiting our arrival. We learned that today *was* the first day of a two-week vacation for the students, but that all the teachers were still on the clock and arriving for the training that we had to offer. She was looking forward to having them trained on how to lead and facilitate their students in the areas of leadership. She then said that they also wanted their pilots to be trained to lead and facilitate others too.

Now the word *"pilots"* caught the attention of more than a few of us. That sounded intriguing. One of the coaches spoke up. In fact, it was probably me. *"Pilots – you have pilots here?"* If I didn't say it, I know I at least thought it along with everyone else.

We all looked on with great interest upon the school's Principal. Before she could answer, Monica, the school's English teacher who would be serving as one of our translators interrupted our thoughts and said, *"Ahh – she means the drivers of our buses for the students."* That generated more than a few chuckles in the room.

Despite the laughter, the eager excitement that was there a moment earlier about training "pilots" quickly left the room. I could tell that the other coaches in the room were not entirely excited about training bus drivers. Training teachers, that's why they had come. Honestly, I didn't blame them. None of us anticipated training bus drivers.

But as I began to think about it – I realized how truly great that was. The school was making a statement. They wanted the first line of connection to their students, the bus drivers, who are the ones that greeted their students every morning and wished them a farewell at the end of the day, to also be trained. Suddenly, I wanted in on that, so I volunteered to train them. My friend Doug Grant followed suit volunteering too. Moments later we found ourselves walking down to the school bus maintenance building, along with Monica, who would serve as our translator.

Their small building and break room sat adjacent to an outdoor parking lot covered with a well-worn artificial grass-like carpet. On both ends of the covered parking lot sat opposing soccer goals. The early morning sun was beaming down on a dew-damped field half-filled with parked cars of the teachers that had arrived earlier.

As we ducked out of the sun into the room where they were waiting, all eyes looked up and locked in. These thirty or so men ranging in age from 25 to 65 years old, sized us up with perhaps a bit of bewilderment and astonishment. Doug and I greeted them. *"¡Hola!"* I shouted. *"¡Buenos Días!"* Doug announced. Our translator Monica simply repeated, *"¡Hola, Buenos Días!"*

Some of them smiled, a few of them chuckled, and others looked puzzled. For them, I'm sure it's not every day two out-of-place, American males; one towering at 6' 4", myself, and the other, ten inches shorter, appear in an employee's break room. I imagine they must have been thinking, *"who are these gringos and what value could they add to us?"*

Round Table #1 – *The Law of Modeling*

With Monica's help, we worked through our introductions and greetings. Following those few minutes of attunement, we asked the same question I asked the day before.

"Today, what things are you truly thankful for?"

We gave them a few moments to chat, and then asked for some volunteers to share their thoughts. After a long pause, one man, who was about fifty years old, finally broke the ice and offered his thoughts. Monica translated for us. *"He says he is thankful for his job. For those in the room."* He was nodding toward his colleagues. *"And he is especially grateful for God and his family."*

Soon, others began to share similar answers. They were thankful for their jobs, for God, and especially their families.

Next, we shifted gears, and dove into our lesson by leading the whole group into a discussion of the *Law of Modeling*, which is about being a positive example for others. For this exercise, we asked for a few volunteers to read, but many of them were apprehensive.

Finally, three people volunteered. With Monica's help, we asked everyone to underline what they liked during the reading.

We then called on a second group to share one thing they underlined and why. No one raised their hand to volunteer. After a short pause, Doug and I tried to hand pick a few. They didn't budge. Finally, two individuals stood up and came up to the front of the room.

What they shared drew the interest of others in the room, but I was concerned. I whispered to Doug. *"I'm not sure we're going to get any more volunteers to share for the next part. We may need to go to Plan B."*

He glanced at me and replied, *"You may be right."* Then after a pregnant pause he asked, *"What's Plan B?"*

I smiled, *"I don't know yet."* I then muttered, *"Plan B is to be ready to pivot. Look to engage. Build trust."*

Doug nodded. *"Yeah. Let's do what we do."*

I knew there was a big soccer game that night in the city stadium that I heard about earlier. Guatemala was playing Argentina. I brought up the game, and then asked them who was watching it. Almost everyone raised their hand, including Doug and Monica. I shared that, because of my connection with Brazil, I couldn't possibly root for Argentina.

They wondered, *"Brazil? But he's American."*

I went on to share my love for the game started when I was young – when I lived as a child in Rio de Janeiro, Brazil. And that I played and coached soccer in the United States. That intrigued them.

Much to their excitement, they were glad to hear that Doug and I would be rooting for Guatemala that night. That was a moment of connection.

We then asked them to evaluate themselves on the Law of Modeling on a scale of 1 to 10, and what would be the impact if they could raise it?

We gave them a few minutes to reflect and think. Then I quietly whispered to Monica, *"I'm not sure we will have enough volunteers for this next part. We may have to have them break into small groups to discuss their self-evaluations."*

She replied, *"I think part of the reason that they are – How do you say ... reluctant? – is that several of them have difficulty reading."*

I hadn't considered that. I'm not sure about Doug, but I remember sending up an arrow prayer.

After a few minutes of them working on their self-evaluations, we asked for some volunteers to share their thoughts. This is where I was expecting no one to step up. However, I was wrong.

Much to my surprise four people promptly jumped up and dashed to the front. What they shared would turn out to be incredible. They were transparent with one another. Three of the volunteers rated themself a 2 or a 3 on this law. They felt they were not a good model for others. They were just bus drivers.

However, the fourth gentleman, Ricardo, who was probably about my age or a little bit older, gave himself a 7. He shared that he liked to be near others who value work and family, and that he saw the men in the room were models to him, and that he saw them as leaders in their jobs and at home.

Quickly some of them started chatting amongst themselves. At this point, Monica leaned over to Doug and me. She told us that this gentleman, Ricardo, was one person in the room that everyone admired. She added, *"he always has a positive attitude. People just want to be near him. He is encouraging."*

We began to sense a shift in the room as the conversations continued. Overhearing the discussions, Monica then whispered to us. *"Most of them are saying that until today, they never saw themself as leaders. They thought they were just bus drivers."*

Upon hearing this, Doug and I knew we needed to build on Ricardo's thoughts. With Doug and Monica's help, I was able to get their attention.

"Men. Ricardo is right. Think about this. As bus drivers, you might be the first person to greet and encourage a student. Right? You may be the only person that will encourage them and wish them a good day. When you encourage someone – you influence someone."

As Monica translated our words, their heads begin to nod. Doug spoke next.

"That's right. Leadership is Influence. If you are influencing someone, then you are a leader." Monica began to echo in translation.

"Position doesn't matter."
    "La posición no importa."

"Age, it doesn't matter."
    "Su edad, no importa."

"How much you make, it doesn't matter."
    "Cuánto gana, no importa."

"Think about it. Each of us has a chance to influence. You are leaders."
    "Piénsalo. Cada uno de nosotros tiene la oportunidad de influir. Ustedes son líderes."

I then added to Doug's thoughts.

"And maybe there is no one with a greater chance to encourage and influence a student than a bus driver."

> *"Y tal vez no haya nadie con mayor chance de alentar e influir en un estudiante que un conductor de autobús."*

"Like Doug and Ricardo said. You are a leader!"

> *"Como dijeron Doug y Ricardo. ¡Tu eres un líder!"*

"Look around you. Everyone in this room is a leader."

> *"Mira a tu alrededor. Todos en esta sala son líderes."*

"The fact that the principal and owner of this school wanted you in this training is proof that you are recognized as leaders!"

> *"¡El hecho de que el director y dueño de esta escuela los haya querido en esta capacitación es prueba de que son reconocidos como líderes!"*

"And you can lead at home, in your community, in your church, or in this school."

> *"Y puede liderar en casa, en tu comunidad, en tu iglesia o en esta escuela."*

Heads were nodding. Everyone appeared attentive. This was clearly a moment where you could see in their eyes renewed hope.

Round Table #2 – *The Value of Listening*

Our next Round Table was on the Value of Listening.

To start, we had them break into smaller groups, encouraging them to pull close to a few others around them. And then we asked them to share what they had learned so far, and what action they would take.

What Doug and I saw was amazing. All these gentlemen quickly formed together into small groups and dove headfirst into discussion.

I want to credit Ricardo again, the man who shared his score of 7 earlier because what he said caused others to reevaluate their own scores. Those that had initially given themselves a 2 or 3 recognized that they shouldn't think so lowly of I, and that they knew they could be a model for others. What took place at that moment was a new image of themselves. Their imagination had been reset.

After that initial round table discussion, they became even more enthused and hungry. Doug and I decided to have everyone stay in their groups and we had them go through the Value of Listening. Afterward, we had a few of them share their insights and thoughts. They became chatterboxes.

Seizing the moment, Doug led them in a cheer, *"¡Transformación está en mí!"* All of them followed along pointing to the air and then pointing to themself as they echoed those words. You could see hope fueling their imagination.

Round Table #3 – *The Value of Forgiveness*

Appealing for more, the group surprisingly wanted to do a third Round Table. So, we did the *Value of Forgiveness*. This was the one lesson that turned out to be the highlight of the day! Some shared that they had held disappointments against others that needed to be forgotten. Others shared personal regrets that they had made, which they needed to forgive themselves. At least five gentlemen shared why and what they needed to forgive.

For most of this morning, Doug and I had been standing in front of them to lead them, but because of what was happening, we realized we needed to sit and value what they were sharing. So, I pulled a well-worn, plastic lawn chair towards me and sat down to listen.

As one gentleman was sharing, my chair began to shift. At first, I didn't think anything of it. I tried to adjust just a little and not cause any noise to disrupt this man's testimony. I thought all was good, but just as he was sharing how the value of forgiveness was something he would now give to his family and neighbors, my chair imploded from underneath me collapsing to the ground along with me. The noise was thunderous. I went down hard.

About a dozen Guatemalan bus drivers instantly leaped from their seats to pull me up. They asked me in Spanish and broken English if I was okay. I smiled. *"Yes. I am okay."* Maria translated, *"Él está bien."* Everyone smiled. Then I started to laugh.

Soon others in the room began to laugh too. I am not sure if they were laughing at me or with me, but it didn't matter. It was the one emotion we had not fully expressed yet – at least to that degree, and the timing couldn't have been better. Nothing pairs up better with forgiveness than the ability to laugh afterward. Laughter helps release Endorphins, but it also increases Serotonin activity.[96] We all needed that moment.

Figure 3 – Serotonin, Pilots, and The Power of Encouragement

I never anticipated training bus drivers that day, but that was an incredible experience. Hope was lifted for all of us! While I can't speak for Monica or Doug, I'm willing to bet that the two of them felt like I did; incredibly honored and blessed to be used to impact the lives of other leaders. These leaders were indeed pilots, pilots leading the lives of others to destinations they could only imagine.

Chapter Summary

Shared imagination might very well be the most potent force on the planet. *Why?* Because it offers others the Power of Encouragement.

Encouragement means *"to pour courage into."* It's about giving others hope, support, and trust. It is a powerful tool for increasing imagination and stimulating collaboration with others. The Power of Encouragement is what influences others to invent the future with you.

Inviting others on the journey is a great way to transfer imagination. Albert Einstein once said, *"we cannot solve our problems with the same thinking we used when we created them."* Our challenge as leaders is to be willing to think differently. Does it really need to be the way we've always done it, or is there a better way?

My friend Diane identifies this struggle as TWWADI Disease, short for *"The Way We've Always Done It"*. She uses it to describe the common struggle that leaders have in making choices (or excuses) when they need to advance a cause.

What I have found as a breakthrough for TWWADI disease is to combine imagination and engagement. Getting another person's perspective is vital for team success. More importantly, leaning in to encourage others is equally as important. It releases a chemical in both the giver and receiver called Serotonin.

Serotonin is what creates the feeling of respect, belonging and self-confidence. It has the power to change how people look at things.

When you begin to think about ways to engage others and encourage them, you become more effective as a leader. This results in Serotonin to be released, which fuels us with a sense of empowerment. I call it the Power of Encouragement.

Each of us has an opportunity to encourage others. When we do, the RAS amongst us unites. Picture multiple imaginations fired up in the pursuit of a common vision. In my world, we would call it distributed computing. Like computers, humans are meant to network together. We are meant to solve common problems and support those we care about. As Imagineers, we should live for this.

Why?

Because if you are a leader, then you are in the hope business.

As you reflect on the impact you can make, ask yourself:

Who can I encourage?

Recognize how others might add value to the future that you are inventing. Try to see everyone in the same boat, rowing with a paddle of hope in the same direction. The Power of Encouragement is mutually beneficial, and it can change the future!

❖ ❖ ❖

Additional tools and resources focused on
Engaging with Others are available at
theimaginebook.com/ch-13

[91] Why did Morpheus's crew enter the Matrix?, https://scifi.stackexchange.com/questions/81041/why-did-morpheuss-crew-enter-the-matrix, last accessed June 28, 2022.

[92] Martin Luenendonk, *11 Leadership Lessons from Napoleon*, https://www.cleverism.com/11-leadership-lessons-from-napoleon-bonaparte/, last accessed June 28, 2022.

[93] RL Carhart-Harris and DJ Nutt, *Serotonin and brain function: a tale of two receptors*, https://www.ncbi.nlm.nih.gov/pmc/articles/PMC5606297/, Aug 31, 2017, last accessed June 28, 2022.

[94] Stephanie Fish, M.D, *Brain Hormones*, https://www.hormone.org/your-health-and-hormones/glands-and-hormones-a-to-z/hormones/Serotonin, last updated Jan 23, 2022, last accessed June 28, 2022.

[95] Nicholas Weiler, *Serotonin Stabilizes Social Memories*, Stanford, https://neurosciencenews.com/serotonin-social-memory-19489/, Oct 18, 2021, last accessed June 28, 2022.

[96] JongEun Yim, *Therapeutic Benefits of Laughter in Mental Health: A Theoretical Review*, ProMed.gov https://pubmed.ncbi.nlm.nih.gov/27439375/, July 2016, last accessed June 28, 2022.

14 – REINVENT CONTINUOUSLY
Understanding the Power of Growth

---

*"Continuous improvement
is better than delayed perfection."*

– Mark Twain

If your heart is still beating, then your brain is still hungry. Think about it. The brain is always "on!" It was designed to be a living, growing organism. Understand that there's something new to discover.

What's powerful about this concept is that if you choose to reinvent continuously, then you allow yourself to step into the person you were called to be. Those who persevere with hope and look to reinvent continuously, create change for themselves and others. They are influencers.

Leonardo DaVinci once said that *"Learning never exhausts the mind."* Learning is what creates understanding and growth, and it is vital for Imagineers.

Remember The Titans

One of my favorite movies is *Remember the Titans* starring Denzel Washington who plays Coach Herman Boone of T.C. Williams High School in Alexandria, Virginia. I love that movie because it takes place in my backyard not far from where I grew up. I went to a Fort Hunt High School, which was less than 10 miles away from T.C. Williams, now called Alexandria City High School. My school was in neighboring Fairfax County as opposed to the city. Still, there was a little bit of rivalry.

It seemed almost every year, our two football teams would play each other in a battle to remember. The battle was always a crazy match up. Both schools had winning programs, and you would never know who was going to come out on top.

Coach Windsor

While I didn't play high school football, I did compete in other sports like soccer and track. As a track athlete, I remember several events that took place at Alexandria City High, including their infamous Track Invitational every spring, which had schools coming from everywhere. The track we competed on circled the very same football field that the Titans played.

As I look back at those years of high school, it was a special time for me, especially the last two years when I transitioned from the game of soccer to the sport of track. Coach Windsor wanted me to be a hurdler and a medium-distance sprinter. I had the height and the stride he needed. But learning to master the hurdles may have been one of the hardest things I have ever experienced. I was stretched in ways that challenged me yet shaped me forever.

I'm not going to lie. Initially, I wanted to quit. But my coach encouraged me and dared me to go beyond myself. He's the one who taught me to imagine not who I was but who I could be. He stretched my thinking, and I can still hear his boisterous voice hollering at me during a meet or a practice to give it my best.

I remember at Alexandria City High; I felt a little off. I wasn't at my peak, and I had a little bit of a muscle strain. Windsor grabbed hold of me by the grandstands and looked at me. He gently asked one question:

If you don't run today,
what excuse will you make tomorrow?

I was a 16-year-old kid. His question initially threw me off. I didn't know how to answer. After what seemed like a minute, but was probably only a few seconds, I said, *"I don't plan to make any excuses, coach."*

With that, he smiled. *"That's the right answer."* Then he said, *"You got the second leg in the mile relay."* He then left me to take his usual position by the side of the track to watch the race.

Despite my physical apprehension, I ended up running one of my best quarter-mile splits. Windsor greeted the team afterward with a warm smile. *"You guys did well – well enough to earn us a few points. Well, done boys! That's what we needed."*

We all smiled, but he wasn't done. *"I want you to think about how you can 'be more' next time. You did good, I'm not complaining, but you are not as good as what you could be."*

He then paused and glanced at our eyes. He seemed to stare at me, but with a supporting smile. *"Now let's hurry up and get on the bus. I've got a lawn to cut."*

In a lot of ways, Coach Windsor was like Titans' Coach Boone – even though they represented different sports and different eras. In the movie, *Remember the Titans* you can see how Boone and his assistant coach Yoast challenged the athletes and team to become more – and to be remembered. He taught his team to be hungry for growth. That's exactly what I learned from Windsor.

The Real Coach Boone

Those who persevere attract others to change. Coach Boone was that coach for his players, just like Coach Windsor was for me.

Some years ago, my family and I had a chance to meet the real Coach Boone, along with many of the members of that championship team of 1971. The event started with an encore showing of the movie. After the viewing, there was a meet and greet event at a nearby restaurant that included a couple of the actors as well. I had a chance to talk with many of the players and Coach Boone.

In my few moments with him, I shared with Coach that I had attended the crosstown rival school just outside the city, Fort Hunt. He looked up from the table where he was signing posters, focused his attention solely on me, and blurted out, *"You went to Fort Hunt?"* He was excited. *"Those boys always gave us trouble. I'll never forget their one running back. What was his name? Rocky...?"*

I laughed and interrupted him with the answer he was looking for, *"Rocky Belk."*

"Yes! Rocky Belk," he fired back. *"I remember playing them at their place in a monsoon. Rained all day. And Rocky was running all over us in the first half."*

In that restaurant backroom, former players started leaning closer to hear their coach. It was as if they were ready to strap their helmet on one more time. The experience of a leader draws in his followers. They are hungry to learn.

He continued, *"But we had to come up with a special play to stop him. Still remember it to this day."*

Boone then grabbed a napkin and Sharpie and drew out the play. *"We called it the 'Special Defense to Stop Rocky Belk'."* He finished drawing the play on the napkin and dug his finger into it. *"That's how we stopped him. But he was a great back. Great back. Went on to play at the U, right?"*

I replied. *"Yup, he sure did. He played at Miami, Coach – then the Browns."*

Then he smiled. *"Yeah, those were the good old days. And your school always fought us hard."*

We exchanged a few more pleasantries, laughed a bit more, and then bid each other farewell. He then handed me the napkin with the infamous play drawn on it, which I now have proudly have on display in my office.

Before my wife and I met Coach Boone that night, I had an image of him looking like the actor that played him, Denzel Washington. The truth is, he didn't look anything like Denzel. But it was clear that Coach Boone was an original like the talented actor who played him. He was a man who persevered as a leader and truly influenced those around him to learn and grow. He could stretch your imagination.

My wife and I ended up talking with other players that night and met one of the actors from the movie. It was an incredible evening meeting the real players of that team.

Upon Further Review

A thought struck me later as I reflected on that night. When you meet someone who has truly learned to persevere, and they share just a tidbit of how they did it, it impacts you – it leaves an impression. **The**

experience of a leader can offer you courage. It can shape your growth and development.

As for his players, you are changed forever when you are under the leadership of someone like that, someone who challenges you to grow and go beyond yourself. If that weren't the case, then all those players would not have been with Coach Boone that night, leaning in to hear about the *"Special Defense to Stop Rocky Belk."*

Coach Windsor is someone who also stretched me. And I'll forever be thankful for his influence in my life. I'll never forget his comment, *"If you don't run today, what excuse will you make for tomorrow?"* It was a subtle way of reminding me that the future starts now.

The Power of Growth

To shape the future, have a hunger for growth. The Power of Growth establishes momentum more quickly than anything else I know. Growth gives you permission to take risks, and grants you passage for reward. The path is not easy, but growth is essential.

James Allen, the author of the book *As a Man Thinketh*, writes, *"Men are anxious to improve their circumstances, but are unwilling to improve themselves; they therefore remain bound."*[97] His comment causes me to wonder. Imagining may seem easy, but only when we pursue what we imagine do we grow! If we don't pursue what we imagine, then we remain bound.

One common limiting belief that might stop us is thinking we ought to know how to do something before we try to do it! When people don't know how to do something, they are often unwilling to progress forward, and they stay stuck.

When we choose to be growth minded, it gives us the gift of resilience. The desire to grow doesn't require a prerequisite to know the *how*. You'll learn the how as you grow. Being growth-minded changes your world; it's what improves the culture of a team, increases your odds for success, and changes the environment from the inside out.

When we are willing to improve ourselves, we are no longer bound to the status quo. Being growth-minded frees us from our current circumstances and unleashes us from the status quo.

You are not as good as what you could be, but when you choose to grow, you can be as good as you want to be.

Stimulate Your Brain – *How to Recreate Yourself*

The science shows that *"every time we learn something new, we are harnessing the power of neuroplasticity."*[98] Neuroplasticity centers on how our brain can adapt, grow, and change.

When we learn a new skill or start to think about something differently, new pathways are created between the neurons in our brain. The more we use these pathways, the greater our skill and ability.

When it comes to learning, a lot happens in your brain. Some of the neurotransmitters that kick into gear include Dopamine, which we discussed earlier, and Glutamate, which may be one of the more common neurotransmitters. Glutamate and its receptors have been *"closely linked to spatial learning and hippocampus-dependent memory processes."*[99]

The hippocampus is embedded deep into the temporal lobe and is responsible for supporting learning and memory. Think of the hippocampus as your inner hard drive.

As you can guess, taking good care of the hippocampus is critical. Those exhibiting deficits in the hippocampus include short-term memory loss and disorientation. Research shows there are three things we can do to improve our hippocampus function:[100]

- Exercise
- Diet
- Stimulate Your Brain

Stimulating the brain starts by looking to create new neural pathways, by stretching yourself, seeking to learn, and exploring new routes. Also, recognize the impact of a great mentor. Coach Windsor and Coach Boone are examples of leaders who stretched and encouraged others. They stimulated their athletes by casting a vision, challenging their thoughts, and creating new opportunities. These coaches and their teams were all about the Power of Growth.

Chapter Summary

This chapter has focused on the Power of Growth. Growth is about *"reaching your potential"* and beyond.[101] It's about looking to increase, develop and learn. **The Power of Growth drives the future.**

I waited to share about the Power of Growth because there may be no better way to finish. The Power of Growth ensures continual improvement and fosters neuroplasticity. When we seek to learn, it transforms our brain and influences others around us.

The OODA Loop itself reflects this principle of continual growth. Growth happens best across all four phases, including when we act.

Think back. When we are young, our intellectual growth matches our physical growth, at least for the most part. However, as we get older, our physical growth begins to slow, and our desire to intellectually grow might also slow. **When curiosity becomes tempered, we choose comfort over courage and cease becoming who we were meant to be.**

It turns out that playing it safe is not safe at all when it comes to learning. We need a hunger for growth!

Philosopher and educator Julia Gulliver echoes this thought, *"Let us never be betrayed into saying we have finished our education; because that would mean we had stopped growing."* The drive to grow is the fuel we need to expand our limits and experience our true potential — no matter what our age. For me, this keeps my candle lit.

When you are intentional, the Power of Growth expands your capability and capacity to influence yourself and those around you. Better yet, ***when you are growth-minded, you never get bored.***[102]

❖ ❖ ❖

Additional tools and resources focused on
Reinventing Continuously are available at
theimaginebook.com/ch-14

[97] James Allen, *As a Man Thinketh*. Mount Vernon, NY, Peter Pauper Press, 1951.

[98] The Digital Learning Consultant, *Neuroplasticity and learning explained*, https://www.youtube.com/watch?v=88OL8NdkV–s, Feb 14, 2018, last accessed June 28, 2022.

[99] Caroline Ménard, Rémi Quirion, *Group 1 metabotropic glutamate receptor function and its regulation of learning and memory in the aging brain*, https://pubmed.ncbi.nlm.nih.gov/23091460/#:~:text=The%20excitatory%20neurotransmitter%20glutamate%20and,of%20adaptation%20regulating%20memory%20formation, last accessed June 28, 2022.

[100] Growth Engineering, *Three Ways To Improve Your Hippocampus Function*, https://www.growthengineering.co.uk/train–your–hippocampus–function/, Feb 25, 2020, last accessed June 28, 2022.

[101] John C. Maxwell, *The 15 Invaluable Laws of Growth: Live Them and Reach Your Potential* (p. 66), Center Street.

[102] Note: This is a statement that I heard John C. Maxwell share February 2012. It changed the course of my life.

Epilogue – Let Imagination Speak Life

"It's crazy to imagine
Words from our lips as the arms of compassion
But look into the eyes of the broken hearted
Watch them come alive as soon as
You speak hope
You speak love
You speak life!"

— TobyMac

In the final research for this book, I reached out to Phil Mahre, the legendary skier who planted the thought of imagination in my mind when I was thirteen. In our exchange, I shared how much those Olympic moments had meant to me, especially the TV interview. Here's what he shared back:

> *Paul,*
>
> *Thank you for the kind words, and the remembering of that moment in time. Visualization was a huge part of my success during my career. If you have an idea as to where you want to be in the distant future, it always helps to see yourself in that moment.*
>
> *Wishing you the best,*
>
> *Phil*

In the multiverse of our imagination, our minds can travel back in time – not just forward in time. Hearing from a legend in my life conjured up the 13-year-old I once was. That younger version of me would be ecstatic to know that he'd hear from a real-life hero in the future. As I look at it now, I think of Phil Mahre as my mentor on the mountain – someone who not only shaped my thinking at an early age but whose pursuit of imagination spoke life into me.

I wrote back to Phil, thanking him for his note and requesting permission to share it with you. He replied enthusiastically.

"By all means go ahead and use it. Good luck with the book."

The email exchange is a reminder that Mahre continues to speak life. We have an opportunity to speak life into others too!

How Will You Speak Life?

In 1906, before he become the Prime Minister of the United Kingdom, Winston Churchill commented, *"Where there is great power there is great responsibility."* If you're like me, you probably thought that was said by Spider-man's uncle imparting wisdom into young Peter Parker. Now we know the truth, it was Churchill. Churchill was Parker's Uncle. :-)

Regardless of who said it, the realization is that once we have gained knowledge on how to shape the future, we have the responsibility to share it with others. Mahre did that with me and the world in 1980, and he did it again in 2022 with his email in just one sentence.

> *"If you have an idea as to where you want to be in the distant future, it always helps to see yourself in that moment."*
> – Phil Mahre

Another mentor in my life was my Uncle Jay. In the late 50s and early 60s, be helped create shipboard computers and the Naval Tactical Data System (NTDS) that the U.S. Navy still uses. A few years before his passing, I had asked him what one thing made the difference for him in inventing the future. I wanted to know his secret. What he shared was profound.

> *"The one thing I've learned is that your outlook drives your output, and your output always comes back around as input."*
> – Jay Kershaw

That was a powerful statement for me. Here was a man who was a mentor in my life, who was like a modern-day MacGyver that could fix just about anything. His strength was finding solutions where others might only see problems. He found joy in using his imagination and encouraging others. He'd often ask, *"what if?"*.

Jay's outlook clearly drove his output. And because of that, it was reciprocated by people who just wanted to be near him. *Why?* Because he spoke life into them.

When it comes to living a life of impact, ask yourself:

Am I allowing what I imagine to speak life into others?

Over the course of the past fourteen chapters, we have identified the necessary tools and techniques for the journey. This includes twelve powerful ways to invent the future using the OODA Loop. Remember to Observe, Orient, Decide, and Act. Recognize that you are more than equipped to shape the world around you.

Incidentally, did you notice the acrostic that was formed from these 14 chapters?

BE THE IMAGINEER

This acrostic sentence represents the components of how we should lead with an imagination mindset.

The table and illustration that follows, provide a recap of the behavior elements that we've explored. Think of this as a declaration for imagining and speaking life.

For each chapter, notice how each element builds on the foundation of the last, yet there is no finish line. Once you reach the final step (ACT), go back to the first (OBSERVE) with your new knowledge and ability and keep imagining. Remember, it's called the OODA Loop for a reason. Rinse and repeat.

Each element of the BE THE IMAGINEER declaration also offers something we can pass on to others. These are behaviors you can model and use to train others. Interwoven into all these behaviors is the element of hope. Real hope is tied to three things: Goals, Systems, and a Just Cause.

Table 1 – *BE THE IMAGINEER Behavior*

Ground Zero	1	BECOME Something More	B
	2	EQUIP Yourself for the Journey	E
Observe	3	TRACE Your Path with the Power of Patterns	T
	4	HUNT Down Misconceptions with the Power of Curiosity	H
	5	EVALUATE The Gains with the Power of Assessment	E
Orient	6	IMAGINE The Possible with the Power of Belief	I
	7	MINIMIZE The Distractions with the Power of Boundaries	M
	8	ALIGN Your Steering with the Power of Values	A
Decide	9	GET Bulletproof with the Power of Resilience	G
	10	INCREASE The Amplitude with the Power of Today	I
	11	NOTICE The Resistance with the Power of Discipline	N
Act	12	ENTER The Matrix with the Power of Movement	E
	13	ENGAGE With Others with the Power of Encouragement	E
	14	REINVENT Continuously with the Power of Growth	R
Epilogue		Let Imagination Speak Life	

IMAGINE

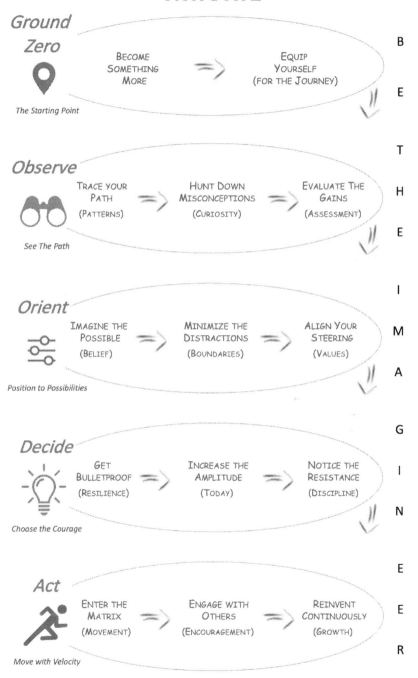

Ground Zero

The Starting Point

BECOME SOMETHING MORE ⟹ EQUIP YOURSELF (FOR THE JOURNEY)

B
E

Observe

See The Path

TRACE YOUR PATH (PATTERNS) ⟹ HUNT DOWN MISCONCEPTIONS (CURIOSITY) ⟹ EVALUATE THE GAINS (ASSESSMENT)

T
H
E

Orient

Position to Possibilities

IMAGINE THE POSSIBLE (BELIEF) ⟹ MINIMIZE THE DISTRACTIONS (BOUNDARIES) ⟹ ALIGN YOUR STEERING (VALUES)

I
M
A

Decide

Choose the Courage

GET BULLETPROOF (RESILIENCE) ⟹ INCREASE THE AMPLITUDE (TODAY) ⟹ NOTICE THE RESISTANCE (DISCIPLINE)

G
I
N

Act

Move with Velocity

ENTER THE MATRIX (MOVEMENT) ⟹ ENGAGE WITH OTHERS (ENCOURAGEMENT) ⟹ REINVENT CONTINUOUSLY (GROWTH)

E
E
R

Goals, Systems, and a Just Cause

Goals reflect the results you want to achieve. *But how do you get there?*

According to best-selling author James Clear. It comes down to systems. *"Systems are about the processes that lead to [desired] results."*[103] Clear adds, *"Goals are good for setting a direction, but Systems are best for making progress."*

Goals help things like your RAS, making them more acutely aware, but Systems like the OODA Loop and OKRs coupled with the right self-reflecting questions allow you to think and process. They are critical for your imagination. This should reinforce the OODA Loop as an important guidance system. But there's one more component that is tied to motivation. It's why Imagineers like Jordan played the game with a mindset of *breaking average.*

Clear states, *"The purpose of setting goals is to win the game. The purpose of building systems is to continue playing the game."* That's an important distinction. We're not just here to win. We need patterns, processes, and systems so that the game we are playing – this game of real hope and value that impacts others – plays on. Simon Sinek calls it an Infinite Game, and this leads us to our third component.

Sinek shares, *"Only when we can imagine in our mind's eye the exact version of the world an organization or leader hopes to advance toward will we know to which organization or to which leader we want to commit our energies and ourselves."* He adds that *"A clear cause is what ignites our passions."*[104]

When it comes to identifying your capacity to influence, ask yourself:

What is my just cause?

Real hope is connected to a *just cause*. I have alluded to this throughout the book. A *just cause*, according to Sinek is a *"specific vision of a future state that does not yet exist; a future state so appealing that people are willing to make sacrifices to help advance toward that vision."*

A *cause* is a catalyst for living and leading. Every *just cause* is tied to hope.

When you take time to understand the value of pursuing hope, three things happen:

- Your belief changes
- Your behavior changes
- Your world changes

If you want proof that hope is essential to strategy, just notice each day. Hope is personified by every sunrise, every new idea, every bird that sings, and every dog that wags its tail. Hope is interwoven throughout your DNA. Don't just look for it; be carriers of it. Remember, BE THE IMAGINEER.

The bottom line is this; if you want to change the world, then speak life. Imagine a *just cause*. Engage with others and pursue the *just cause*. Stand up and be courageous.

Become Hope

Speaking life takes courage. There's a great scene in one of the *Spider-Man* movies a few years back that offers an example of a *just cause*. Gwen Stacy, Peter Parker's girlfriend, is giving the valedictorian address at her high school, and she shares these words:

> *"Fight for what matters to you, no matter what.*
> *Because even if you fall short,*
> *what better way is there to live?*
>
> *It's easy to feel hopeful on a beautiful day like today,*
> *But there will be dark days ahead of us too.*
> *And there'll be days where you feel all alone,*
> *And that's when hope is needed most.*
> *Keep it alive. No matter how buried it gets,*
> *or lost you feel, you must promise me,*
> *That you will hold on to hope and keep it alive.*
>
> *We must be greater than what we suffer.*
> *My wish for you is to become hope.*
> *People need that."*[105]

This paints for us an example of a *just cause* and exemplifies a person who was brave enough to share it. It reminds me of another story, that changed everything for me.

See Hope

When my oldest son was almost four years old, he was going through some noticeable challenges walking and using his left hand. This was a result of a mild stroke that occurred before his birth. Despite the struggle, he found a way to plug in and participate. I remember one time I was heading to a local bike shop to look at some gear and he wanted to tag along. So, I took him with me.

When we arrived at the shop, Michael, who was fully charged with the Power of Curiosity, cased the joint wandering around the small store and looking at all the bikes. An older gentleman who was there looking to buy a part took notice of Michael. After a few minutes, he came up to me and initiated a conversation. *"Excuse me, I couldn't help but notice your son's gait and that he is a toe walker."*

At first, I was taken back. Why would some come up and be so forward about my son? In that moment, I may have wanted to slap him like Will Smith, but instead, I held back my emotion.

He continued, *"I'm sorry. I should have introduced myself. My name is Dr. Anderson, and I am a pediatrician in town. I just want you to know that in my thirty-plus years of practice I've had the privilege to treat children with similar conditions as I noticed with your son."*

He then asked me a few questions about Michael, including what he enjoyed and what we had done to help him. After I shared a little bit, he put his hand on my shoulder and said something I would never forget.

"I want you to know that there's hope. There are lots of things they can do now. And I have personally seen children with conditions much like your son – maybe worse – who work through it and do extremely well."

He went on to add, *"Let me tell you, there's nothing more satisfying than to one day see them on their day of graduation walk up to receive their diploma without ever noticing the limp."* He then added, *"Don't ever think that your son can't do it – because one day he will!"*

Fast-forward eighteen years later to Blacksburg, Virginia. It's graduation day at Virginia Tech in 2015. A day when that good doctor's words proved to be prophetic. In an auditorium filled with graduates and their families and friends, you would have easily found me, my wife Barb, and my youngest son Ryan proudly watching Michael walking up in procession to receive his diploma. The limp is forgotten; it's without notice. And when they called his name to receive his diploma, I was the dad who stood up to his feet shouting at the top of lungs, *"You Go Michael!"*. It was uncharacteristic of me, but I simply couldn't help myself. I was witnessing hope realized!

What that doctor did for me and my whole family is spoke life by seeing hope and sharing it. Isn't that what a *just cause* is all about? All these years later, I realize it's my mission to do the same, but I can't do it alone. I need people like you.

It's Your Turn

There's a terrific Netflix Series called *Losers* that caught my attention recently. One of the opening lines is this statement:

> *"We always say that we learn more*
> *from defeat than from victory.*
> *So, if we learn from defeat,*
> *we should pay more attention*
> *to those who lose."*[106]

"Ahh!" I thought. *"That's an interesting point. We should take notice of how people got back up."* I then started thinking about all those who have gone before us who possessed the powers of imagination and shared this gift of hope with others who had a *just cause*. That's when I realized that those who achieve much often endure much. Their cause is greater than what they may suffer.

Think of the stories we've explored: The Mahre Brothers, The Wright Trio, Elon Musk, Tyler Perry, Victor Frankl, Corrie Ten Boom, Andy Grove, Michael J. Fox, Steve Jobs, Herman Boone, and my oldest son. They all reflect successful individuals that endured disappointment, doubt, and defeat.

To discover winning, sometimes we need to succeed at losing. After all, those that persevere through the losses eventually find the wins.

What's interesting is how they did this.

In all our stories, what we see in common is that they leverage imagination and perseverance by choosing to live with hope. Hope fulfilled requires imagination, experimentation, evaluation, and integrity. Those who persist with these qualities are the ones that find a win!

More importantly, at a very young age, there's a call on all of us to be Imagineers – to make a difference. We're created to imagine and create. Our imagination in these early years is strong and reflects this call, but the desire can be lost and forgotten over time. *What if though, it's still there?*

Hear the call to be an Imagineer. There's a *just cause* worth pursuing that can bring new experiences, capabilities, and realities to life. Recognize how your brain is already at work. There are neurons and synapses firing thoughts that give you a glimpse of what can be, and yet we suppress it. What you imagine matters. What if you shared that hope with others? What if you pursued that hope?

Only when you pursue what's in your imagination can it be ever realized. **What you imagine has the potential to ignite a generation.**

Your imagination holds your attention, but it can also captivate other people's attention. Think about what Martin Luther King, Jr. did with his *"I Have a Dream"* speech on the steps of the Lincoln Memorial, or what John F. Kennedy did with his moonshot speech at Rice University. Those speeches changed our world.

Nothing is as impactful as a person bringing hope into awareness for someone else. Focused imagination creates awareness, and awareness can bring something new to life. Sharing a vision of hope is a pattern exemplified by Imagineers.

I like to think that when God created the universe, he spoke what he imagined into being. What if we're called to do the same? What if we're called to speak what we imagine into our sphere of influence and those we encounter?

What you imagine matters!

It's been said that *"To the world, you may be one person, but to one person you may be the world."* With one idea – one *"just cause"* – you can change the world. That is what it means to imagine.

❖ ❖ ❖

Additional tools and resources
on *Imagination* are available at
theimaginebook.com/epilogue

---

[103] James Clear, *Atomic Habits* (p. 23), Penguin Publishing Group.

[104] Sinek, Simon. *The Infinite Game* (p. 40), Penguin Publishing Group.

[105] *The Amazing Spider–Man 2*. Burbank, Calif.: Sony Pictures Home Entertainment, 2014.

[106] Topic Studios, *Losers*, A Netflix Original Documentary Series, 2019, Storyline: In a "winning is everything" society, how do we handle failure? This series profiles athletes who have turned the agony of defeat into human triumph.

Acknowledgments

While this book was written during nights and weekends over the last four years – and even longer as I look back at old journals. There was some heavy influence and direction that I sought along the way. I can't possibly identify and thank everyone, but please know that if you and I had an engaging conversation over the last four years, it probably influenced me as I shaped and carved out this book. For that, I thank you.

When COVID came on us, I felt a greater tug to write this book. The world seemed to need a fresh message on hope. Something that could encourage us because I needed to be reminded of that message myself. It's been my *just cause.* As I wrote, I wanted to be a vessel to capture that hope and deliver a clear cause to others. But it's been the people I encountered on the path that inspired me to share it.

First and foremost, I want to acknowledge my wife, Barb. She has been a sounding board and a rock. She has encouraged me just like she did all those years ago when I was struggling in my final year of college. She continues offering me a glimpse of what can be, and I owe her my life. *Valentine, thank you for your powerful influence, love, and support in my life. This book is also dedicated to you because you are committed to helping others, and that inspires me! You are the Imagineer that inspires me and our whole family!*

I also want to thank my grown children, Ryan, Michael, and Wani. *You inspire me more than you'll ever know. Keep imagining. Be all that you hope for and desire. The world needs you. Never be afraid to speak life!*

To my Wednesday morning Men's Group (aka *The Thought Leader Jedis*), thank you for your support and influence. Richard, Barry, Dave, Doug, Daniel, Fu, John, Big Mike, Joe, Hub, and Stig. *You guys are amazing. I enjoy connecting with you guys.* Shout out also to Rick Morris, Mike Harbour, and Joe Dutkiewicz. *I have always enjoyed our conversations. You keep me fresh! Joe D., special thanks for all the help in editing this book. You have been a rock star!*

Closer to home, I want to thank my incredible SimVentions family. Especially the leadership team that I work with every day. Joe, Megan, Larry, Blaine, Ryan, and Robert – and the team behind them. What an amazing group. I love the SimV family and all our team members. *Together we are called to "Imagine. Create. Explore. Discover."*

I also want to thank Phil Mahre for inspiring me not once but twice. *Phil, thank you for speaking life into me when I was 13 and again all these decades later. You and your brother Steve aren't just Olympians; you are Imagineers.*

In addition, I want to thank Mark Batterson. *Pastor Mark, you inspire me and thousands of others with excellent books and insights that activate our imagination. Thank you. And thank you also for the foreword you offered to help open this book. You are also a true Imagineer!*

To you, the reader, you matter the most. *Thank you for investing your time in digesting this book. I truly hope you found encouragement and helpful insight. Please let me know how it impacts you.*

As a person of faith, I want to also thank God for giving us the powers of our imagination. Faith, for me, is a critical component to all of this. If you want to amplify the OODA Loop, lean into your faith. If you lack wisdom, *ask*. If you need hope, *seek*. If you want opportunities, *knock*. He promises that the door will be opened to you. What's in front of each of us is a path to imagining new possibilities, breaking average, and blessing others with a *just cause*.

Finally, to inspire you to pursue this *just cause*, I leave you with another great quote from Albert Einstein.

"There comes a point in your life when you need to stop reading other people's books and write your own."

All the best,

Paul

Appendix A –
The Imagineer Assessment Tool

I want to leave you with a helpful tool to assess your imagination capability, specifically your Imagineering Type.

Research Background

I am often wary of assessments because I don't want the labels to limit the leadership. Now and then, however, a good assessment can offer us awareness of strengths and how we can best serve. Because I pulled in a ton of research, I was able to come up with a compelling assessment that I think you'll like.

The assessment is based on some of the research in the behavioral science space regarding visual thinkers. A published article in June 2014 explored a set of capability scales for imagination and creativity using a group of students.[107] They presented an intriguing collection of questions to identify imaginative capacity across three facets, which respectfully map with the three different Imagineering types.

Table 2 – Imagineering Facets

Facets	Imagineering Type
Initiating imagination	Dreamer
Conceiving imagination	Designer
Transforming imagination	Implementer

Each of us is one or more of these three types of Imagineers. Dreamers are those who formulate brand new ideas – they initiate. Designers expand on an idea and figure out how to make it work – they help conceive the design. Finally, Implementers help execute the plan and bring it to life – they help bring about transformation.

Imagineering Types Assessment

To identify the Imagineering Type, I have scaled the number of questions evenly for each Imagineering type resulting in 21 questions total (7 per type). Also, the questions have been modified slightly to address a broader group of participants beyond the original target audience.

Each question should be responded to with a value between 1 and 5, with 1 being least likely true and 5 being most likely true. A self-assessment is more than adequate to perform the test, as you know yourself best. The key is not to take too much time to think about your rating for any one question. Respond with the first inclination that comes to mind.

DREAMER – Initiating Imagineer

Please read each of the following items carefully. Briefly think about how it relates to your behavior, and then identify how true it is for you. Use the following scale to respond.

Never	Rarely	Sometimes	Often	Always
1	2	3	4	5

Table 3 – The DREAMER Scorecard

	Characteristics	Value	Score
1	I get excited when I see the opportunity for a new idea.	1 2 3 4 5	
2	I am emotionally stable because I expect to overcome challenges and difficulties.	1 2 3 4 5	
3	I focus on a project until ideas are formed.	1 2 3 4 5	
4	I formulate an approach quickly to meet a specific user need.	1 2 3 4 5	
5	I set goals in accordance with my abilities.	1 2 3 4 5	
6	I absorb and integrate diverse perspectives and can connect seemingly unrelated concepts.	1 2 3 4 5	
7	I can understand the implications of a concept by organizing fragmented information.	1 2 3 4 5	
	TOTAL =	____ / 35	

Take a moment to add up your DREAMER score.

DESIGNER – Concept Imagineer

Please read each of the following items carefully. Briefly think about how it relates to your behavior, and then identify how true it is for you. Use the following scale to respond.

Never	Rarely	Sometimes	Often	Always
1	2	3	4	5

Table 4 – The DESIGNER Scorecard

	Characteristics	Value	Score
1	I formulate unique ideas more frequently than other people do.	1 2 3 4 5	
2	I frequently develop ideas by examining unconventional perspectives.	1 2 3 4 5	
3	I generate new ideas by combining previous experiences.	1 2 3 4 5	
4	I frequently have a rich diversity of ideas.	1 2 3 4 5	
5	I consistently formulate different approaches to complete a project.	1 2 3 4 5	
6	I am proficient at adapting existing resources into a novel concept.	1 2 3 4 5	
7	I form mental images to address a problem or challenge.	1 2 3 4 5	
	TOTAL =	____ / 35	

Take a moment to add up your DESIGNER score.

IMAGINEER ASSESSMENT TOOL

IMPLEMENTER – Transformation Imagineer

Please read each of the following items carefully. Briefly think about how it relates to your behavior, and then identify how true it is for you. Use the following scale to respond.

Never	Rarely	Sometimes	Often	Always
1	2	3	4	5

Table 5 – The IMPLEMENTER Scorecard

	Characteristics	Value	Score
1	I perceive the world through various sensorial perceptions and personal experiences.	1 2 3 4 5	
2	I enjoy testing and trying out products to learn how they function.	1 2 3 4 5	
3	I express abstract concepts by using examples from daily life.	1 2 3 4 5	
4	I can explain unfamiliar concepts and provide examples relevant to a target audience.	1 2 3 4 5	
5	I use concrete images to explain difficult concepts.	1 2 3 4 5	
6	I apply my experiences to resolve new problems.	1 2 3 4 5	
7	I resolve daily life problems by applying what I have learned.	1 2 3 4 5	
	TOTAL =	____ / 35	

Finally, take a moment to add up your IMPLEMENTER score.

Evaluate and Improve Your Imagineering Type

Go back and tally up your scores for each of the tree types. One of the three will likely be higher than the rest. The score doesn't really matter, it's all about the relative delta among the three areas that matter. It tells you your default IMAGINEERING TYPE.

Table 6 – The Imagineering Results

DREAMER Score	DESIGNER Score	IMPLEMENTER Score

Circle the Imagineering Type that stands out above the rest.

A mark above 25 for any one type is significant result. This likely means you are highly imaginative as that type.

A score below 15, for any one type is not unusual, nor something to be concerned about. Low scores don't disqualify you from being an IMAGINEER. It just means you are stronger in one or two of the other Imagineering Types. The most important part of this assessment is to look at your comparative numbers across the three types, not necessarily the score itself, but the relative values to one another. How do you measure as a Dreamer relative to a Designer? A Designer relative to an Implementer? And a Dreamer relative to an Implementer?

We know that leadership may not be a born trait and that it needs to be cultivated, but imagination is a born trait. We are all born to be imaginative, the only problem is we may have not learned how to fully harness our imagination.

If we can learn to better leverage our imagination, then it will help us lead ourselves. If we can learn to be good at leading ourselves using the powers of our imagination, then we will find we can be better at leading others. Top leaders are good at being either a Dreamer, Designer, or Implementer. Leaders should learn to be good at more than one type and look to find others who can complement you and strengthen you.

If you want to "up" your score, identify the areas where you can improve as an Imagineer, by asking yourself three similar questions:

- What characteristics do I want to improve as a Dreamer?
- What characteristics do I want to improve as a Designer?
- What characteristics do I want to improve as an Implementer?

Every one of us can get better as an Imagineer. It starts with identifying what areas we want or need to improve. Use the Imagineering Target Improvement Chart provided to identify how you to want to get better as an Imagineer.

Table 7 – Imagineering Target Improvement Chart

What characteristics do I want to improve as a Dreamer?	What characteristics do I want to improve as a Designer?	What characteristics do I want to improve as an Implementer?

Spend some time capturing your thoughts and thinking through these. Maybe, for one or more of them it is an area where you want to seek out a coach or a mentor to guide you.

Here are some strategies to help you.

Strategy #1 - Improving THE DREAMER

A dreamer is someone who can come up with *"new ideas and form mental images"* to address a problem or challenge. They are known as an Initiating Imagineer. If you score high in this area you are regarded as someone who can play a crucial role in the ideation stage, which is the practice of coming up with unique ideas. Some of the qualities exhibited for an Initiating Imagineer include the following:

- Shows excitement regarding the potential for a new idea (they see the usefulness and value)
- Formulates an approach to bring the idea to life
- Set goals in accordance with their passions and strengths
- Frequently stay focused on a project without distraction until ideas are formed
- Frequently maintain composure when they face extreme difficulties
- Frequently connect seemingly unrelated concepts and integrate diverse perspectives

Think about the areas you scored high, and how you might be able to take advantage of those strengths. If you scored lower than what you hoped, identify the two areas where you are strongest and one area you would like to shore up and strengthen.

Be sure to capture your thoughts in the space provided below, or in a personal notebook or journal.

Strategy #2 - Improving THE DESIGNER

A designer is someone who can take a good idea after it has been seeded and conceive a plan to bring it to life. They are known as a Concept Imagineer. If you score high in this area you are regarded as someone who can play a crucial role in formulating an approach. Not only that, but a Concept Imagineer also has the capability to formulate a mental picture of one or more use-cases. They see the value and usefulness. Some of the attributes of a Concept Imagineer include the following:

- Frequently is the one who dreams up a unique idea (Steve Job called them the crazy ones)
- Frequently formulates ideas by looking at unconventional perspectives
- Frequently formulates new ideas by combining previous experiences
- Frequently comes up with different approaches to solve a problem

Again, think about the areas you scored high, and how you might be able to take advantage of those strengths. If you scored lower than what you hoped, identify the two areas where you are strongest and one area you would like to shore up and strengthen.

Be sure to capture your thoughts in the space below provided below, or in a personal notebook or journal.

Strategy #3 - Improving THE IMPLEMENTOR

An implementer is someone who can take a solution and explore its potential value and transform it into something usable. They are known as a Transformation Imagineer. Some of the qualities of a Transformation Imagineer include the following:

- Frequently enjoy deepening an understanding of concepts through personal experiences
- Frequently enjoy testing new things to learn how they function
- Frequently can explain unfamiliar or difficult concepts and share concrete examples relevant to an audience
- Frequently apply their own experiences to resolve new problems
- Frequently can apply similar concepts to different projects

Again, think about the areas you scored high, and how you might be able to take advantage of those strengths. If you scored lower than what you hoped, identify the two areas where you are strongest and one area you would like to shore up and strengthen.

Be sure to capture your thoughts in the white space provided, or in a personal notebook or journal.

Additional tools and resources focused on
Assessments are available at
theimaginebook.com/append-a

---

[107] Hsu (National Central University, Taiwan), Li–Pie Peng, Wang and Liang (National Taiwan University), *The Imaginative Capability and Creative Capability Scales: Testing the Relationship between Imagination and Creativity among Agriculture Students*, 2014.

APPENDIX B – WHAT ABOUT FAITH?

> *"Faith is to believe what you do not see;*
> *the reward of this faith is to see what you believe."*
>
> — Saint Augustine

Before we close the lid on the topic of imagination, there is one more important matter. For this book to be complete, we need to address the aspect of faith as it relates to the imagination.

By and large, each chapter has tried to separate the elements of physiology from theology, but it was clear throughout my research that faith is a contributing factor and a primary driver of imagination for millions worldwide. It just can't be ignored. It turns out that faith and imagination may be opposite sides of the same coin.

The Power of Faith

One question that repeatedly surfaced during my research was, ***"What does faith say about imagination?"*** I wondered if there might be some gaps or deficiencies missing that faith might reveal.

The results, in some ways, surprised me. While I expected to find that imagination and faith would be wired together through things like the RAS, I didn't expect to see the Power of Faith activate imagination across multiple cultures, religions, and beliefs.

The Power of Faith is important to at least 89% of Americans alone.[108] The numbers are staggering. 56% of Americans believe in God as described in the Bible. And 33% believe in some higher power or spiritual force, which they may still describe as God. Only 10% of Americans don't believe in the Power of Faith.

Expressions of faith relating to the imagination can be found in art, books, blogs, music, memes, movies, sermons, prayers, and podcasts.

But it was clear one source needed to be explored more than any other – the Bible. It is the most read and quoted book of all time.

Ronald Reagan, America's 40th President, once remarked, *"Inside the Bible's pages lay ALL the answers to the problems man has ever known."* He adds, *"It is my firm belief that the enduring values presented in its pages have a great meaning for each of us and for our nation. The Bible can touch our hearts, order our minds, and refresh our souls."*

Thought leaders like Reagan inspire us to use our imagination, and this comment spurred me to explore the Bible further. I wondered, *"what 'great meaning' does the Bible offer as it relates to the imagination?"* I was curious!

I discovered something interesting. The Bible is a foundational resource for various faiths and religions, including Christianity, Judaism, and Samaritanism. It has influenced or is embraced by other beliefs too.

Additionally, the Bible has been instrumental in the establishment of numerous colleges, companies, and countries.

- Some of the more well-known colleges in the world that got their start based on Biblical principles include *Harvard, Boston College, Princeton, Notre Dame, Baylor University, Pepperdine University*, and many more.

- Companies built on the foundation of Biblical principles include *Chick-fil-A, Hobby Lobby, Interstate Battery, Tyson Foods, SimVentions* (where I work), and many more.

- Examples of countries founded on biblical principles include the United States, Israel, The Vatican (yes, that is a nation), England, Denmark, Norway, Argentina, and many more.

The Scripture from the Bible appears to be a valuable guidebook for individuals, teams, and societies worldwide.

My objective for this last component is simple, *"What does the Bible say about imagination and faith that we can leverage?"*

And *"How much are the two related?"*

What the Bible Says About Imagination

The Bible reveals that the God who created the universe seeks to engage our imagination. He spurs our imagination through creation, art, literature, music, and film.[109] Furthermore, **God encourages us to use our imagination to test His will.**[110] That, I think, is profound.

When you explore the variations of the word *imagine* as it relates to the original Hebrew and Greek languages found in the Bible, you discover several ancient words that correlate it with the idea of *thinking* and *meditating*. These words are *Chashabh*, *Hagah*, and *Meletao*. Those words don't quite roll off the tongue. So let me explain what they mean.

Chashabh (Hebrew) means *"to think, plan, devise, esteem, calculate, invent."*[111] In the NAS version of the Bible, this verb is linked to 122 verses in the Old Testament.[112]

Hagah (Hebrew) and *Meletao* (Greek) both mean *"to meditate"*.[113] *Hagah* is linked multiple times in the Old Testament[114], whereas *Meletao* is used in the New Testament.[115]

Here's a simple exercise to try. If you see the phrases "***think***", "***think about***", "***think of***", "***meditate***", and "***mediate on***" in the Bible, replace them with the word "***imagine.***" Additionally, if you see the noun phrase "***thoughts***", replace it with the word "***imagination.***" This reveals one part of the connection between faith and imagination.

Here are just a handful of examples with this treatment:

- For as he *imagines* in his heart, so is he. – Proverbs 23:7 (NKJV)
- I stay awake through the night, *imagining* your promise. – Psalm 119:148 (NLT)
- Look! I am creating new heavens and a new earth, and no one will even *imagine* the old ones. – Isaiah 65:17 (NLT)
- *Imagine* the things of heaven, not the things of earth. – Colossians 3:2 (NLT)
- Those who are dominated by the sinful nature *imagine* sinful things, but those who are controlled by the Holy Spirit *imagine* things that please the Spirit. – Romans 8:5 (NLT)

- And now, dear brothers and sisters, one final thing. Fix your *imagination* on what is true, and honorable, and right, and pure, and lovely, and admirable. *Imagine* things that are excellent and worthy of praise. – Philippians 4:8 (NLT)

- Let us *imagine* ways to motivate one another to acts of love and good works. – Hebrews 10:4 (NLT)

- *Imagine* these things; give yourself entirely to them, that your progress may be evident to all. – 1 Timothy 4:15 (NKJV)

While I am no theologian, the Bible tells us that it's important to be careful with what we imagine – and how we imagine.[116]

Imagination is vital for a person of faith as it relates to our journey, yet it can be a tripping hazard as it relates to our challenges. **How we think and what we meditate on matters.** The key is understanding more about how faith is tied to imagination.

What the Bible Says About Faith

The Bible offers a crystal-clear definition of faith. *"Faith is the assurance of things hoped for, and the conviction of things not seen."*[117]

Things hoped for. Things not seen. That sure sounds like imagination, doesn't it?

If faith is the assurance of things hoped for, and it's the conviction of things not seen, then it seems we have a definition of faith that is universal. It's a definition that works for different cultures, brain types and Imagineers.

You might argue that faith is just another layer of imagination. At one time, I might have nodded in agreement. I understand. I've been there.

My response today is two sets of questions:

1. *How does one possess imagination without faith?*

2. *For your imagination to work, don't you need to believe in something?*

Imagination brings into our awareness things outside of the physical that we believe in. Faith isn't just another layer of imagination, it's the basis of belief.

To test this theory, just open the Bible to the very beginning. It declares something profound.

"In the beginning, God created the heavens and the earth."[118]

Whether you personally believe in the creation story or not is secondary to the language of what's stated. The first verse in the Bible paints a picture that triggers the imagination right out of the gates. It's an origin story that invites you to wonder and think about the creation of the universe and the plan intended for all humanity – you included.

The Bible then takes us on a journey. We learn about the story of Adam, Noah, Abraham, Joseph, Moses, Joshua, Ruth, Samson, David, Daniel, Esther, Mary, Jesus, the Disciples, and more. Each story ties to this common definition of faith. **Those who step forward with trust and a conviction of faith shape the future.** It's why we still talk about them.

What might be more interesting is the story of God himself. The Bible makes it clear that he's not just some builder of the universe that walked away after he was done. He appears to be the object of faith in each of the stories we read about throughout history. The Bible, which is one of the all-time best history books, tells us more about faith and how it ties to our imagination.

The 21 "Wills"

Like a scientist, let's look through the lens of a microscope into the fabric of faith. If you search for the phrase *"God will"* in the Bible, you will discover 110 results in the New King James Version (NKJV), 138 results in the New International Version (NIV), and 190 results in the New Living Testament (NLT).

Most of these verses cast a light of hope and promise. They speak of faith, but not just any kind of faith, a faith in God visualized by the powers of imagination. Here are just a handful:

1. "God will provide…" – Genesis 22:8 (NLT)
2. "God will fight for you." – Deuteronomy 3:22 (NLT)
3. "God will bless you in all your work…" – Deuteronomy 15:10 (NIV)
4. "God will be with you where you go." – Joshua 1:9 (NIV)
5. "God will deliver." – Joshua 8:7 (NKJV)
6. "God will redeem me." – Psalm 49:15 (NIV)

7. "God will stand with me." – Psalm 59:10 (NLT)
8. "God will hold your right hand…" – Isaiah 41:13 (NLT)
9. "God will help me." – Isaiah 50:9 (NKJV)
10. "God will hear me." – Micah 7:7 (NIV)
11. "God will intervene." – Zechariah 2:7 (NKJV)
12. "God will blow the trumpet." – Zechariah 9:14 (NKJV)
13. "God will rescue his people." – Zechariah 9:16 (NLT)
14. "God will give you the right words at the right time." – Matt 10:19 (NLT)
15. "God will never fail." – Luke 1:37 (NLT)
16. "God will reward you." – Luke 14:14 (NLT)
17. "God will give you whatever you ask." – John 11:22 (NIV)
18. "God will give us many opportunities to speak." – Colossians 4:3 (NLT)
19. "God will meet all your needs." – Philippians 4:19 (NIV)
20. "God will answer your prayers." – Philemon 1:22 (NLT)
21. "God will wipe away every tear…" – Revelation 21:4 (NKV)

For a person of faith, these promises are profound. They activate the RAS. They make you look for successful outcomes.

On the other end of the scale, the Bible also clarifies that imagination tied to doubt, fear, and a lack of integrity will often paint a different outcome.[119] What's required is faith that overcomes the doubt.

What is Doubt?

Jesus makes a profound statement in the gospel of Mark.

> *"Have faith in God. Truly I tell you, if anyone says to this mountain, 'Go, throw yourself into the sea,' and does not doubt in their heart but believes that what they say will happen, it will be done."*

Jesus then emphasizes a key point.

> *"I tell you, whatever you ask for in prayer, believe that you have received it, and it will be yours."*[120]

Later, James, the younger half-brother of Jesus, reemphasizes this key point in one of his letters.

> *"When you ask, you must believe and **not doubt** because the one who **doubts** is like a wave of the sea, blown and tossed by the wind."*

James then shares that doubt makes us *"double-minded and unstable."*

So, what is doubt?

Doubt is unbelief. Doubt is rejection. Doubt is uncertainty, hesitation, skepticism, and a lack of conviction.

Have you ever experienced doubt?

It turns out that **the antidote for doubt is action.** When you step forward with courage despite the fear, the opposite of doubt is there to experience.

The opposite of doubt is belief and trust. More precisely, the opposite of doubt is faith in action.

James declares that faith without works is dead. That it's not enough to believe, it is essential to also act. I would add that faith without imagination is dead too. Faith needs imagination and action. Without action to follow the imagination, you never finish the OODA Loop.

Dopamine, Prayer, and Good Health

There is an interesting discovery about Dopamine that is worth knowing. It relates back to the story of the prayer that John Maxwell offered me in the hallway at the Leadership conference shared in Chapter 9.

That prayer, rather than casting a vision of doom and gloom, offered a vision of a hope and a future. It was a prayer reflective of a Lead Bulletproof Mindset, which I would say has helped me acknowledge, persevere, and overcome my health challenges.

The research shows that a prayer like the one John Maxwell shared, does the body good – or in this case, the brain. A study by researchers at the University of Pennsylvania revealed that **praying increases our levels of Dopamine.**[121] Furthermore, studies show that a benefit of prayer tied to a belief in God is that it improves our *"response to medical treatment."* Those who lean on their faith *"have better mental health and adapt more quickly"* to health challenges.[122]

This provides evidence that Imagination drives Faith, Faith promotes Prayer, Prayer increases Dopamine, Dopamine spurs Hope, and Hope fuels Health. It goes full circle.

Faith vs. Imagination – *Which Came First?*

Before we close the book on this topic, there are three questions that I invite you to consider:

- *Can faith exist without imagination?*
- *Can imagination exist without faith?*
- *Which came first?*

Let's explore each of these topics.

Can faith exist without imagination?

Let's presume for a moment that faith requires imagination. If we explore some of the promises from the Bible, we can see how some of the powers of imagination feed our faith. Here are a few that stood out:

1. Imagining with the Power of Belief validates our faith and future:

   "For I know the plans I have for you, declares the Lord, plans to prosper you not to harm you, plans to give you a hope and a future."
   - Jeremiah 29:11 (NIV)

2. Imagining with the Power of Belief strengthens us in our faith walk:

   "God is able to do far more than we could ever ask for or imagine. He does everything by his power that is working in us."
   - Ephesians 3:20 (NIRV)

3. Imagining with the Power of Curiosity activates our faith with knowledge:

   "Tune your ears to wisdom and concentrate on understanding. Cry out for insight and ask for understanding. Search for them as you would for silver; seek them like hidden treasures." - Proverbs 2:2-4 (NLT)

4. Imagining with the Power of Boundaries emboldens our faith journey:

"Keep on asking, and you will receive what you ask for. Keep on seeking, and you will find. Keep on knocking, and the door will be opened to you. For everyone who asks, receives. Everyone who seeks, finds. And to everyone who knocks, the door will be opened." – Matthew 7:7 (NLT)

5.   Imagining with the Power of Values strengthens our faith focus:

"Whatever is true, whatever is honorable, whatever is just, whatever is pure, whatever is lovely, whatever is commendable, if there is any excellence, if there is anything worthy of praise, think about these things." – Philippians 4:8 (ESV)

Notice how several of these Bible passages offers guidance on how we should imagine, which leads us to the next question:

Can imagination exist without faith?

This second question may be tougher to answer since faith is personal, and our beliefs may differ. Using the Bible as a guide, we can at least explore how faith might activate various powers of imagination. Here are another five that stood out:

6.   Faith fuels the Power of Belief by instilling trust:

"Trust in the LORD with all your heart, and do not lean on your own understanding. In all your ways acknowledge him, and he will make straight your paths." – Proverbs 3:5-6 (ESV)

7.   Faith readies us with the Power of Discipline by testing our ability:

"Count it all joy, my brothers, when you meet trials of various kinds, for you know that the testing of your faith produces steadfastness. And let steadfastness have its full effect, that you may be perfect and complete, lacking in nothing." – James 1:2-4 (ESV)

8.   Faith empowers us with the Power of Resilience by protecting our mind:

"We are afflicted in every way, but not crushed; perplexed, but not driven to despair; persecuted, but not forsaken; struck down, but not destroyed." – 2 Corinthians 4:8-9 (ESV)

9.   Faith emboldens us with the Power of Encouragement by reminding us we are not alone:

"Have I not commanded you? Be strong and courageous. Do not be frightened, and do not be dismayed, for the LORD your God is with you wherever you go." - Joshua 1:9 (ESV)

10. Faith reminds us of the Power of Belief by comforting with us peace:

"Even though I walk through the valley of the shadow of death, I will fear no evil, for you are with me..." - Psalm 23:4 (ESV)

It seems **a healthy imagination requires faith** – at least a belief in something. Faith means trust, confidence, and reliance. A more personal question worthy of asking might be, *what faith do you believe in?*

Faith, as it relates to religion, is clearly a personal choice. But recognize **we all have faith in something**. Whether you believe in God or not is a matter of choice.

But what you will find is that Bible seems to indicate that imagination can't survive for long in an atmosphere not tied to faith. It also offers "lead bulletproof" encouragement to embolden you in your faith and imagination.

What's clear is that faith matters. Faith offers hope and encouragement. **Faith fosters imagination.**

Or is it the other way around?

Which came first?

As to which one came first, imagination or faith, I am naturally inclined to think that imagination came first. The question that I ponder is, *"How can faith be established in the mind's eye without imagination?"* The definition of faith in the Bible points to the importance of imagination. It's like a prerequisite to faith.

My thoughts on this also center on how we are physically created. What separates humankind from any other living being is our imagination. There's no other living being on the planet that imagines quite like us; no other being that creates songs, music, art, movies, and more. When you really think about it, what if religion has been created by man to define who God is and to express our faith? If so, that seems limiting. What if it wasn't meant that way? What if God created imagination to define who we are and to expand our faith?

I like to think the evidence of God's creation is everywhere. I'm reminded of that every time I go to Colorado, or the beach, or in a kayak with my paddle, which represents hope. The good news is that through imagination, God created a way to get us out of our box.

While man created religion to try to put God in a box,
maybe God created imagination to get us out of our own.
After all, what is faith without imagination?

Our capacity to imagine is a differentiator that makes faith possible. Imagination expands our faith. But you could argue that faith is what makes imagination possible.

So, which comes first?

Maybe they coexist. Like the two sides of a coin, maybe we can't have one without the other. Faith and imagination are opposite sides of the same coin.

Chapter Summary

This bonus chapter has focused on the Power of Faith. The Power of Faith is instrumental for Dreamers, Designers, and Implementers alike who are ready to invent the future.

The testimonies are out there, and the research shows that imagination is something that directs our faith. But faith also influences our imagination. For millions, faith is what creates better alignment, clearer boundaries, and greater resilience. Faith can offer a person like you and me the confidence we need to step into the future and pursue the unknown.

How?

Because a faith–minded person believes they are not alone. That means they should be more courageous. Faith at this level offers us trust and strength. Courage isn't the absence of fear; it's the presence of faith. It is this type of faith that can't live without imagination.

Finally, the Bible makes it clear. *"As a man thinketh, so is he."*[123] It adds that there's, *"A hope and a future."*[124] And it encourages us to *"be transformed by the renewing of our mind."*[125] These embolden us – no matter who we are – to create the future by imagining the unseen and believing that *"all things are possible."*[126]

I love that thought because isn't that what faith is all about?

The first step of faith is to *"just imagine."* The equivalent step of imagination is to *"have faith!"* They are partners in a dance. The music they dance to is a song of Hope.[127]

Additional tools and resources focused on
the Faith Factor are available at
theimaginebook.com/append-b

---

[108] Dalia Fahmy, *Key findings about Americans' belief in God*, April 25, 2018
https://www.pewresearch.org/fact-tank/2018/04/25/key-findings-about-americans-belief-in-god/,
last accessed July 10, 2022.

[109] Paul M. Gould, Cultural Apologetics (p. 102). Zondervan Academic.

[110] The Bible, "Do not conform to the pattern of this world, but be transformed by the renewing of your mind. Then you will be able to test and approve what God's will is—his good, pleasing and perfect will.". Romans 12:2.

[111] Bible Hub, *Imagine*, https://biblehub.com/topical/i/imagine.htm, last accessed June 28, 2022.

[112] Brown, Driver, Briggs and Gesenius. "Hebrew Lexicon entry for Chashab",
https://www.biblestudytools.com/lexicons/hebrew/nas/chashab.html,
last accessed June 28, 2022.

[113] International Standard Bible Online, *Meditation*,
https://www.internationalstandardbible.com/M/meditation.html, last accessed June 28, 2022.

[114] Bible Hub, *Meditate*, https://biblehub.com/topical/m/meditate.htm, last accessed June 28, 2022.

[115] Thayer and Smith. "Greek Lexicon entry for Meletao". "The NAS New Testament Greek Lexicon" 1999, https://www.biblestudytools.com/lexicons/greek/nas/meletao.html, last accessed June 28, 2022.

[116] The Bible, "...everything they think or imagine is bent toward evil from childhood. – Genesis 8:21 (NLT).

[117] The Bible, "Now faith is the assurance of things hoped for, the conviction of things not seen." – Hebrews 11:1 (ESV).

[118] The Bible, Genesis 1:1 (NIV).

[119] There are too many verses to list in the confines of this book to highlight the consequence of improper imagination. Discover more at http://theimaginebook.com.

[120] The Bible, Mark 11:22–24 (NIV).

[121] Sanjana Gupta, *9 Scientifically Proven Ways In Which Praying Is Actually Good For Your Health!*, https://www.indiatimes.com/health/healthyliving/9–ways–in–which–praying–is–actually–good–for–your–health–backed–by–science–245787.html, published May 6 2016, last accessed June 28, 2022.

[122] Rev. Catherine Duncan, MA, BCC, *Prayer* https://www.takingcharge.csh.umn.edu/prayer, last accessed July 10, 2022. Look for the heading "Is there evidence for benefits of prayer".

[123] The Bible, Proverbs 23:7 (NJKV).

[124] The Bible, Jeremiah 29:11 (NIV).

[125] The Bible, Romans 12:2 (NIV).

[126] The Bible, Matthew 19:26 (NIV).

[127] For millions worldwide. Hope has a name; Hope is God. Hope is also reflected in the name Messiah, Emmanuel, and Jesus. In the Old and New Testament God himself is attributed to the name Hope, and in the book of Isaiah reveals a Hope to come in the form of a coming Messiah identified as Emmanuel, which means "God is With Us." The gospels of Matthew, Mark, Luke, and John reveal that the Messiah prophesized is Jesus. The Greek name Jesus comes from the Hebrew word Yeshua, which means "to rescue or to deliver." Jesus is a descendent of King David. David's father's name was Jesse, which means a "gift of hope." The Hope that is identified in Isaiah 40:31 assures us those who hope in the Lord will renew their strength. Lord here refers to God, but it could also refer to the Messiah. The book of Isaiah, after all, is sometimes referred to as the 5th Gospel, which is the first account of the Messiah. Finally, God is identified as Hope by the Apostle Paul in Romans 5:1–13. He writes "May the God of hope fill you with all joy and peace as you trust in him, so that you may overflow with hope by the power of the Holy Spirit." The Holy Spirit offers another source of Hope intent to help us. Belief in Jesus promises us eternal life (John 3:16), and that's great, but don't discount the promise of the Holy Spirt while we are still here on earth (John 15:26-27). The Apostle Paul writes as if he knows the Holy Spirit taps into our RAS. He even shares how it writes on our mind (Hebrews 10:15-16). This takes us back to the OODA Loop where the Holy Spirit is a guide. *What do we observe? How should we orient? What decision do we need to make? What action is necessary?* Every step we take is a step of faith.

APPENDIX C — QUOTES THAT INSPIRE

If you are like me, a good quote can give you the perspective you seek when you need it the most. In addition to what was offered in the chapters, I want to share with you some of my other favorites that not only captivate the imagination but might inspire you too. These are quotes organized by the phases of the OODA Loop.

OBSERVE – See the Hope

The quotes below are offered to encourage you to leverage the Power of Patterns, the Power of Curiosity, and the Power of Assessment.

1. *"Hope is a waking dream."* – Aristotle

2. *"The happiness of your life depends upon the quality of your thoughts."* – Marcus Aurelius

3. *"Never deprive someone of hope; it might be all they have."* – H. Jackson Brown, Jr.

4. *"Learn from yesterday, live for today, hope for tomorrow. The important thing is not to stop questioning."* – Albert Einstein

5. *"To me, hope is informed optimism."* – Michael J. Fox

6. *"My hope still is to leave the world a bit better than when I got here."* – Jim Henson

7. *"Everything that is done in the world is done by hope."* – Martin Luther

8. *"Out of the mountain of despair, a stone of hope."* – Martin Luther King. Jr.

9. *"If you concentrate on what you don't have, you will never have enough."* – Oprah Winfrey

10. *"Whatever your beliefs, you should never be without hope, because everything good in life begins with it."* – Nick Vujicic

ORIENT – Position to Possibilities

The quotes below are selected to encourage you to leverage the Power of Belief, the Power of Boundaries, and the Power of Values.

1. *"The world of reality has its limits; the world of imagination is boundless."* – Jean-Jacques Rousseau

2. *"The human brain has more potential than even the brain itself can imagine."* – William Shatner

3. *"You are never too old to set another goal or to dream a new dream."* – C.S. Lewis

4. *"To invent, you need a good imagination and a pile of junk."* – Thomas Edison

5. *"The imagination paints pictures in our mind that help us see reality more clearly."* – Paul M. Gould

6. *"The world will ask you who you are, and if you don't know, the world will tell you."* – Carl Jung

7. *"All successful men and women are big dreamers. They imagine what their future could be..."* – Brian Tracy

8. *"I see possibilities in everything. For everything that's taken away, something of greater value has been given."* – Michael J. Fox

9. *"We all have possibilities we don't know about. We can do things we don't even dream we can do."* – Dale Carnegie

10. *"Our lives are always moving in the direction of our strongest thoughts. What we think shapes who we are."* – Craig Groeschel

DECIDE – Choose the Courage

The quotes below are selected to encourage you to leverage the Power of Resilience, the Power of Today, and the Power of Discipline.

1. *"The best way to predict the future is to invent it."*
   – Ed Catmull

2. *"When you have a dream, you've got to grab it and never let go."* –
   Carol Burnett

3. *"If a door is shut, go up and wiggle it a little don't assume it's locked."* – Bob Goff

4. *"I learned that courage isn't the absence of fear, but the triumph over it …The brave man is not he who does not feel afraid, but he who conquers that fear."* – Nelson Mandela

5. *"All you need is the plan, the road map, and the courage to press on to your destination."* – Earl Nightingale

6. *"No one can make you feel inferior without your consent."*
   – Eleanor Roosevelt

7. *"Hope lies in dreams, in imagination, and in the courage of those who dare to make dreams into reality."* – Jonas Salk

8. *"Sometimes the hurdles aren't really hurdles at all. They're welcome challenges, tests."* – Paul Walker

9. *"Your greatest regret at the end of your life will be the lions you didn't chase. You will look back longingly on risks not taken, opportunities not seized, and dreams not pursued. Stop running away from what scares you most and start chasing the God-ordained opportunities that cross your path."* – Mark Batterson

10. *"Nothing is impossible. The word itself says 'I'm possible!'"*
    – Audrey Hepburn

ACT – Move with Velocity

The quotes below are selected to encourage you to leverage the Power of Movement, the Power of Encouragement, and the Power of Growth.

1. *"Life is like riding a bicycle. To keep your balance, you must keep moving."* – Albert Einstein

2. *"It ain't about how hard you hit. It's about how hard you can get hit and keep moving forward."* – Sylvester Stallone

3. *"Success is not final; failure is not fatal: it is the courage to continue that counts."* – Winston Churchill

4. *"Passionate living is the soul of success."* – Daniel Amen, M.D.

5. *"There comes a moment when you must quit talking to God about the mountain in your life and start talking to the mountain about your God."* – Mark Batterson

6. *"What is now proved was once only imagined."* – William Blake

7. *"Everyone has inside of him a piece of good news. The good news is that you don't know how great you can be! How much you can love! What you can accomplish! And what your potential is!"* – Anne Frank

8. *"Imagination is not only the uniquely human capacity to envision that which is not, ... it is the power that enables us to empathize with humans whose experiences we have never shared."* – J. K. Rowling

9. *"Imagination is the beginning of creation. You imagine what you desire, you "will" what you imagine and at last you create what you will."* – George Bernard Shaw

10. *"Success is when reality catches up with your imagination."* – Simon Sinek

APPENDIX D – RECOMMENDED RESOURCES

At the conclusion of each chapter, I included notes and source citations. I want to also include a few recommended books and movie resources to help you further unpack the powers of imagination.

Here are a few that I recommend:

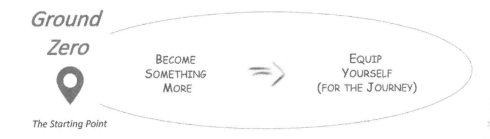

1. Become Something More

- *No Hill Too Fast,* by John Fry, Phil Mahre, and Steve Mahre
- *Aspire,* by Kevin Hall
- *Life without Limits,* by Nick Vujicic
- *The Infinite Game,* by Simon Sinek

2. Equip Yourself for the Journey

- *The Wright Brothers,* by David McCullough
- *The Circle Maker,* by Mark Batterson
- *Boyd: The Fighter Pilot Who Changed the Art of War,* by Robert Coram
- *Peak Mind,* by Amishi P. Jna

Phase One

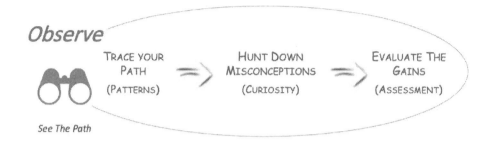

Observe

TRACE YOUR PATH (PATTERNS) ⟹ HUNT DOWN MISCONCEPTIONS (CURIOSITY) ⟹ EVALUATE THE GAINS (ASSESSMENT)

See The Path

3. The Power of Patterns

- *Atomic Habits,* by James Clear
- *A Pattern Language,* by Christopher Alexander
- *Four Patterns of Healthy People,* by Matt Norman
- *Analysis Patterns,* by Martin Fowler

4. The Power of Curiosity

- *Man's Search for Meaning,* by Victor Frankl
- *Get off Your 'But': How to End Self-Sabotage and Stand Up for Yourself,* by Sean Stephenson
- *The Power of Curiosity: How to Have Real Conversations That Create Collaboration, Innovation and Understanding,* by Kathy Taberner
- *The Brain is Always Listening,* by Dr. Daniel Amen

5. The Power of Assessment

- *Soundtracks,* by John Acuff
- *Seven Habits of Highly Effective People,* by Steven Covey
- *Measure What Matters,* by John Doerr
- *The Power of Habits,* by Charles Duhigg

Phase Two

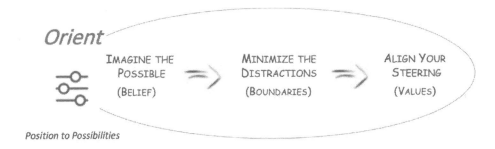

Orient

IMAGINE THE POSSIBLE (BELIEF) ⇒ MINIMIZE THE DISTRACTIONS (BOUNDARIES) ⇒ ALIGN YOUR STEERING (VALUES)

Position to Possibilities

6. The Power of Belief

- *Elon Musk,* by Ashlee Vance
- *Believe It,* by Jamie Kern Lima
- *Permission to be Bold,* by Barbara Valentine Gustavson
- *The Biology of Belief,* by Bruce Lipton

7. The Power of Boundaries

- *Boundaries for Leaders,* by Dr. Henry Cloud
- *Indistractable,* by Nir Eyal
- *Scrum: The Art of Doing Twice the Work in Half the Time,* by Jeff Sutherland

8. The Power of Values

- *The Hiding Place,* by Corrie ten Boom
- *Good to Great,* by Jim Collins
- *Drive,* by Daniel Pink
- *Principles,* by Ray Dalio

Phase Three

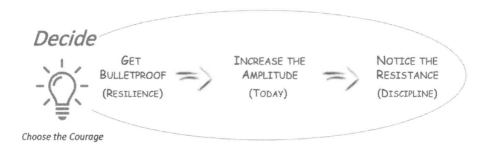

Decide

GET
BULLETPROOF ⟹
(RESILIENCE)

INCREASE THE
AMPLITUDE ⟹
(TODAY)

NOTICE THE
RESISTANCE
(DISCIPLINE)

Choose the Courage

9. The Power of Resilience

- *Lucky Man*, by Michael J. Fox
- *Dopamine Nation*, by Anna Lembke, M.D.
- *Tiny Habits*, by B.J. Fogg
- *Micro-resilience*, by Bonnie St. John
- *Option B,* by Sheryl Sandberg and Adam Grant

10. The Power of Today

- *Steve Jobs,* by Walter Isaacson
- *Today Matters,* by John C. Maxwell
- *Win the Day,* by Mark Batterson
- *The 5 Minute Journal,* by Intelligent Change

11. The Power of Discipline

- *The 21 Irrefutable Law of Leadership*, specifically the chapter titled "The Law of Big Mo" by John C. Maxwell
- *Only the Paranoid Survive: How to Exploit the Crisis Points That Challenge Every Company,* by Andy Grove
- *The Four Disciplines of Execution*, by McChesney, Covey, and Huling

Phase Four

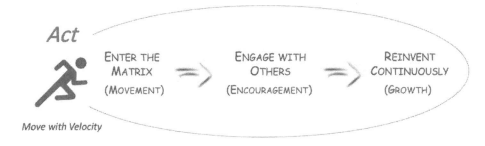

Move with Velocity

12. The Power of Movement

- *The Matrix*, Warner Brothers (movie)
- *Think Again,* by Adam Grant
- *Thinking, Fast and Slow*, by Daniel Kahneman,
- *The Potential Principle*, by Mark Sanborn

13. The Power of Encouragement

- *Who Not How,* by Dan Sullivan
- *Encouragement Changes Everything*, by John C. Maxwell
- *Leaders Eat Last*, by Simon Sinek

14. The Power of Growth

- *Remember the Titans*, Disney (movie)
- *15 Invaluable Laws of Growth*, by John C. Maxwell
- *Make Your Bed*, by William McRaven

ABOUT THE AUTHOR

Paul Gustavson

Paul Gustavson is a co-founder and CTO of *SimVentions, Inc.*, a technology firm supporting today's military and decision makers with innovative engineering solutions. *SimVentions* has been recognized as one of Virginia's Best Places to Work and was named by *Inc. Magazine* as one of "The Best Places to Work" in 2016 and 2022.

As the CTO, Paul leads in identifying and contributing to the company's capability and influencing the strategic vision. Paul is also the author of the books *Breaking Average, Leaders Press On,* and *Speech Blueprint* and co-host of the *Breaking Average Podcast*. He is an active member of the simulation and virtual reality communities.

You can connect with Paul at the following links:

- https://www.simventions.com
- https://breakingaverage.com
- Twitter: @PaulGustavson
- Instagram: @paul.gustavson

❖ ❖ ❖

Additional tools and resources are available at
theimaginebook.com

LEAD EDGE PRESS BOOKS

Books By PAUL GUSTAVSON

Leaders Press On
Discovering the Power of Perseverance

Speech Blueprint
Using Simon Sinek's TED Talk
as a Model to "Inspire Action"

Breaking Average
The Seven Critical Factors to
Team Strong Leadership

Imagine
The Surprising Truth About Hope and
The 12 Powerful Ways to Invent the Future

Books By BARBARA VALENTINE GUSTAVSON

Permission to be BOLD:
A Guide to Loving Yourself, Living Fully,
and Leaving Your Mark in the World

Lead Edge
PRESS

Made in the USA
Columbia, SC
22 December 2022

966f411f-ae66-4d8e-ac07-4860c705809cR01